KT-199-795

TOP 10

OF EVERYTHING

2009

TOP 10

OF EVERYTHING

Russell Ash **2009**

hamlyn

Contents

Produced for Hamlyn by
Palazzo Editions Ltd
2 Wood Street, Bath, BA1 2JQ

Publishing director: Colin Webb
Art director: Bernard Higton
Managing editor: Sonya Newland
Picture researcher: Sophie Hartley

First published in Great Britain in 2009 by
Hamlyn, a division of
Octopus Publishing Group Ltd
2–4 Heron Quays, London E14 4JP

Copyright © Octopus Publishing
Group Ltd 2009
Text copyright © Russell Ash 2009

The right of Russell Ash to be identified as
the author of this work has been asserted
by him in accordance with the Copyright,
Designs and Patents Act 1988.

All rights reserved. No part of this work
may be reproduced or utilized in any form
or by any means, electronic or mechanical,
including photocopying, recording, or by
any information storage and retrieval
system, without the prior written
permission of the publisher.

ISBN 9780600617396

A CIP catalogue record for this book is
available from the British Library.

Printed and bound in China.

10 9 8 7 6 5 4 3 2 1

Introduction

MAGIC NUMBERS

Although 10 is the magic number as far as this book is concerned, the number 20 is not without its appeal: there were 20 days in an Aztec month, there are 20 bottles in a Nebuchadnezzar and 20 numbers on a dartboard; we refer to 20/20 vision and the 'Roaring '20s', play Twenty20 cricket and the quiz 20 Questions, while 2020 is widely predicted as the year the world hits peak oil production. And 20 is now the number of years *Top 10 of Everything* has been published.

When I compiled the first edition in 1989, it was not intended to be an annual, but it has been ever since. A shelf of the complete set with one copy of each year's would be over 50 cm (20 in) long – mine, with all the versions now published around the world, is considerably longer!

IT WAS 20 YEARS AGO...

Alongside the array of Top 10 lists, the often dramatic changes over the past 20 years or so are reflected in the 'Now & Then' lists presented here for the first time. They show such developments as population changes, oil consumers and car owners, the tallest skyscrapers, the largest cities and film budgets, the busiest airports, longest life expectancy, most expensive paintings and the most popular names of people and pets.

THIS EVER-CHANGING WORLD

While the 'Now & Then' lists show what has altered over the past 20 years, pretty much every list changes from year to year – even 'fixed' list such as those of tallest mountains are revised as more sophisticated measuring techniques are used, or deepest caves, as deeper branches are discovered. The minimum entry requirements for Top 10 lists are in a constant state of flux as, for example, rich people get increasingly richer and build ever-bigger yachts, films with bigger and bigger budgets are released and achieve higher-earning opening weekends (three films have now made more than $1 billion worldwide). And just as the tallest building in the world nears completion, plans are announced for one more than twice as tall, the proposed 1,609-m (5,280-ft) Mile-High Tower in Jeddah, Saudi Arabia.

IT'S A FACT

Top 10 lists provide a shorthand glimpse at what is happening with the world economy, global warming, deforestation, the countries that will have the most people and the densest populations in the future, and other issues that concern us all. At the same time, it conveys a fascinating and entertaining overview of the amazing diversity of our planet and its people, with lists on such subjects as longest place names and the people on the FBI's 'Most Wanted' list, the largest diamonds and the largest snails, the heaviest and the oldest people, the richest dead celebrities, the largest shopping malls and the most powerful computers, the most common and the most unusual phobias, the most borrowed and the most translated authors, the leading chocolate consumers and the most overweight countries.

MADE TO MEASURE

The ground rules are that all the Top 10s in the book are measurable: biggests, fastests, richests, firsts, oldests, and so on. There are no 'bests', except bestsellers, and 'worsts' are of disasters and murders where they are measured by numbers of victims. Unless otherwise stated, film lists are based on cumulative global earnings, irrespective of production or marketing budgets and, as is standard in the industry, inflation is not taken into account – which inevitably means that recent releases feature more prominently.

'Countries' are independent countries, not dependencies or overseas territories. All the lists are all-time and global unless a specific year or territory is noted. If the UK does not figure in a country-based list, it is generally added as an extra entry.

SOURCES

My sources encompass international organizations, commercial companies and research bodies, specialized publications and a network of people around the world who have shared their knowledge of everything from snakes and skyscrapers to ships and spiders. As ever, I gladly acknowledge their invaluable contribution (see page 255 for a full list of credits), as well everyone who has been involved with the book at all stages of its development on this and the previous 19 annual editions.

OVER TO YOU

I hope you enjoy the book. Your comments, corrections and suggestions for new lists are always welcome. Please contact me via the publisher or visit the *Top 10 of Everything* website www.top10ofeverything.com or my own www.RussellAsh.com

Russell Ash

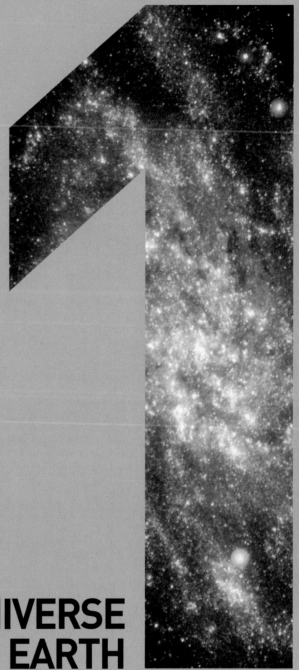

THE UNIVERSE
& THE EARTH

Elementary

TOP 10 **MOST COMMON ELEMENTS IN THE EARTH'S CRUST**

	ELEMENT	SYMBOL	PARTS PER MILLION*
1	Oxygen	O	461,000
2	Silicon	Si	282,000
3	Aluminium	Al	82,300
4	Iron	Fe	56,300
5	Calcium	Ca	41,500
6	Sodium	Na	23,600
7	Magnesium	Mg	23,300
8	Potassium	K	20,900
9	Titanium	Ti	5,650
10	Hydrogen	H	1,400

* Mg per kg, based on average percentages of elements in igneous rock

At an atomic level, out of every million atoms, some 200,000 are silicon, 63,000 aluminium and 31,000 hydrogen – although in the Universe as a whole, hydrogen is by far the most common element, comprising some 930,000 out of every million atoms, followed by helium at 72,000 per million.

TOP 10 **MOST COMMON ELEMENTS ON THE MOON**

	ELEMENT	SYMBOL	%
1	Oxygen	O	40.0
2	Silicon	Si	19.2
3	Iron	Fe	14.3
4	Calcium	Ca	8.0
5	Titanium	Ti	5.9
6	Aluminium	Al	5.6
7	Magnesium	Mg	4.5
8	Sodium	Na	0.33
9	Potassium	K	0.14
10	Chromium	Cr	0.002

This list is based on the analysis of the 20.77 kg (45.8 lb) of rock samples brought back to Earth by the crew of the 1969 *Apollo 11* lunar mission. One of the minerals they discovered at Tranquility Base was named Armalcolite in honour of the three astronauts **Arm**strong, **Al**drin and **Col**lins. It contains magnesium, iron, titanium and oxygen. In all, the six *Apollo* missions brought back 382 kg (842 lb) of lunar rocks and other samples.

TOP 10 **MOST COMMON ELEMENTS IN THE SUN**

	ELEMENT	SYMBOL	% OF ATOMS
1	Hydrogen	H	92.1
2	Helium	He	7.8
3	Oxygen	O	0.061
4	Carbon	C	0.030
5	Nitrogen	N	0.0084
6	Neon	Ne	0.0076
7	Iron	Fe	0.0037
8	Silicon	Si	0.0031
9	Magnesium	Mg	0.0024
10	Sulphur	S	0.0015

A total of 99.9 per cent of all the atoms in the Sun are made up of two elements, hydrogen and helium. Helium was in fact discovered in the Sun before it was detected on Earth, its name coming from *helios*, the Greek word for 'Sun'. More than 70 elements have been detected in the Sun, the most common of which correspond closely to those found in the Universe as a whole, but with some variations in their ratios, including a greater proportion of the principal element, hydrogen. The atoms of hydrogen in the Universe outnumber those of all the other elements combined.

TOP 10 MOST COMMON ELEMENTS IN THE OCEANS

	ELEMENT	SYMBOL	AMOUNT (TONNES PER CU KM)
1	Oxygen*	O	857,000,000
2	Hydrogen*	H	107,800,000
3	Chlorine	Cl	19,870,000
4	Sodium	Na	11,050,000
5	Magnesium	Mg	1,326,000
6	Sulphur	S	928,000
7	Calcium	Ca	422,000
8	Potassium	K	416,000
9	Bromine	Br	67,300
10	Carbon	C	28,000

* Combined as water

A typical cubic kilometre (a billion tonnes) of seawater is a treasury of often valuable elements – there are reckoned to be 5,000 million million tonnes of solids dissolved in the world's oceans, but sodium and chlorine (combined as sodium chloride – common salt) are the only two that are extracted in substantial quantities. The costs of extracting elements such as gold (even though as much as 500 kilos of it may be found in the average cubic kilometre of seawater) would be so expensive that with current technology it is not economic to do so.

TOP 10 MOST COMMON ELEMENTS IN THE UNIVERSE

	ELEMENT	SYMBOL	PARTS PER MILLION*
1	Hydrogen	H	750,000
2	Helium	He	230,000
3	Oxygen	O	10,000
4	Carbon	C	5,000
5	Neon	Ne	1,300
6	Iron	Fe	1,100
7	Nitrogen	N	1,000
8	Silicon	Si	700
9	Magnesium	Mg	600
10	Sulphur	S	500

* Mg per kg

In his element
Einsteinium was named after Albert Einstein, winner of the 1921 Nobel Prize for Physics.

THE 10 FIRST ELEMENTS TO BE NAMED AFTER REAL PEOPLE

	ELEMENT	SYMBOL	NAMED AFTER	YEAR
1	Samarium*	Sm	Vasili Samarsky-Bykhovets (Russia, 1803–70)	1879
2	Gadolinium#	Gd	Johan Gadolin (Finland, 1760–1852)	1880
3	Curium	Cm	Pierre† and Marie Curie† (France, 1859–1906; Poland, 1867–1934)	1944
4	Einsteinium	Es	Albert Einstein† (German, 1879–1955)	1952
5	Fermium	Fm	Enrico Fermi† (Italian, 1901–54)	1953
6	Nobelium	No	Alfred Nobel (Sweden, 1833–96)	1958
7	Lawrencium	Lr	Ernest Lawrence† (USA, 1901–58)	1961
8	Rutherfordium	Rf	Ernest Rutherford† (UK, 1871–1937)	1969
9	Seaborgium	Sg	Glenn T. Seaborg† (USA, 1912–99)	1974
10	Bohrium	Bh	Niels Bohr† (Denmark, 1885–62)	1981

* Named after mineral samarskite, which was named after Samarsky-Bykhovets
\# Named after mineral gadolinite, which was named after Gadolin
† Awarded Nobel Prize

The Universe

TOP 10 BRIGHTEST GALAXIES

GALAXY/NO.	DISTANCE FROM EARTH (MILLIONS OF LIGHT YEARS)	APPARENT MAGNITUDE
1 Large Magellanic Cloud	0.17	0.91
2 Small Magellanic Cloud	0.21	2.70
3 Andromeda Galaxy/NGC 224 M31	2.6	4.36
4 Triangulum Galaxy/NGC 598 M33	2.8	6.27
5 Centaurus Galaxy/NGC 5128	12.0	7.84
6 Bode's Galaxy/NGC 3031 M81	12.0	7.89
7 Silver Coin Galaxy/NGC 253	8.5	8.04
8 Southern Pinwheel Galaxy/NGC 5236 M83	15.0	8.20
9 Pinwheel Galaxy/NGC 5457 M101	24.0	8.31
10 Cigar Galaxy/NGC 55	4.9	8.42

Messier (M) numbers are named after French astronomer Charles Messier, who compiled the first catalogue of galaxies, nebulae and star clusters in 1781. From 1888 onwards, these were replaced by New General Catalogue (NGC) numbers. As well as the official names that have been assigned to them, galaxies discovered prior to the change are identified by both M and NGC numbers.

TOP 10 MOST FREQUENTLY SEEN COMETS

COMET	YEARS BETWEEN APPEARANCES
1 Encke 1	3.29
2 NEAT (Near Earth Asteroid Tracking) 22	4.20
3 Helfenzrieder 1	4.35
4 Catalina 3	4.42
5 LINEAR (Lincoln Near-Earth Asteroid Research) 30	4.85
6 LINEAR 46	4.86
7 = Grigg-Skjellerup 1	4.98
= NEAT 10	4.98
9 LONEOS (Lowell Observatory Near-Earth-Object Search) 6	5.01
10 Blanpain 1	5.10

Source: NASA, Planetary Data System Small Bodies Node

The comets in the Top 10, and several others, return with regularity (although with some notable variations), while others have such long periods that they may not be seen again for many thousands, or even millions, of years. The most frequent visitor is Encke's Comet, named not after its 1786 discoverer (French astronomer Pierre Méchain), but the German astronomer Johann Franz Encke, who in 1818 calculated the period of its elliptical orbit. It had been first observed shortly before his birth, but without its orbit being calculated, and has been seen on almost all its subsequent returns.

TOP 10 STARS NEAREST EARTH

STAR*	LIGHT YEARS	DISTANCE FROM EARTH KM (MILLIONS)	MILES (MILLIONS)
1 Proxima Centauri	4.22	39,923,310	24,792,500
2 Alpha Centauri	4.39	41,531,595	25,791,250
3 Barnard's Star	5.94	56,195,370	34,897,500
4 Wolf 359	7.78	73,602,690	45,707,500
5 Lalande 21185	8.31	78,616,755	48,821,250
6 Sirius	8.60	81,360,300	50,525,000
7 Luyten 726-8	8.72	82,495,560	51,230,000
8 Ross 154	9.69	91,672,245	56,928,750
9 Ross 248	10.32	97,632,360	60,630,000
10 Epsilon Eridani	10.49	99,240,645	61,628,750

* Excluding the Sun

Source: Peter Bond, Royal Astronomical Society

A spaceship travelling at 40,237 km/h (25,000 mph) – faster than any human has yet reached in space – would take more than 113,200 years to reach Earth's closest star, Proxima Centauri. Even this distance and those of the others in this Top 10 are dwarfed by those of stars within the Milky Way up to 2,500 light years away, while our own galaxy may span as much as 100,000 light years.

TOP 10 LARGEST ASTEROIDS

NAME	NO.	DISCOVERED	MAX. DIAMETER* KM	MILES
1 Ceres	1	1 Jan 1801	940	584
2 Vesta	4	29 Mar 1807	576	357
3 Pallas	2	28 Mar 1802	538	334
4 Hygeia	10	12 Apr 1849	430	267
5 Interamnia	704	2 Oct 1910	338	210
6 Davida	511	30 May 1903	324	201
7 Cybele	65	8 Mar 1861	308	191
8 Europa	52	4 Feb 1858	292	181
9 Sylvia	87	16 May 1866	282	175
10 Patienta	451	4 Dec 1899	280	173

* Most asteroids are irregular in shape

Asteroids, now often known as 'minor planets', are fragments of rock orbiting between Mars and Jupiter. Ceres is large enough to be regarded as a 'dwarf planet' (bodies over 750 km/466 miles in diameter), along with Pluto and Eris. Up to August 2007, some 161,988 asteroids had been identified. Each of the four Beatles has an asteroid named after him (4,147–4,150), as do Elvis Presley (17,059), the Rolling Stones (19,383), James Bond (9,007) and the members of the Monty Python team (9,617–9,622).

TOP 10 **LARGEST BODIES IN THE SOLAR SYSTEM**

		MAX. DIAMETER		SIZE COMPARED
	BODY	KM	MILES	WITH EARTH
1	Sun	1,392,140	865,036	109.136
2	Jupiter	142,984	88,846	11.209
3	Saturn	120,536	74,898	9.449
4	Uranus	51,118	31,763	4.007
5	Neptune	49,528	30,775	3.883
6	Earth	12,756	7,926	1.000
7	Venus	12,104	7,521	0.949
8	Mars	6,805	4,228	0.533
9	Ganymede	5,262	3,270	0.413
10	Titan	5,150	3,200	0.404

Most of the planets are visible with the naked eye and have been observed since ancient times. The exceptions are Uranus, discovered on 13 March 1781 by the British astronomer Sir William Herschel; Neptune, found by German astronomer Johann Galle on 23 September 1846 (Galle was led to his discovery by the independent calculations of the French astronomer Urbain Le Verrier and the British mathematician John Adams); and, outside the Top 10, former planet Pluto, located using photographic techniques by American astronomer Clyde Tombaugh.

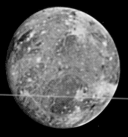
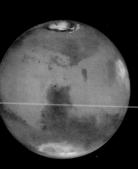

Worlds apart
The Sun (top) and, in descending order of size, the Solar System's largest bodies. Mercury and ex-planet Pluto are smaller than Jovian satellite Ganymede and Saturn's Titan.

To Boldly Go...

TOP 10 COUNTRIES WITH THE MOST SPACEFLIGHT EXPERIENCE

	COUNTRY	ASTRONAUTS/ COSMONAUTS	TOTAL DURATION OF MISSIONS* DAYS	HRS	MINS
1	USSR/Russia	211	17,738	17	4
2	USA	750	11,434	19	36
3	Germany	14	494	0	12
4	France	17	383	21	50
5	Kazakhstan	4	349	7	26
6	Canada	13	146	1	31
7	Japan	10	102	2	24
8	Italy	7	86	4	22
9	Ukraine	2	64	22	48
10	Switzerland	4	42	11	31
	UK	*1*	*7*	*21*	*13*

* To 27 March 2008

The USSR, and now Russia, has clocked up its considerable lead on the rest of the world – with 57.3 per cent of the total time spent by humans in space – largely through the long-duration stays of its cosmonauts on board the *Mir* space station. The USA has had more than three times as many astronauts in space – principally aboard the Space Shuttle – but its missions have been of shorter duration.

TOP 10 MOST EXPERIENCED US ASTRONAUTS*

	NAME	MISSIONS	TOTAL DURATION DAYS	HRS	MINS
1	C. Michael Foale	6	373	18	8
2	Michael López-Alegria	4	257	22	46
3	Carl E. Walz	4	230	13	4
4	Chiao Leroy	4	229	8	41
5	Daniel Bursch	4	226	22	16
6	William S. McArthur	4	224	22	19
7	Shannon Lucid	5	223	2	50
8	Kenneth Bowersox	5	211	14	12
9	Susan J. Helms	5	210	23	6
10	Edward Lu	3	205	23	18

* To 27 March 2008

TOP 10 MOST EXPERIENCED COSMONAUTS*

	COSMONAUT	MISSIONS	TOTAL DURATION DAYS	HRS	MINS
1	Sergei Krikalyov	6#	803	9	39
2	Sergei Avdeyev	3	747	14	14
3	Valeri Polyakov	2	678	16	32
4	Anatoly Solovyov	5#	651	0	2
5	Alexander Kaleri	4	609	21	53
6	Viktor Afanasyev	4	555	18	33
7	Yuri Usachev	4#	552	22	25
8	Musa Manarov	2	541	0	28
9	Alexander Viktorenko	4	489	1	33
10	Nikolai Budarin	3#	444	1	25

* To 27 March 2008; all Soviet/Russian
# Including flights aboard US Space Shuttles

All the missions listed were undertaken by the USSR (and, latterly, Russia). In recent years a number of US astronauts added to their space logs by spending time on board the Russian Mir space station, and latterly on the International Space Station, but none has matched the endurance records set by Russian cosmonauts. Krikalyov established the cumulative record aboard the ISS during his sixth mission in 2005.

Mission patch
STS-102 carried Krikalyov, Helms and Usachev, three of the most experienced of all astronauts and cosmonauts.

Walking round the world
During their record duration spacewalk from the International Space Station, US astronaut James S. Voss, accompanied by Susan J. Helms, orbited the Earth more than five times.

TOP 10 MOST EXPERIENCED NON-US AND NON-RUSSIAN ASTRONAUTS AND COSMONAUTS*

NAME / COUNTRY	MISSIONS	TOTAL DURATION DAYS	HRS	MINS
1 Thomas A. Reiter Germany	2	350	5	35
2 Talgat A. Musabayev Kazakhstan	3	341	9	48
3 Jean-Pierre Haigneré France	2	209	12	25
4 Léopold Eyharts France	2	69	21	31
5 Ulf D. Merbold Germany	3	49	21	36
6 Jean-Loup J. M. Chrétien France	3	43	11	19
7 Claude Nicollier Switzerland	4	42	12	5
8 Takao Doi Japan	2	31	10	45
9 Joseph J.-P. M. Garneau Canada	3	29	2	1
10 Dafydd Rhys Williams Canada	2	28	15	46

* To 27 March 2008

Claudie Haigneré, the wife of Jean-Pierre Haigneré, here in third place, has been on two Soyuz missions but just fails to make the list with a total time in space of 25 days 14 hours and 22 minutes. Asteroid 135268, discovered in France in 2001, was named Haigneré in honour of the country's most experienced space couple.

TOP 10 LONGEST SPACEWALKS*

ASTRONAUTS# / SPACECRAFT	DATE	DURATION HR:MIN
1 James S. Voss, Susan J. Helms STS-102/ISS†	11 Mar 2001	8:56
2 Thomas Akers, Richard Hieb, Pierre J. Thuot STS-49	13–14 May 1992	8:29
3 John M. Grunsfeld, Steven L. Smith STS-103	22–23 Dec 1999	8:15
4 C. Michael Foale, Claude Nicollier STS-103	23–24 Dec 1999	8:10
5 John M. Grunsfeld, Steven L. Smith STS-103	24–25 Dec 1999	8:08
6 = James F. Reilly, John D. Olivas STS-117	15–16 Jun 2007	7:58
= Stanley G. Love, Rex J. Walheim STS-122	11 Feb 2008	7:58
8 = Daniel Barry, Tamara Jernigan STS-96/ISS	30 May 1999	7:55
= Michael López–Alegria, Sunita Williams Soyuz TMA-9/ISS	31 Jan 2007	7:55
10 Jeffrey A. Hoffman, F. Story Musgrave STS-61	5 Dec 1993	7:54

* To 27 March 2008
# All US
† International Space Station

Bodies of Water

TOP 10 DEEPEST OCEANS AND SEAS

OCEAN/SEA	AVERAGE DEPTH M	FT
Southern Ocean	4–5,000	13,123–16,404
Pacific Ocean	4,028	13,215
Indian Ocean	3,963	13,002
Atlantic Ocean	3,926	12,999
Caribbean Sea	2,647	8,684
South China Sea	1,652	4,150
Red Sea	1,611	5,285
Bering Sea	1,547	5,075
Gulf of Mexico	1,486	4,875
Mediterranean Sea	1,429	4,688
World ocean average	*3,730*	*12,237*

TOP 10 LARGEST OCEANS AND SEAS

	NAME	APPROX. AREA* SQ KM	SQ MILES
1	Pacific Ocean	155,557,000	60,060,900
2	Atlantic Ocean	76,762,000	29,637,977
3	Indian Ocean	68,556,000	26,469,622
4	Southern Ocean#	20,327,000	7,848,299
5	Arctic Ocean	14,056,000	5,427,053
6	Caribbean Sea	2,718,200	1,049,503
7	Mediterranean Sea	2,510,000	969,117
8	South China Sea	2,319,000	895,371
9	Bering Sea	2,291,900	884,908
10	Gulf of Mexico	1,592,800	614,984

* Excluding tributary seas
\# Defined by the International Hydrographic Organization, 2000

The Shrinking Sea

Fifty years ago, the Aral Sea in Kazakhstan and Uzbekistan was the fourth-biggest inland sea in the world, with a water surface area of 66,100 sq km (25,521 sq miles) and islands of 2,200 sq km (849 sq miles), a total of 68,300 sq km (26,371 sq miles). By 2004, as a result of two feeder rivers being diverted to irrigate cotton crops, it had shrunk to 17,158 sq km (6,625 sq miles), with ships beached and former fishing villages 100 km (62 miles) inland, and it is heavily polluted. The recent construction of a dam has began the process of refilling the northern part, which has expanded by over 1,000 sq km (386 sq miles) since 2005.

TOP 10 DEEPEST LAKES

	LAKE	LOCATION	GREATEST DEPTH M	FT
1	Baikal	Russia	1,741	5,712
2	Tanganyika	Burundi/Tanzania/Dem. Rep. of Congo/Zambia	1,471	4,825
3	Caspian Sea	Azerbaijan/Iran/ Kazakhstan/Russia/ Turkmenistan	1,025	3,363
4	Malawi (Nyasa)	Malawi/Mozambique/ Tanzania	706	2,316
5	Issyk-kul	Kyrgyzstan	668	2,191
6	Great Slave	Canada	614	2,015
7	Matana	Sulawesi, Indonesia	590	1,936
8	Crater	Oregon, USA	589	1,932
9	Toba	Sumatra, Indonesia	529	1,736
10	Hornindalsvatnet	Norway	514	1,686

TOP 10 **LARGEST LAKES**

LAKE	LOCATION	APPROX. AREA SQ KM	SQ MILES
1 Caspian Sea	Azerbaijan/Iran/ Kazakhstan/Russia/ Turkmenistan	371,000	143,244
2 Michigan/ Huron*	Canada/USA	117,436	45,342
3 Superior	Canada/USA	82,103	31,700
4 Victoria	Kenya/Tanzania/Uganda	69,485	26,828
5 Tanganyika	Burundi/Tanzania/ Dem. Rep. of Congo/ Zambia	32,893	12,700
6 Baikal	Russia	31,494	12,160
7 Great Bear	Canada	31,153	12,028
8 Malawi (Nyasa)	Malawi/Mozambique/ Tanzania	29,600	11,429
9 Great Slave	Canada	28,568	11,030
10 Erie	Canada/USA	25,745	9,940

* Now considered two lobes of the same lake

Regarded geologically and hydrologically as two lobes of the same lake, Michigan/Huron is the world's largest freshwater lake. A depth of 1,741 m (5,712 ft) near Olkhon, off Cape Ukhan, established Lake Baikal as the world's deepest, although subsequent research has failed to record soundings greater than 1,620 m (5,315 ft).

Victorious Victoria
The world's largest tropical lake, Victoria's fishing industry is a mainstay of the economy of the surrounding region. The lake was unknown to Europeans until its discovery by John Hanning Speke in 1858.

TOP 10 **LARGEST LAKES IN THE UK**

LAKE	COUNTRY	AREA SQ KM	SQ MILES
1 Lough Neagh	Northern Ireland	381.74	147.39
2 Lower Lough Erne	Northern Ireland	105.08	40.57
3 Loch Lomond	Scotland	71.12	27.46
4 Loch Ness	Scotland	56.64	21.87
5 Loch Awe	Scotland	38.72	14.95
6 Upper Lough Erne	Northern Ireland	31.73	16.60
7 Loch Maree	Scotland	28.49	11.00
8 Loch Morar	Scotland	26.68	10.30
9 Loch Tay	Scotland	26.39	10.19
10 Loch Shin	Scotland	22.53	8.70

Despite its size, Lough Neagh is ranked as the 31st largest lake in Europe; it is also among the shallowest, with an average depth of 9 m (29.5 ft). The largest lake in England is Windermere, 14.74 sq km/5.69 sq miles and the largest in Wales is Lake Vyrnwy, at 8.03 sq km/3.10 sq miles.

Go with the Flow

TOP 10 LARGEST RIVER DRAINAGE BASINS

	RIVER BASIN	CONTINENT	APPROX. DRAINAGE AREA SQ KM	SQ MILES
1	Amazon	South America	6,144,727	2,372,492
2	Congo	Africa	3,730,474	1,440,344
3	Nile	Africa	3,254,555	1,256,591
4	Mississippi-Missouri	North America	3,202,230	1 236 388
5	Plata	South America	3,100,000	1,196,917
6	Ob'	Asia	2,972,497	1,147,688
7	Paraná	South America	2,582,672	997,175
8	Yenisei	Asia	2,554,482	986,291
9	Lena	Asia	2,306,772	890,650
10	Niger	Africa	2,261,763	873,272

Drainage basins are the areas of land into which water from rain or melting snow drain into a body of water, such as a river or lake, or to the sea. Endorheic basins are those where the water does not ultimately enter the sea. As they are important in providing water for agriculture, and domestic and industrial uses, the management of water resources is often based on defined drainage basins.

TOP 10 GREATEST* RIVER SYSTEMS

	RIVER SYSTEM	CONTINENT	AVERAGE DISCHARGE AT MOUTH (CU M/SEC)	(CU FT/SEC)
1	Amazon	South America	219,000	7,733,912
2	Congo (Zaïre)	Africa	41,800	1,476,153
3	Yangtze (Chang Jiang)	Asia	31,900	1,126,538
4	Orinoco	South America	30,000	1,059,440
5	Paraná	South America	25,700	907,587
6	Yenisei-Angara	Asia	19,600	692,168
7	Brahmaputra (Tsangpo)	Asia	19,200	678,042
8	Lena	Asia	17,100	603,881
9	Madeira-Mamoré	South America	17,000	600,349
10	Mississippi-Missouri	North America	16,200	572,098

* Based on rate of discharge at mouth

Frozen river
Discovered by Ernest Shackleton in 1908, the vast Beardmore glacier was named after Sir William Beardmore, the sponsor of his expedition.

TOP 10 LONGEST GLACIERS

	GLACIER / LOCATION	APPROX. LENGTH: KM	MILES
1	Lambert Antarctica	400	249
2	Bering Alaska, USA	190	118
3	Beardmore Antarctica	160	99
4	Byrd Antarctica	136	85
5	Nimrod Antarctica	135	84
6	Amundsen Antarctica	128	80
7	Hubbard Alaska, USA	122	76
8	Slessor Antarctica	120	75
9	Denman Antarctica	112	70
10	= Recovery Antarctica	100	62
	= Shackleton Antarctica	100	62

TOP 10 **LONGEST RIVERS**

	RIVER / LOCATION (SOURCE TO MOUTH)	APPROX. LENGTH: KM	MILES
1	**Nile** Tanzania – Egypt	6,650	4,132
2	**Amazon** Peru – Brazil	6,400	3,976
3	**Yangtze (Chang Jiang)** China	6,300	3,915
4	**Mississippi-Missouri** USA	6,275	3,899
5	**Yenisei-Angara-Selenga** Mongolia – Russia	5,539	3,441
6	**Huang He (Yellow)** China	5,464	3,395
7	**Ob-Irtysh** Kazkhakstan – China	5,410	3,362
8	**Congo-Chambeshi** Tanzania – Angola	4,700	2,920
9	**Amur-Argun** Russia – China	4,444	2,761
10	**Lena** Russia	4,400	2,734

Above: Slow boat in China
Historically one of China's major transport arteries, the Yangtze retains its importance in the twenty-first century.

TOP 10 **HIGHEST WATERFALLS**

	WATERFALL / RIVER	LOCATION	TOTAL DROP M	FT
1	Angel Carrao	Venezuela	979	3,212*
2	Tugela Tugela	South Africa	948	3,110
3	Ramnefjellsfossen Jostedal Glacier	Nesdale, Norway	800	2,625
4	Mongefossen Monge	Mongebekk, Norway	774	2,540
5	Gocta Cataracta Cocahuayco	Peru	771	2,531
6	Mutarazi Mutarazi River	Zimbabwe	762	2,499
7	Yosemite Yosemite Creek	California, USA	739	2,425
8	Østre Mardøla Foss Mardals	Eikisdal, Norway	656	2,152
9	Tyssestrengane Tysso	Hardanger, Norway	646	2,120
10	Cuquenán Arabopo	Venezuela	610	2,000

* Longest single drop 807 m (2,648 ft)

TOP 10 **WIDEST WATERFALLS**

	WATERFALL / RIVER / COUNTRY	WIDTH M	FT
1	Chutes de Khône, Mekong River, Laos	10,783	35,376
2	Salto Pará, Rio Caura, Venezuela	5,608	18,400
3 =	Salto del Guaíra, Rio Paraná, Brazil	4,828	15,840
=	Chutes de Livingstone, Congo River, Congo	4,828	15,840
5	Celilo Falls, Columbia River, USA	3,219	10,560
6	Kongou Falls, Ivindo River, Gabon	3,200	10,500
7	Salto de Iguaçu, Rio Iguaçu, Argentina/Brazil	2,700	8,858
8 =	Saltos dos Patos e Maribondo, Rio Grande, Brazil	2,012	6,600
=	Salto do Urubupungá, Rio Paraná, Brazil	2,012	6,600
10	Victoria Falls, Zambezi River, Zimbabwe/Zambia	1,737	5,700

Islands

TOP 10 HIGHEST ISLANDS

	ISLAND / HIGHEST POINT	HIGHEST ELEVATION M	FT
1	New Guinea, Indonesia/Papua New Guinea; Puncak Jaya (Mount Carstensz)	4,884	16,023
2	Hawaii, USA; Mauna Kea	4,205	13,795
3	Borneo, Indonesia/Malaysia; Mount Kinabalu	4,101	13,454
4	Taiwan; Jade Mountain (Yu Shan)	3,952	12,965
5	Sumatra, Indonesia; Mount Kerinci	3,805	12,480
6	Ross, Antarctica; Mount Erebus	3,794	12,447
7	Honshu, Japan; Mount Fuji	3,776	12,388
8	New Zealand; Aorakim (Mount Cook)	3,755	12,319
9	Lombok, Indonesia; Mount Rinjani	3,726	12,224
10	Tenerife, Spain; Pico de Teide	3,718	12,198

Some of the tallest island mountains were formed by tectonic activity, while others are volcanic in origin, including dormant volcanoes Mauna Kea and Fuji and active volcanoes Erebus and Rinjani, and Teide, the highest European island mountain.

TOP 10 LARGEST ISLAND COUNTRIES

	COUNTRY	AREA SQ KM	SQ MILES
1	Indonesia	1,904,569	735,358
2	Madagascar	587,713	226,917
3	Papua New Guinea	462,840	178,703
4	Japan	377,873	145,897
5	Malaysia	329,847	127,354
6	Philippines	300,000	115,830
7	New Zealand	270,534	104,453
8	Cuba	110,861	42,803
9	Iceland	103,000	39,768
10	Sri Lanka	65,610	25,332

All the countries on this list are self-contained island countries. Because Ireland and Northern Ireland share an island, the UK and Ireland are both excluded from this list. Had it been included, the UK (excluding the Isle of Man and the Channel Islands) would take eighth place with an area of 242,900 sq km (93,784 sq miles). Although larger than all these islands, as a province of Denmark, Greenland is not eligible for this list.

TOP 10 LARGEST CORAL ISLANDS

	ISLAND / LOCATION	AREA SQ KM	SQ MILES
1	Lifou, Loyalty Islands, New Caledonia	1,146.2	442.6
2	Muyua, Trobriand Islands, Papua New Guinea	873.9	337.4
3	Rennell, Solomon Islands	660.1	248.9
4	Mare, Loyalty Islands, New Caledonia	656.6	253.5
5	Grande Terre, Guadeloupe	639.0	246.7
6	Guam	541.0	208.9
7	Acklins, Bahamas	507.5	195.9
8	Crooked, Bahamas	282.1	109.9
9	Kiriwina, Trobriand Islands, Papua New Guinea	266.5	102.9
10	Niue	263.7	101.8

Source: United Nations Environment Programme (UNEP)

These islands are all believed to be either raised coral or limestone atolls, although some may be combined with older volcanic structures – as is the largest, Lifou, which formed round a submerged volcano, and Guam, which comprises both a limestone plateau and dormant volcanoes.

TOP 10 LARGEST GREAT LAKE ISLANDS

	ISLAND	LAKE	LOCATION	AREA SQ KM	SQ MILES
1	Manitoulin	Huron	Ontario	2,766	1,068
2	Isle Royale	Superior	Michigan	536	207
3	St Joseph	Huron	Ontario	365	141
4	Drummond	Huron	Michigan	347	134
5	Saint Ignace	Superior	Ontario	274	106
6	Michipicoten	Superior	Ontario	184	71
7	Beaver	Michigan	Michigan	145	56
8	Cockburn	Huron	Ontario	139	54
9	Sugar	George/Nicolet	Michigan	128	49
10	Wolfe	Ontario	Ontario	124	48

Manitoulin, the largest of the Great Lakes' approximately 35,000 islands, is ranked 31st largest in Canada and 173rd in the world. It has more lakes within it than any other island in the world – a total of 110. Some of these, in turn, have their own islands. Manitoulin's 12,600 population expands to some 50,000 in the summer, making it the most populated lake island: other Great Lake islands have a low – or, in the case of Isle Royale no – permanent population.

Peak activity
Mount Kerinci, an active volcano, dominates the Kerinci Seblat National Park in Sumatra, the world's sixth-largest island.

TOP 10 **LARGEST ISLANDS**

ISLAND / LOCATION	AREA*	
	SQ KM	SQ MILES
1 Greenland (Kalaatdlit Nunaat)	2,175,600	840,004
2 New Guinea, Papua New Guinea/ Indonesia	785,753	303,381
3 Borneo, Indonesia/Malaysia/Brunei	748,168	288,869
4 Madagascar	587,713	226,917
5 Baffin Island, Canada	503,944	194,574
6 Sumatra, Indonesia	443,065	171,068
7 Honshu, Japan	227,413	87,805
8 Great Britain	218,077	84,200
9 Victoria Island, Canada	217,292	83,897
10 Ellesmere Island, Canada	196,236	75,767

* Mainlands, including areas of inland water, but excluding offshore islands

Australia is regarded as a continental land mass rather than an island, otherwise it would rank first, at 7,618,493 sq km (2,941,517 sq miles), or 35 times the size of Great Britain.

TOP 10 **LARGEST VOLCANIC ISLANDS**

ISLAND / LOCATION / TYPE	AREA	
	SQ KM	SQ MILES
1 Sumatra, Indonesia Active volcanic	443,065.8	171,068.7
2 Honshu, Japan Volcanic	225,800.3	87,182.0
3 Java, Indonesia Volcanic	138,793.6	53,588.5
4 North Island, New Zealand Volcanic	111,582.8	43,082.4
5 Luzon, Philippines Active volcanic	109,964.9	42,457.7
6 Iceland Active volcanic	101,826.0	39,315.2
7 Mindanao, Philippines Active volcanic	97,530.0	37,656.5
8 Hokkaido, Japan Active volcanic	78,719.4	30,394.7
9 New Britain, Papua New Guinea Volcanic	35,144.6	13,569.4
10 Halmahera, Indonesia Active volcanic	18,039.6	6,965.1

Source: United Nations Environment Programme (UNEP)

Mountains & Land Features

TOP 10 HIGHEST MOUNTAINS

MOUNTAIN / LOCATION FIRST ASCENT / TEAM NATIONALITY	HEIGHT* M	FT
1 Everest, Nepal/China 29 May 1953, British/New Zealand	8,850	29,035
2 K2 (Chogori), Pakistan/China 31 Jul 1954, Italian	8,611	28,251
3 Kangchenjunga, Nepal/India 25 May 1955, British	8,586	28,169
4 Lhotse, Nepal/China 18 May 1956, Swiss	8,516	27,940
5 Makalu I, Nepal/China 15 May 1955, French	8,485	27,838
6 Cho Oyu, Nepal/China 19 Oct 1954, Austrian	8,188	26,864
7 Dhaulagiri I, Nepal 13 May 1960, Swiss/Austrian	8,167	26,795
8 Manaslu I (Kutang I), Nepal 9 May 1956, Japanese	8,163	26,781
9 Nanga Parbat (Diamir), Pakistan, 3 Jul 1953, German/Austrian	8,125	26,657
10 Anapurna I, Nepal 3 Jun 1950, French	8,091	26,545

* Height of principal peak; lower peaks of the same mountain are excluded

TOP 10 LONGEST MOUNTAIN RANGES

RANGE / LOCATION	LENGTH KM.	MILES
1 Andes, South America	7,242	4,500
2 Rocky Mountains, North America	6,035	3,750
3 Himalayas/Karakoram/Hundu Kush, Asia	3,862	2,400
4 Great Dividing Range, Australia	3,621	2,250
5 Trans-Antarctic Mountains, Antarctica	3,541	2,200
6 Brazilian East Coast Range, Brazil	3,058	1,900
7 Sumatran/Javan Range, Sumatra, Java	2,897	1,800
8 Tien Shan, China	2,253	1,400
9 Eastern Ghats, India	2,092	1,300
10 = Altai, Asia	2,012	1,250
= **Central New Guinean Range**, Papua New Guinea	2,012	1,250
= **Urals**, Russia	2,012	1,250

This Top 10 includes only ranges that are continuous (the Sumatran/Javan Range is divided only by a short interruption between the two islands). The Aleutian Range extends for 2,655 km (1,650 miles), but is fragmented across numerous islands of the north-west Pacific. As well as these ranges that lie above the surface of the Earth, there are also several submarine ranges that are even longer.

TOP 10 LARGEST DESERTS

DESERT / LOCATION / APPROX. AREA (SQ KM/SQ MILES)

This Top 10 presents the approximate areas and ranking of the world's great deserts, which are often broken down into smaller desert regions – the Australian Desert into the Gibson, Great Sandy, Great Victoria and Simpson, for example. The world total is more than double that of the Top 10, at some 35,264,000 sq km (13,616,000 sq miles), or about a quarter of the world's land area.

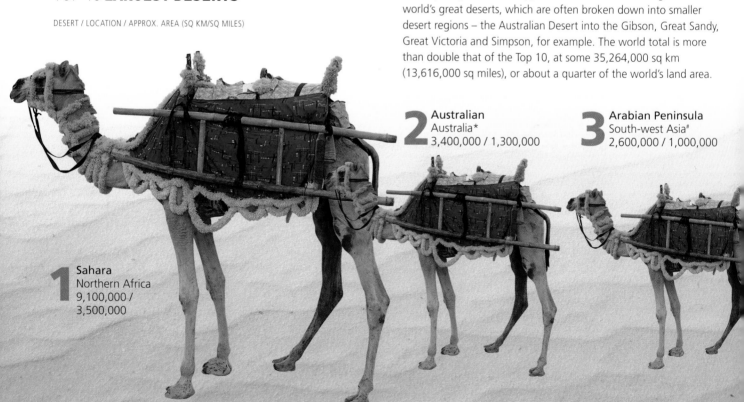

2 Australian
Australia*
3,400,000 / 1,300,000

3 Arabian Peninsula
South-west Asia#
2,600,000 / 1,000,000

1 Sahara
Northern Africa
9,100,000 /
3,500,000

TOP 10 **LONGEST CAVES**

CAVE / LOCATION	TOTAL KNOWN LENGTH KM	MILES
1 Mammoth Cave System, Kentucky, USA	590.6	367
2 Jewel Cave, South Dakota, USA	225.4	140
3 Optimisticeskaja, Ukraine	215.0	134
4 Wind Cave, South Dakota, USA	200.8	125
5 Lechuguilla Cave, New Mexico, USA	196.0	122
6 Hölloch, Switzerland	194.2	121
7 Fisher Ridge System, Kentucky, USA	177.3	110
8 Sistema Ox Bel Ha*, Mexico	164.4	102
9 Sistema Sac Actun*, Mexico	157.5	98
10 Siebenhengste-hohgant, Switzerland	154.0	96

* Underwater cave

The World's Deepest Cave

At 2,190 m (7,185 ft) the Voronya or Krubera Cave, Georgia, is the world's deepest cave. In January 2001 a team of Ukrainian cave explorers found a branch that extended to a record 1,710 m (5,610 ft). Progressively deeper penetrations have taken its extent to more than seven times the height of the Eiffel Tower.

* Includes Gibson, Great Sandy, Great Victoria and Simpson
\# Includes an-Nafud and Rub al-Khali
† Includes Kara-Kum and Kyzylkum
§ Includes Great Basin, Mojave, Sonorah and Chihuahuan

Mammoth cave
The Mammoth Cave System, Kentucky, is the world's most extensive. It became a US National Park in 1941 and was designated a World Heritage Site in 1981.

4 Turkestan
Central Asia†
1,900,000 / 750,000

5 = Gobi
Central Asia
1,300,000 / 500,000

= North American Desert
USA/Mexico§
1,300,000 / 500,000

7 Patagonia
Southern Argentina
670,000 / 260,000

8 Thar
North-west India/
Pakistan
600,000 / 230,000

9 Kalahari
South-western Africa
570,000 / 220,000

10 Takla Makan
North-western China
480,000 /
185,000

World Weather

TOP 10 **WETTEST PLACES – AVERAGE**

LOCATION* / AVERAGE ANNUAL RAINFALL# (MM / IN)

* Maximum of two places per country listed
# Annual rainfall total, averaged over a long period of years

Source: Philip Eden

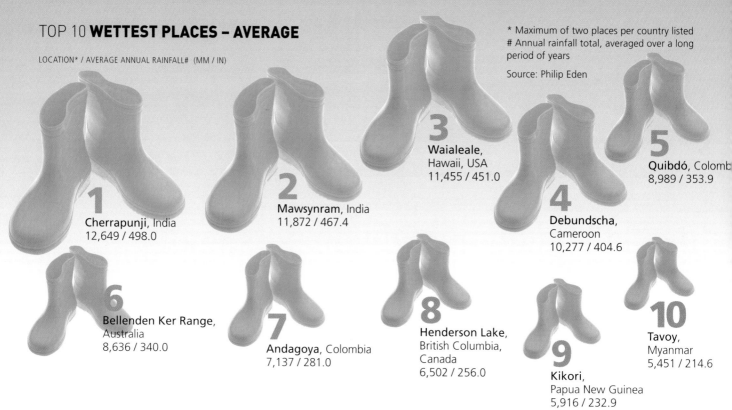

1
Cherrapunji, India
12,649 / 498.0

2
Mawsynram, India
11,872 / 467.4

3
Waialeale,
Hawaii, USA
11,455 / 451.0

4
Debundscha,
Cameroon
10,277 / 404.6

5
Quibdó, Colomb
8,989 / 353.9

6
Bellenden Ker Range,
Australia
8,636 / 340.0

7
Andagoya, Colombia
7,137 / 281.0

8
Henderson Lake,
British Columbia,
Canada
6,502 / 256.0

9
Kikori,
Papua New Guinea
5,916 / 232.9

10
Tavoy,
Myanmar
5,451 / 214.6

TOP 10 **PLACES WITH THE HEAVIEST DAILY DOWNPOURS***

LOCATION# / HIGHEST RAINFALL RECORDED IN 24 HOURS (MM / IN)

* Based on limited data
# Maximum of two places per country listed

Source: Philip Eden

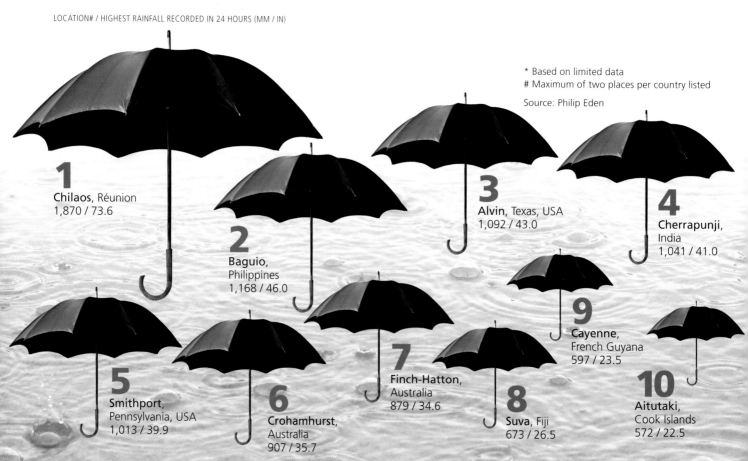

1
Chilaos, Réunion
1,870 / 73.6

2
Baguio,
Philippines
1,168 / 46.0

3
Alvin, Texas, USA
1,092 / 43.0

4
Cherrapunji,
India
1,041 / 41.0

5
Smithport,
Pennsylvania, USA
1,013 / 39.9

6
Crohamhurst,
Australia
907 / 35.7

7
Finch-Hatton,
Australia
879 / 34.6

8
Suva, Fiji
673 / 26.5

9
Cayenne,
French Guyana
597 / 23.5

10
Aitutaki,
Cook Islands
572 / 22.5

TOP 10 COLDEST PLACES – AVERAGE*

	LOCATION#	AVERAGE TEMPERATURE °C	°F
1	Plateau†, Antarctica	-56.7	-70.0
2	Amundsen-Scott†, Antarctica	-49.0	-56.2
3	Northice†, Greenland	-30.0	-22.0
4	Eismitte†, Greenland	-29.2	-20.5
5	Resolute, NWT, Canada	-24.2	-11.6
6	Eureka, NWT, Canada	-19.7	-3.5
7	Ostrov Bol'shoy, Lyakhovskiy, Russia	-14.7	5.5
8	Barrow Point, Alaska, USA	-12.3	9.8
9	Barter Island, Alaska, USA	-12.1	10.2
10	Ostrov Vrangela, Russia	-11.7	11.0

* Lowest long-term temperature averaged throughout the year
# Maximum of two places per country listed
† Present or former scientific research base

Source: Philip Eden

TOP 10 PLACES WITH THE MOST CONTRASTING SEASONS*

	LOCATION#	WINTER °C	°F	SUMMER °C	°F	DIFFERENCE °C	°F
1	Verkhoyansk, Russia	-50.3	-58.5	13.6	56.5	63.9	115.0
2	Yakutsk, Russia	-45.0	-49.0	17.5	63.5	62.5	112.5
3	Manzhouli, China	-26.1	-15.0	20.6	69.0	46.7	84.0
4	Fort Yukon, Alaska, USA	-29.0	-20.2	16.3	61.4	45.3	81.6
5	Fort Good Hope, Northwest Territory, Canada	-29.9	-21.8	15.3	59.5	45.2	81.3
6	Brochet, Manitoba, Canada	-29.2	-20.5	15.4	59.7	44.6	80.2
7	Tunka, Mongolia	-26.7	-16.0	16.1	61.0	42.8	77.0
8	Fairbanks, Alaska, USA	-24.0	-11.2	15.6	60.1	39.6	71.3
9	Semipalatinsk, Kazakhstan	-17.7	0.5	20.6	69.0	38.3	68.5
10	Jorgen Bronlund Fjørd, Greenland	-30.9	-23.6	6.4	43.5	37.3	67.1

* Biggest differences between mean monthly temperatures in summer and winter
# Maximum of two places per country listed

Source: Philip Eden

TOP 10 HOTTEST PLACES – AVERAGE

	LOCATION*	AVERAGE TEMPERATURE# °C	°F
1	Dalol, Ethiopia	34.6	94.3
2	Assab, Eritrea	30.4	86.8
3	Néma, Mauritania	30.3	86.5
4	Berbera, Somalia	30.1	86.2
5	Hombori, Mali	30.1	86.1
6	Perm Island, South Yemen	30.0	86.0
7	Djibouti, Djibouti	29.9	85.8
8	Atbara, Sudan	29.8	85.7
9	=Bender Qaasim, Somalia	29.7	85.5
	=Kamaran Island, North Yemen	29.7	85.5

* Maximum of two places per country listed
# Highest long-term temperature averaged throughout the year

Source: Philip Eden

TOP 10 DRIEST PLACES – AVERAGE

	LOCATION*	AVERAGE ANNUAL RAINFALL# MM	IN
1	Arica, Chile	0.7	0.03
2	=Al'Kufrah, Peru	0.8	0.03
	=Aswân, Egypt	0.8	0.03
	=Luxor, Egypt	0.8	0.03
5	Ica, Peru	2.3	0.09
6	Wadi Halfa, Sudan	2.6	0.10
7	Iquique, Chile	5.0	0.20
8	Pelican Point, Namibia	8.0	0.03
9	=Aoulef, Algeria	12.0	0.32
	=Callao, Peru	12.0	0.32

* Maximum of two places per country listed
# Annual total averaged over a long period of years

Source: Philip Eden

Natural Disasters

THE 10 COUNTRIES WITH THE MOST DEATHS FROM NATURAL DISASTERS*

COUNTRY / EST. DEATHS FROM NATURAL DISASTERS, 1900–2007

China
12,619,280

India
9,108,609

Soviet Union
3,868,434

Bangladesh
2,970,175

Ethiopia
415,837

Indonesia
237,091

Japan
221,719

Uganda
203,611

Niger
193,999

Pakistan
169,471

UK 4,884
World total 31,849,838

* Includes deaths from drought, earthquakes, epidemics, extreme
temperatures, floods, insect infestations, landslides, volcanoes,
waves/surges, wildfires, windstorms

Source: EM-DAT, CRED, University of Louvain, Belgium

THE 10 WORST HURRICANES, TYPHOONS AND CYCLONES

	LOCATION	DATE	ESTIMATED NO. KILLED
1	Ganges Delta, Bangladesh	13 Nov 1970	500,000–1,000,000
2	Bengal, India	7 Oct 1737	>300,000
3 =	Coringa, India	25 Nov 1839	300,000
=	Haiphong, Vietnam	8 Oct 1881	300,000
5	Bengal, India	31 Oct 1876	200,000
6	Ganges Delta, Bangladesh	29 Apr 1991	138,000
7	Bombay, India	6 Jun 1882	>100,000
8	Southern Japan	23 Aug 1281	68,000
9	North-east China	2–3 Aug 1922	60,000
10	Calcutta, India	5 Oct 1864	50,000–70,000

The cyclone of 1970 hit the Bay of Bengal with winds of over 190
km/h (120 mph). Loss of life was worst in the Bhola region, as a
result of which it is often known as the Bhola cyclone. The cyclone
that struck India in 1737 churned the river and sea into a 12-m
(40-ft) storm surge, flooding land and destroying 20,000 ships.

THE 10 WORST EARTHQUAKES

	LOCATION	DATE	EST. NO. KILLED
1	Near East/Mediterranean	20 May 1202	1,100,000
2	Shenshi, China	2 Feb 1556	820,000
3	Calcutta, India	11 Oct 1737	300,000
4	Antioch, Syria	20 May AD 526	250,000
5	Tang-shan, China	28 Jul 1976	242,419
6	Nan-Shan, China	22 May 1927	200,000
7	Yeddo, Japan	30 Dec 1703	190,000
8	Kansu, China	16 Dec 1920	180,000
9	Messina, Italy	28 Dec 1908	160,000
10	Tokyo/Yokohama, Japan	1 Sep 1923	142,807

There are some discrepancies between the 'official' death tolls in
many of the world's worst earthquakes and the estimates of other
authorities. A figure of 750,000 is sometimes quoted for the Tang-
shan earthquake of 1976. Several other earthquakes in China and
Turkey resulted in deaths of 100,000 or more. In recent times, the
Armenian earthquake of 7 December 1988 and that which struck
north-west Iran on 21 June 1990 resulted in the deaths of over
55,000 (official estimate 28,854) and 50,000 respectively. One
of the most famous earthquakes – that which destroyed San
Francisco on 18 April 1906 – killed between 500 and 1,000,
mostly in the fires that followed the shock.

THE 10 **WORST VOLCANIC ERUPTIONS**

Aftermath
The devastation and death toll of the eruption of Mont Pelée, Martinique, was the worst of the twentieth century.

LOCATION	DATE	EST. NO. KILLED

1 Tambora, Indonesia — 5–12 Apr 1815 — 92,000
The cataclysmic eruption of Tambora on the island of Sumbawa killed about 10,000 islanders immediately, with a further 82,000 dying subsequently from disease and famine resulting from crops being destroyed. An estimated 1.7 million tonnes of ash were hurled into the atmosphere.

2 Krakatoa, Sumatra/Java — 26–27 Aug 1883 — 36,380
After a series of eruptions over the course of several days, the uninhabited island of Krakatoa exploded with what may have been the biggest bang ever heard by humans, audible up to 4,800 km (3,000 miles) away.

3 Mont Pelée, Martinique — 8 May 1902 — 27,000
After lying dormant for centuries, Mont Pelée began to erupt in April 1902. Assured that there was no danger, the residents of the main city, St Pierre, stayed in their homes and were there when at 7.30 a.m. on 8 May the volcano burst apart.

4 Nevado del Ruiz, Colombia — 13 Nov 1985 — 22,940
The Andean volcano gave warning signs of erupting, but by the time local inhabitants began to evacuate, it was too late.

5 Mount Etna, Sicily — 11 Mar 1669 — up to 20,000
Europe's largest volcano (3,280 m/10,760 ft) has erupted frequently, but the worst instance occurred in 1669 when the lava flow engulfed the town of Catania – according to some accounts killing as many as 20,000.

6 Mount Etna, Sicily — 1169 — >15,000
Large numbers died in Catania cathedral, where they believed they would be safe, and more were killed when a tsunami caused by the eruption hit the port of Messina.

7 Unzen, Japan — 1 Apr 1792 — 14,300
During a period of intense volcanic activity in the area, the island of Unzen (or Unsen) completely disappeared, killing all its inhabitants.

8 Laki, Iceland — Jan–Jun 1783 — 9,350
Iceland is one the most volcanically active places on Earth, but being sparsely populated eruptions seldom result in major loss of life. The worst exception occurred at the Laki volcanic ridge, culminating on 11 June with the largest lava flow ever recorded.

9 Kelut, Indonesia — 19 May 1919 — 5,110
Dormant since 1901, Kelut erupted without warning, ejecting a crater lake that killed inhabitants by drowning or in resultant mudslides. The volcano remains active, erupting as recently as 2007.

10 Galunggung, Indonesia — 8 Oct 1882 — 4,011
Galunggung erupted suddenly, spewing boiling mud, burning sulphur, ash and rocks before finally exploding, destroying a total of 114 villages. A further eruption in 1982 killed 68 people.

2

LIFE ON EARTH

Extinct & Endangered

TOP 10 **HEAVIEST DINOSAURS EVER DISCOVERED**

	NAME	ESTIMATED WEIGHT (TONNES)
1	Bruhathkayosaurus	175–220
2	Amphicoelias	122
3	= Argentinosaurus	80–100
	= Puertasaurus	80–100
5	Argyrosaurus	>80
6	Paralititan	65–80
7	Antarctosaurus	69
8	Sauroposeidon	50–60
9	Brachiosaurus	48–56
10	Supersaurus	40–50

Right: Long leg
Femur of a gigantic Antarctosaurus dinosaur, found in Argentina.

Below: Jumbo sized
Another former inhabitant of Argentina, after which it is named, Argentinosaurus may have weighed as much as ten 10-tonne elephants.

THE 10 **FIRST DINOSAURS TO BE NAMED**

	NAME / MEANING	NAMED BY	YEAR
1	Megalosaurus Great lizard	William Buckland	1824
2	Iguanodon Iguana tooth	Gideon Mantell	1825
3	Hylaeosaurus Woodland lizard	Gideon Mantell	1833
4	Macrodontophion Long tooth snake	A. Zborzewski	1834
5	Palaeosaurus Ancient lizard	Samuel Stutchbury and Henry Riley	1836
6	Thecodontosaurus Socket-toothed lizard	Henry Riley and Samuel Stutchbury	1836
7	Plateosaurus Flat lizard	Hermann von Meyer	1837
8	Poekilopleuron Varying side	Jacques Armand and Eudes-Deslongchamps	1838
9	Cetiosaurus Whale lizard	Richard Owen	1841
10	Cladeiodon Branch tooth	Richard Owen	1841

The name Megalosaurus was proposed by William Buckland (1784–1856), an English geologist. The Iguanodon was identified by Gideon Algernon Mantell (1790–1852). In 1822 he (or perhaps his wife Mary) found teeth that resembled enormous versions of those of the Central American iguana lizard, and hence – first in a letter dated 12 November 1824, and then in an article in *Philosophical Transactions* – suggested the name Iguanodon. A number of dinosaurs had been named before the word 'dinosaur' itself had been coined: 'dinosauria' ('fearfully great lizards') was proposed as a name for the group by Richard Owen in 1842.

Under threat
Indigenous to Borneo, Indonesia, orangutans (whose name means 'man of the forest') are among the country's mammal species in danger of extinction as a result of poaching and habitat destruction.

THE 10 COUNTRIES WITH THE MOST THREATENED BIRD SPECIES

	COUNTRY / TOTAL NO. OF THREATENED BIRDS
1	Brazil 122
2	Indonesia 116
3	Peru 94
4	Colombia 87
5	China 86
6	India 75
7	USA 74
8	New Zealand 70
9	Ecuador 68
10	Philippines 67
	UK 3

Source: 2007 IUCN Red List of Threatened Species

THE 10 COUNTRIES WITH THE MOST THREATENED REPTILE AND AMPHIBIAN SPECIES

	COUNTRY	THREATENED REPTILES	AMPHIBIANS	TOTAL
1	Mexico	95	198	293
2	Colombia	15	209	224
3	Ecuador	10	163	173
4	China	31	85	116
5	India	25	63	88
6	Peru	6	80	86
7	=Australia	38	47	85
	=USA	32	53	85
9	Madagascar	20	55	75
10	Malaysia	21	46	67
	UK	0	0	0

Source: 2007 IUCN Red List of Threatened Species

THE 10 COUNTRIES WITH THE MOST THREATENED MAMMAL SPECIES

	COUNTRY / TOTAL NO. OF THREATENED MAMMALS
1	Indonesia 146
2	India 89
3	China 83
4	Brazil 73
5	Mexico 72
6	Australia 64
7	Papua New Guinea 58
8	Philippines 51
9	Malaysia 50
10	Madagascar 47
	UK 9

Source: 2007 IUCN Red List of Threatened Species

The IUCN Red List system classifies the degree of threat posed to wildlife on a sliding scale from Vulnerable (high risk of extinction in the wild), through Endangered (very high risk of extinction in the wild), to Critically Endangered (facing an extremely high risk of extinction in the wild), with mammals in these countries under threat in any of these categories. The actual threats are many and varied, and include both human activities and natural events, ranging from habitat loss and degradation, invasions by alien species, hunting and accidental destruction to persecution, pollution and natural disasters.

Sea Creatures

TOP 10 FASTEST FISH

	FISH / SCIENTIFIC NAME	MAX. RECORDED SPEED KM/H	MPH
1	Sailfish (*Istiophorus platypterus*)	112	69
2	Striped marlin (*Tetrapturus audax*)	80	50
3	Wahoo (peto, jack mackerel) (*Acanthocybium solandri*)	77	48
4	Southern bluefin tuna (*Thunnus maccoyii*)	76	47
5	Yellowfin tuna (*Thunnus albacares*)	74	46
6	Blue shark (*Prionace glauca*)	69	43
7 =	Bonefish (*Albula vulpes*)	64	40
=	Swordfish (*Xiphias gladius*)	64	40
9	Tarpon (ox-eye herring) (*Megalops cyprinoides*)	56	35
10	Tiger shark (*Galeocerdo cuvier*)	53	33

Source: Lucy T. Verma

Jaws of death
The great white shark, star of the Jaws films, is rightly feared as the type responsible for 38 per cent of all recorded attacks and 47 per cent of fatalities.

TOP 10 LONGEST-LIVED MARINE ANIMALS

	ANIMAL / SCIENTIFIC NAME	MAX. LIFESPAN (YEARS)
1	Quahog (marine clam) (*Arctica islandica*)	220*
2	Bowhead whale (*Balaena mysticetus*)	200
3 =	Alligator snapping turtle (*Macrochelys temminckii*)	150
=	Whale shark (*Rhincodon typus*)	150
5	Sea anemone (*Actina mesembryanthemum*, etc.)	90
6	European eel (*Anguilla anguilla*)	88
7	Lake sturgeon (*Acipenser fulvescens*)	82
8	Freshwater mussel (*Palaeoheterodonta* – various)	80
9	Dugong (*Dugong dugon*)	73
10	Spiny dogfish (*Squalus acanthias*)	70

* Claim of 405-year old specimen caught off Iceland in 2007

At the other end of the scale, several fish have lifespans that are completed within a year, among them the white goby, top minnow, seahorse, dwarf pygmy goby and ice fish, while the tropical killifish seldom lives for more than about eight months.

Ancient Ocean Quahog

Although a 220-year-old quahog clam found in 1982 holds the official record as the longest-lived animal, a specimen of *Arctica islandica*, the ocean quahog, discovered off the Iceland coast and studied at Bangor University, Wales, in 2007, was found to have some 405 annual growth rings, indicating it may have been alive when Shakespeare was writing *Hamlet*.

THE 10 TYPES OF SHARK THAT HAVE KILLED THE MOST HUMANS

SHARK SPECIES   UNPROVOKED ATTACKS* TOTAL / FATALITIES#

1 Great white 237 / 64

2 Tiger 88 / 28

3 Bull 77 / 23

4 Requiem (species) 30 / 8

5 Blue 12 / 4

6 = Sand tiger 30 / 2

= Shortfin mako 8 / 2

8 = Blacktip 28 / 1

= Oceanic whitetip 5 / 1

= Dusky 3 / 1

= Galapagos 1 / 1

* 1580–2007   # Where fatalities are equal, entries are ranked by total attacks

Source: International Shark Attack File, Florida Museum of Natural History

Aquatic acrobatics
A vulnerable species numbering some 70,000 worldwide, the surprisingly agile humpback whale may weigh as much as 36 tonnes.

TOP 10 **LARGEST WHALES**

SPECIES / SCIENTIFIC NAME	LENGTH (RANGE)	
	M	FT
1 Blue whale (*Balaenoptera musculus*)	21–27	69–88.5
2 Fin whale (*Balaenoptera physalus*)	18–22	59–72.25
3 Bowhead whale (*Balaena mysticetus*)	14–18	46–59
4 Sei whale (*Balaenoptera borealis*)	12–16	39.5–52.5
5 = Northern/Southern right whale (*Eubalaenaglacialis/Eubalaena australis*)	11–18	36–59
= Sperm whale (*Physeter macrocephalus*)	11–18	36–59
7 Gray whale (*Eschrichtius robustus*)	12–14	39.5–46
8 Humpback whale (*Megaptera novaeangliae*)	11.5–15	37.75–49.25
9 Bryde's whale (*Balaenoptera brydei*)	11.5–14.5	37.75–47.5
10 Baird's beaked whale (*Berardius bairdii*)	10.7–12.8	35–42

TOP 10 **HEAVIEST SPECIES OF SALTWATER FISH CAUGHT**

SPECIES / SCIENTIFIC NAME	ANGLER / LOCATION / DATE	WEIGHT			
		KG	G	LB	OZ
1 Great white shark (*Carcharodon carcharias*)	Alfred Dean, Ceduna, South Australia, 21 Apr 1959	1,208	380	2,664	0
2 Tiger shark (*Galeocerdo cuvier*)	Kevin James Clapson, Ulladulla, Australia, 28 Mar 2004	809	975	1,785	11
3 Greenland shark (*Somniosus Microcephalus*)	Terje Nordtvedt, Trondheimsfjord, Norway, 18 Oct 1987	774	991	1,708	9
4 Black marlin (*Istiompax marlina*)	Alfred C. Glassell Jr, Cabo Blanco, Peru, 4 Aug 1953	707	610	1,560	0
5 Bluefin tuna (*Thunnus thynnus*)	Ken Fraser, Aulds Cove, Nova Scotia, Canada, 26 Oct 1979	678	580	1,496	0
6 Atlantic blue marlin (*Makaira nigricans*)	Paulo Amorim, Vitoria, Brazil, 29 Feb 1992	636	993	1,402	2
7 Pacific blue marlin (*Makaira nigricans*)	Jay W. de Beaubien, Kaaiwi Point, Kona, 31 May 1982	624	140	1,376	0
8 Sixgilled shark (*Hexanchus griseus*)	Clemens Rump, Ascension Island, 21 Nov 2002	588	760	1,298	0
9 Great hammerhead shark (*Sphyrna mokarran*)	Bucky Dennis, Boca Grande, Florida, USA, 23 May 2006	580	598	1,280	0
10 Shortfin mako shark (*Isurus oxyrinchus*)	Luke Sweeney, Chatham, Massachusetts, USA, 21 Jul 2001	553	840	1,221	0

Source: International Game Fish Association

Land Mammals

THE 10 SLOWEST MAMMALS

	MAMMAL / SCIENTIFIC NAME	AVERAGE SPEED*	
		KM/H	MPH
1	Three-toed sloth (*Bradypus variegatus*)	0.1–0.3	0.06–0.19
2	Short-tailed (giant mole) shrew (*Blarina brevicauda*)	2.2	1.4
3	= Pine vole (*Microtus pinetorum*)	4.2	2.6
	= Red-backed vole (*Clethrionomys gapperi*)	4.2	2.6
5	Opossum (order *Didelphimorphia*)	4.4	2.7
6	Deer mouse (order *Peromyscus*)	4.5	2.8
7	Woodland jumping mouse (*Napaeozapus insignis*)	5.3	3.3
8	Meadow jumping mouse (*Zapus hudsonius*)	5.5	3.4
9	Meadow mouse or meadow vole (*Microtus pennsylvanicus*)	6.6	4.1
10	White-footed mouse (*Peromyscus leucopus*)	6.8	4.2

* Of those species for which data available

TOP 10 LAND ANIMALS WITH THE BIGGEST BRAINS

	ANIMAL SPECIES	AVERAGE BRAIN WEIGHT		
		G	LB	OZ
1	Elephant	6,000	13	4
2	Adult human	1,350	3	0
3	Camel	762	1	11
4	Giraffe	680	1	8
5	Hippopotamus	582	1	4
6	Horse	532	1	3
7	Gorilla	500	1	1
8	Polar bear	498	1	1
9	Cow	445	0	15
10	Chimpanzee	420	0	15

Brain power
Elephant brain (background) in comparison with the brain of an adult human (red) and a chimpanzee (blue).

TOP 10 SLEEPIEST MAMMALS

ANIMAL / SCIENTIFIC NAME / AVERAGE HOURS OF SLEEP PER DAY

 = Lion (*Panthera leo*) 20
= Three-toed sloth (*Bradypus variegatus*) 20

 Little brown bat (*Myotis lucifugus*) 19.9

 Big brown bat (*Eptesicus fuscus*) 19.7

 = Opossum (*Didelphis virginiana*) 19.4
= Water opossum (Yapok) (*Chironectes minimus*) 19.4

 Giant armadillo (*Priodontes maximus*) 18.1

 Koala (*Phascolarctos cinereus*) up to 18

 Nine-banded armadillo (*Dasypus novemcinctus*) 17.4

 Southern owl monkey (*Aotus azarai*) 17.0

The list excludes periods of hibernation, which can last up to several months among creatures such as the ground squirrel, marmot and brown bear. Marsupials such as the pygmy possum may remain dormant for a year.

Weighty weight
The lengthy gestation of an African elephant is
380 days longer than the average for a human.

TOP 10 **FASTEST MAMMALS**

MAMMAL / SCIENTIFIC NAME / MAX. RECORDED SPEED* KM/H / MPH

Cheetah (*Acinonyx jubatus*) 114 / 71

1

Pronghorn antelope (*Antilocapra americana*) 95 / 57

2

= Blue wildebeest (brindled gnu)
(*Connochaetes taurinus*) 80 / 50
= Lion (*Panthera leo*) 80 / 50
= Springbok (*Antidorcas marsupialis*) 80 / 50

3

= Brown hare (*Lepus capensis*) 77 / 48
= Red fox (*Vulpes vulpes*) 77 / 48

6

= Grant's gazelle (*Gazella granti*) 76 / 47
= Thomson's gazelle
(*Gazella thomsonii*) 76 / 47

8

Horse (*Equus caballus*) 72 / 45

10

* Of those species for which data available

TOP 10 **MAMMALS WITH THE LONGEST GESTATION PERIODS**

MAMMAL / SCIENTIFIC NAME	AVERAGE GESTATION (DAYS)
1 African elephant (*Loxodonta africana*)	660
2 Asiatic elephant (*Elephas maximus*)	600
3 White rhinoceros (*Ceratotherium simum*)	490
4 Walrus (*Odobenus rosmarus*)	480
5 = Black rhinoceros (*Diceros bicornis*)	450
= Giraffe (*Giraffa camelopardalis*)	450
7 Bactrian camel (dromedary) (*Camelus bactrianus*)	410
8 Tapir (*Tapirus*)	400
9 Arabian camel (dromedary) (*Camelus dromedarius*)	390
10 Grant's zebra (*Equus quagga*)	365

Fastest feline
The cheetah is capable of accelerating faster than
most sports cars, and holds the world record
speed for a land animal over short distances.

Creepy Crawlies

Long story
For over a century naturalists have sought to confirm the existence of giant anacondas, so far without success.

TOP 10 **LONGEST SNAKES**

SNAKE / SCIENTIFIC NAME	MAX. LENGTH M	FT
1 Reticulated (royal) python (*Python reticulatus*)	10.0	32
2 Anaconda (*Eunectes murinus*)	8.5	28
3 Indian python (*Python molurus molurus*)	7.6	25
4 Diamond python (*Morelia spilota spilota*)	6.4	21
5 King cobra (*Opiophagus hannah*)	5.8	19
6 Boa constrictor (*Boa constrictor*)	4.9	16
7 Bushmaster (*Lachesis muta*)	3.7	12
8 Giant brown snake (*Oxyuranus scutellatus*)	3.4	11
9 Diamondback rattlesnake (*Crotalus atrox*)	2.7	9
10 Indigo or gopher snake (*Drymarchon corais*)	2.4	8

US president and hunting enthusiast Theodore Roosevelt offered $1,000 reward for an anaconda of more than 9 m (30 ft). The prize now stands at $50,000, but remains unclaimed. The four largest snakes are all constrictors; the king cobra is the longest venomous snake.

THE 10 **DEADLIEST SNAKES**

SNAKE / SCIENTIFIC NAME	EST. LETHAL DOSE FOR HUMANS (MG)	AVERAGE VENOM PER BITE (MG)	POTENTI HUMA KILL PER B
1 Coastal taipan (*Oxyuranus scutellatus*)	1	120	12
2 Common krait (*Bungarus caeruleus*)	0.5	42	8
3 Philippine cobra (*Naja naja philippinensis*)	2	120	6
4 = King cobra (*Ophiophagus hannah*)	20	1,000	5
= Russell's viper (*Daboia russelli*)	3	150	5
6 Black mamba (*Dendroaspis polyepis*)	3	135	4
7 Yellow-jawed tommygoff (*Bothrops asper*)	25	1,000	4
8 = Multibanded krait (*Bungarus multicinctus*)	0.8	28	3
= Tiger snake (*Notechis scutatus*)	1	35	3
10 Jararacussu (*Bothrops jarararcussu*)	25	800	3

Source: Russell E. Gough

This list takes account of the various factors that determine the relative danger posed by poisonous snakes, including the strength of the venom (and hence the estimated lethal dose for an adult), and the typical amount injected per bite.

Along came a spider
The Heteropoda maxima *huntsman spiders of Laos have a legspan of up to 30 cm (1 ft).*

TOP 10 **MOST COMMON INSECTS***

SPECIES / SCIENTIFIC NAME	APPROX. NO. OF KNOWN SPECIES
1 Beetles (*Coleoptera*)	400,000
2 Ants, bees and wasps (*Hymenoptera*)	250,000
3 Butterflies and moths (*Lepidoptera*)	190,000
4 True flies (*Diptera*)	120,000
5 True bugs (*Hemiptera*)	100,000
6 Crickets, grasshoppers and locusts (*Orthoptera*)	20,000
7 Caddisflies (*Trichoptera*)	12,627
8 Dragonflies and damselflies (Odonata)	5,600
9 Lice (*Phthiraptera/Psocoptera*)	5,000
10 Lacewings (*Neuroptera*)	4,700

* By number of known species

Triton's trumpet trumps
The Triton's trumpet sea snail is among the biggest marine snails. The largest land gastropod, the giant Ghana snail, measures barely half its size.

TOP 10 **LARGEST SNAILS**

SNAIL / SCIENTIFIC NAME	LENGTH	
	MM	IN
1 Australian trumpet (*Syrinx aruanus*)	770	30.3
2 Horse conch (*Pleuroploc filamentosa*)	580	22.8
3 = Baler shell (*Voluta amphora*)	480	18.8
= Triton's trumpet (*Charonia tritonis*)	480	18.8
5 Beck's volute (*Voluta becki*)	470	18.5
6 Umbilicate volute (*Voluta umbilicalis*)	420	16.5
7 Madagascar helmet (*Cassis madagascariensis*)	409	16.1
8 Spider conch (*Lambis truncata*)	400	15.7
9 Knobbly trumpet (*Charonia nodifera*)	390	15.3
10 Goliath conch (*Strombus goliath*)	380	14.9

TOP 10 **LARGEST SPIDERS**

	SPECIES	LEGSPAN	
		MM	IN
1	Huntsman spider (*Heteropoda maxima*)	300	11.8
2	Brazilian salmon pink (*Lasiodora parahybana*)	270	10.6
3	Brazilian ginat tawny red (Grammostola mollicoma)	260	10.2
4	= Goliath tarantula or bird-eating spider (*Theraphosa blondi*)	254	10.0
	= Wolf spider (*Cupiennius sallei*)	254	10.0
6	= Purple bloom bird-eating (*Xenesthis immanis*)	230	9.1
	= Xenesthis monstrosa	230	9.1
8	Hercules baboon (*Hysterocrates hercules*)	203	8.0
9	Hysterocrates sp.	178	7.0
10	Tegenaria parietin	140	5.5

It should be noted that although these represent the average legspans of the world's largest spiders, their body size is often considerably smaller: that of the *Lasiodora*, found in Brazil, is around 92 mm (3.6 in), while that of the *Tegenaris parietina*, the largest spider found in Britain, may measure as little as 18 mm (0.7 in).

Birdlife

TOP 10 **HEAVIEST FLIGHTED BIRDS***

BIRD / SCIENTIFIC NAME	WEIGHT		
	KG	LB	OZ
1 Mute swan (*Cygnus olor*)	22.50	49	6
2 Kori bustard (*Ardeotis kori*)	19.00	41	8
3 = Andean condor (*Vultur gryphus*)	15.00	33	1
= Great white pelican (*Pelecanus onocrotalus*)	15.00	33	1
5 Eurasian black vulture (*Aegypius monachus*)	12.50	27	5
6 Sarus crane (*Grus antigone*)	12.24	26	9
7 Himalayan griffon (vulture) (*Gyps himalayensis*)	12.00	26	5
8 Wandering albatross (*Diomedea exulans*)	11.30	24	9
9 Steller's sea eagle (*Haliaeetus pelagicus*)	9.00	19	8
10 Marabou stork (*Leptoptilos crumeniferus*)	8.90	19	6

* By species

Source: Chris Mead

Biggest Bird

Aepyornis maximus, the so-called elephant bird, was the largest known bird. It was flightless and stood some 3 m (10 ft) tall, and weighed about 454 kg (1,000 lb). Its eggs, the biggest on record, measured 30 cm (12 in) in length and had a volume equivalent to more than seven ostrich eggs or 180 chicken's eggs. It lived only on the island of Madagascar and probably became extinct sometime during the seventeenth century.

Heavyweight champion
Exceptionally large specimens of the mute swan establish it as the heaviest of all flighted birds, with a wingspan of more than 2 m (6 ft 7 in).

TOP 10 **FASTEST BIRDS IN FLIGHT**

BIRD / SCIENTIFIC NAME	MAX. RECORDED FLYING SPEED	
	KM/H	MPH
1 Common eider (*Somateria mollissima*)	76	47
2 Bewick's swan (*Cygnus columbianus*)	72	44
3 = Barnacle goose (*Branta leucopsis*)	68	42
= Common crane (*Grus grus*)	68	42
5 Mallard (*Anas platyrhynchos*)	65	40
6 = Red-throated diver (*Gavia stellata*)	61	38
= Wood pigeon (*Columba palumbus*)	61	38
8 Oystercatcher (*Haematopus ostralegus*)	58	36
9 = Ring-necked pheasant (*Phasianus colchichus*)	54	33
= White-fronted goose (*Anser albifrons*)	54	33

Source: Chris Mead

TOP 10 **MOST COMMON BREEDING BIRDS IN THE UK**

BIRD / SCIENTIFIC NAME	ESTIMATED NO. OF PAIRS (2000)*
1 Wren (*Troglodytes troglodytes*)	8,512,000
2 Chaffinch (*Fringilla coelebs*)	5,974,000
3 Robin (*Erithacus rubecula*)	5,895,000
4 Blackbird (*Turdus merula*)	4,935,000
5 House sparrow (*Passer domesticus*)	2,100,000–3,675,000
6 Blue tit (*Cyanistes caeruleus*)	3,535,000
7 Wood pigeon (*Columba palumbus*)	2,570,000–3,160,000
8 Willow warbler (*Phylloscopus trochilus*)	2,125,000
9 Northern lapwing (*Vanellus vanellus*)	1,600,000–2,100,000
10 Great tit (*Parus major*)	2,074,000

* Ranked by upper estimate

Source: 'Population estimates of birds in Great Britain and the United Kingdom', *British Birds*, January 2006

Winged wonder
The wandering albatross has a wingspan equal to the height of two 2-m (6-ft) humans.

TOP 10 **BIRDS WITH THE LARGEST WINGSPANS**

BIRD* / SCIENTIFIC NAME	MAX. WINGSPAN CM	IN
1 Wandering albatross# (*Diomedea exulans*)	370	146
2 Great white pelican (*Pelecanus onocrotalus*)	360	141
3 Andean condor (*Vultur gryphus*)	320	126
4 Himalayan griffon (vulture) (*Gyps himalayensis*)	310	122
5 Eurasian black vulture (*Aegypius monachus*)	295	116
6 Marabou stork (*Leptoptilos crumeniferus*)	287	113
7 Lammergeier (*Gypaetus barbatus*)	282	111
8 Sarus crane (*Grus antigone*)	280	110
9 Kori bustard (*Ardeotis kori*)	270	106
10 Steller's sea eagle (*Haliaeetus pelagicus*)	265	104

* By species
# Royal albatross, a close relative, is the same size

Source: Chris Mead

The measurements given are, as far as can be ascertained, for wingtip to wingtip for live birds measured in a natural position – much larger wingspans have been claimed for many species, but dead specimens may easily be stretched by 15 to 20 per cent.

TOP 10 **LONGEST-LIVED RINGED WILD BIRDS**

BIRD / SCIENTIFIC NAME	AGE* YEARS	MONTHS
1 Royal albatross (*Diomedea epomophora*)	50	0
2 Fulmar (*Fulmarus glacialis*)	40	11
3 Manx shearwater (*Puffinus puffinus*)	37	0
4 Gannet (*Morus bassanus*)	36	4
5 Oystercatcher (*Haematopus ostralegus*)	36	0
6 White (Fairy) tern (*Gygis alba*)	35	11
7 Common eider (*Somateria mollissima*)	35	0
8 Lesser Black-backed gull (*Larus fuscus*)	34	10
9 Pink-footed goose (*Anser brachyrhynchus*)	34	2
10 Great frigate bird (*Fregata minor*)	33	9

* Elapsed time between marking and report

Source: Chris Mead

Only by ringing can the true age of a wild bird be reliably monitored. Hard rings, likely to last as long as the bird, started to be used over 50 years ago. Land-based songbirds do not live as long as the slow-breeding seabirds. In general, big birds live longer than small ones, so the tiny Fairy tern (*Sterna nereis*) and Storm petrel (*Hydrobates pelagicus*), at 31 years 11 months, are particularly noteworthy. Records of birds in captivity are even more impressive.

Cats & Dogs

TOP 10 PEDIGREE CAT BREEDS IN THE UK

BREED / NO. REGISTERED BY CAT FANCY (2007)

1. British shorthair 6,618
2. Siamese 3,780
3. Bengal 2,915
4. Persian 2,715
5. Burmese 2,356
6. Ragdoll 2,067
7. Maine coon 2,027
8. Birman 1,619
9. Norwegian forest 1,206
10. Oriental short hair 1,085

Source: The Governing Council of the Cat Fancy

This Top 10 is based on a total of 31,483 cats registered with the Governing Council of the Cat Fancy in 2007.

TOP 10 CATS' NAMES IN THE UK

1. Molly
2. Felix
3. Smudge
4. Sooty
5. Tigger
6. Charlie
7. Alfie
8. Oscar
9. Millie
10. Misty

Source: RSPCA 2006 survey

TOP 10 BESTSELLING BRANDS OF CAT FOOD

BRAND / MANUFACTURER / % BRAND SHARE BY VALUE

1. Whiskas (Mars) 14.4
2. Friskies (Nestlé) 12.4
3. Iams (Procter & Gamble) 5.6
4. Felix (Nestlé) 4.6
5. Hill's Science Diet (Colgate-Palmolive) 4.4
6. Kitekat (Mars) 4.3
7. = Cat Chow (Nestlé) 2.9
   = Sheba (Mars) 2.9
9. Fancy Feast (Nestlé) 1.9
10. = Meow Mix (Meow Mix) 1.8
    = 9 Lives (Del Monte Foods) 1.8

Source: Euromonitor International

The world market for prepared cat food grew by 10.4 per cent in the period 2000–05. An estimated 5.2 million tonnes, worth a total of $16.2 billion, were sold globally in 2005.

Left: Top cat
The increasingly popular Maine coon is one of the largest of all domestic cats. Its name derives from the myth that they are the offspring of a cat and a raccoon.

TOP 10 **DOGS' NAMES IN THE UK***

2007		1987
Molly	1	Ben
Jack	2	Sam
Holly	3	Susie
Max	4	Benji
Buster	5	Max
Lucy	6	Lucy
Jake	7	Kim
Barney	8	Lady
Charlie	9	Shelly
Sam	10	Judy

* Including variants (Sam/Sammy, Susie/Suzie, etc.)

Source: Gallup National Dog Survey/Spillers/RSPCA

As was observed in the first *Top 10 of Everything*, 'In the past decade, there has been a definite move away from traditional dogs' names. Ten years ago, the Top 10 list included such evergreen (and specifically canine) names as Shep, Brandy, Whisky, Patch, Butch, Rex and, of course, Rover. Now most of the names could equally be those of people.' Twenty years on, it is clear that this trend has continued.

TOP 10 **PEDIGREE DOG BREEDS IN THE UK**

BREED / NO. REGISTERED BY KENNEL CLUB (2007)

1. Labrador retriever   45,079
2. Cocker spaniel   20,883
3. English springer spaniel   14,702
4. Staffordshire bull terrier   12,167
5. German shepherd dog (Alsatian)   12,116
6. Cavalier King Charles spaniel   11,422
7. Golden retriever   9,557
8. Border terrier   8,814
9. West Highland white terrier   8,309
10. Boxer   8,191

Source: The Kennel Club

TOP 10 **BESTSELLING BRANDS OF DOG FOOD**

BRAND / MANUFACTURER / % BRAND SHARE BY VALUE

1 Pedigree (Mars) 13.2
2 Hill's Science Diet (Colgate-Palmolive) 5.7
3 Iams (Procter & Gamble) 4.7
4 Dog Chow (Nestlé) 4.0
5 Friskies (Nestlé) 2.7
6 Pal (Mars) 2.3
7 Eukanuba (Procter & Gamble) 2.2
8 Alpo (Nestlé) 2.1
9 Royal Canin (Mars) 2.0
10 Cesar (Mars) 1.8

The world market for dog food grew by 17.7 per cent in the period 2000–05. Globally, some 12.6 million tonnes, worth $25.9 billion, were sold in 2005.

Source: Euromonitor International

Livestock

TOP 10 **TYPES OF LIVESTOCK**

ANIMAL / WORLD STOCKS

1 animal represents approx. 500,000,000

1 Chickens 16,365,353,100   **2** Cattle 1,364,950514   **3** Sheep 1,059,810,132   **4** Ducks 1,032,257,000   **5** Pigs 943,762,330

Source (all livestock lists): Food and Agriculture Organization of the United Nations (latest available year)

TOP 10 **CHICKEN COUNTRIES**

	COUNTRY	CHICKENS
1	China	4,214,748,000
2	USA	1,970,000,000
3	Indonesia	1,149,374,000
4	Brazil	1,100,000,000
5 =	India	425,000,000
=	Mexico	425,000,000
7	Russia	328,338,000
8	Iran	290,000,000
9	Japan	284,926,000
10	Turkey	277,533,000
	UK	*157,780,000*
	World total	*16,365,353,100*

TOP 10 **CATTLE COUNTRIES**

	COUNTRY	CATTLE
1	Brazil	204,512,736
2	India	185,500,000
3	China	112,536,523
4	USA	94,888,000
5	Argentina	50,768,000
6	Sudan	38,325,000
7	Ethiopia	38,102,688
8	Mexico	31,700,000
9	Australia	27,460,000
10	Colombia	24,950,000
	UK	*10,551,000*
	World total	*1,364,950,514*

TOP 10 **SHEEP COUNTRIES**

	COUNTRY	SHEEP
1	China	157,330,215
2	Australia	101,300,000
3	India	62,500,000
4	Iran	54,000,000
5	Sudan	48,000,000
6	New Zealand	39,271,000
7	UK	35,848,000
8	Turkey	25,431,000
9	South Africa	25,360,000
10	Pakistan	24,700,000
	World total	*1,059,810,132*

Cash cows
Brazil's ranking as the worlds No.1 cattle country has been achieved at huge cost, as forests have been cleared to create pastureland.

Goats 790,028,397   **7** Rabbits 526,412,890   **8** Geese 295,127,500   **9** Turkeys 276,552,000   **10** Buffaloes 171,954,765

TOP 10 **PIG COUNTRIES**

	COUNTRY	PIGS
1	China	472,895,791
2	USA	60,443,700
3	Brazil	33,085,300
4	Germany	26,495,000
5	Vietnam	26,143,728
6	Spain	24,894,956
7	Poland	16,987,900
8	Russia	15,979,833
9	France	15,004,320
10	Mexico	14,625,199
	UK	*5,161,000*
	World total	*943,762,330*

TOP 10 **TURKEY COUNTRIES**

	COUNTRY	TURKEYS
1	USA	88,000,000
2	France	33,648,000
3	Chile	25,700,000
4	Italy	25,000,000
5	Brazil	16,200,000
6	Germany	9,000,000
7	UK	8,300,000
8	Portugal	7,000,000
9	Slovakia	5,800,000
10	Canada	5,520,000
	World total	*276,552,000*

TOP 10 **DUCK COUNTRIES**

	COUNTRY	DUCKS
1	China	710,361,000
2	Vietnam	59,000,000
3	India	33,000,000
4	Indonesia	32,572,000
5	France	22,870,000
6	Ukraine	20,000,000
7	Malaysia	16,000,000
8	Thailand	15,649,000
9	Bangladesh	11,700,000
10	Philippines	10,211,000
	UK	*1,970,000*
	World total	*1,032,257,000*

Ducks in a row
A major item on the national menu, two of
every three of the world's ducks are in China.

Living off the Land

TOP 10 **FRUIT CROPS**

CROP / ANNUAL PRODUCTION (TONNES)

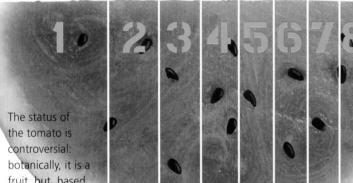

Tomatoes 124,422,207	Watermelons 95,618,577	Bananas 72,653,442	Grapes 67,099,739	Oranges 64,260,568	Apples 63,399,721	Coconuts 54,660,767	Plantains 32,976,476	Cantaloupes and other melons 27,336,989	Mangoes 27,181,020
1	2	3	4	5	6	7	8	9	10

The status of the tomato is controversial: botanically, it is a fruit, but, based on its use in cooking, for legal and import duty purposes certain countries consider it a vegetable.

TOP 10 **VEGETABLE CROPS**

CROP* / ANNUAL PRODUCTION (TONNES)

* Excluding cereals; including only vegetables grown for human and animal consumption

Sugar cane 1,332,144,140	Potatoes 330,300,700	Sugar beets 249,118,499	Soybeans 206,461,698	Sweet potatoes 127,228,146	Cabbages 68,134,983	Onions (dry) 56,922,514	Cucumbers and gherkins 40,947,625	Yams 39,881,003	Aubergines 30,119,664
1	2	3	4	5	6	7	8	9	10

TOP 10 **BANANA-PRODUCING COUNTRIES**

COUNTRY / ANNUAL PRODUCTION (TONNES)

#	Country	Production
1	India	16,820,000
2	Brazil	6,583,564
3	China	6,245,900
4	Ecuador	6,038,077
5	Philippines	5,631,200
6	Indonesia	4,874,439
7	Costa Rica	2,220,000
8	Mexico	2,100,000
9	Thailand	2,000,000
10	Burundi	1,600,000

World total 72,653,442

TOP 10 **CEREAL CROPS**

CROP / ANNUAL PRODUCTION (TONNES)

1 Maize 724,589,004
2 Wheat 632,594,726
3 Rice (paddy) 606,267,950
4 Barley 154,138,969
5 Sorghum 58,710,952
6 Millet 27,768,243
7 Oats 26,055,792
8 Rye 17,651,640
9 Triticale (wheat/rye hybrid) 13,874,440
10 Mixed grain 5,420,259

Source (all lists this page): Food and Agriculture Organization of the United Nations (latest available year)

TOP 10 SUNFLOWER SEED-PRODUCING COUNTRIES

	COUNTRY	ANNUAL PRODUCTION (TONNES)
1	Russia	4,800,710
2	Argentina	3,100,000
3	Ukraine	3,050,100
4	China	1,750,000
5	Romania	1,557,813
6	France	1,461,508
7	India	1,224,000
8	Hungary	1,186,180
9	Bulgaria	1,078,832
10	USA	929,690
	World total	*26,366,554*

Source: Food and Agriculture Organization of the United Nations (latest available year)

Bearing fruit
Of all countries, the USA has undergone the greatest increase in organic acreage as, despite high costs and low yields, the demand for organically grown crops such as strawberries escalates.

TOP 10 ORGANIC FARMING COUNTRIES

	COUNTRY	TOTAL ORGANIC FARMING LAND HECTARES	ACRES
1	Australia	11,800,000	29,158,390
2	Argentina	3,099,427	7,658,839
3	China	2,300,000	5,683,415
4	USA	1,620,351	4,003,968
5	Italy	1,067,102	2,636,862
6	Brazil	842,000	2,080,624
7	Spain	807,569	1,995,543
8	Germany	807,406	1,995,141
9	Uruguay	759,000	1,875,527
10	UK	619,852	1,531,685
	World total	*30,558,183*	*75,510,798*

Source: International Federation of Organic Agriculture Movements, *The World of Organic Agriculture*, 2007

Starting some 70 years ago as a reaction to the use of artificial fertilizers, and for long a minority movement, organic farming has gained such momentum and widespread public support in recent years that the world total area of land devoted to organic production is now, at 305,582 sq km (117,985 sq miles), greater than the size of Italy.

TOP 10 ORGANIC CROPS*

	CROP	TOTAL ORGANIC FARMING LAND HECTARES	ACRES
1	Olives	354,480	875,938
2	Coffee	309,585	765,000
3	Fruits and nuts	168,793	417,096
4	Grapes	103,667	256,166
5	Tropical fruits	98,810	244,164
6	Cocoa	76,726	189,594
7	Citrus fruit	33,508	82,800
8	Tea	30,780	76,059
9	Sugar cane	10,644	26,302
10	Medicinal and aromatic plants	1,744	4,310
	Special crops (oil palm, hops, etc.)	*20,307*	*50,180*
	Other permanent crops	*188,414*	*455,580*

* Permanent crops only

Source: International Federation of Organic Agriculture Movements, *The World of Organic Agriculture*, 2007

In addition to these permanent crops, which occupy a total of 1,393,595 hectares (3,443,643 acres), some 1,445,462 hectares (3,571,809 acres) worldwide are devoted to cereal production.

Trees & Forests

TOP 10 **DEFORESTING COUNTRIES***

COUNTRY / ANNUAL FOREST LOSS (2000–05) SQ KM/SQ MILES

1 AXE REPRESENTS APPROX. 1,000 SQ KM (386 SQ MILES)

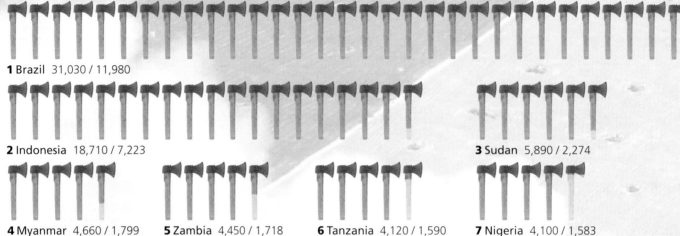

1 Brazil 31,030 / 11,980

2 Indonesia 18,710 / 7,223

3 Sudan 5,890 / 2,274

4 Myanmar 4,660 / 1,799

5 Zambia 4,450 / 1,718

6 Tanzania 4,120 / 1,590

7 Nigeria 4,100 / 1,583

8 Dem. Rep. of Congo
3,190 / 1,231

9 Zimbabwe
3,130 / 1,208

10 Venezuela 2,880 / 1,111

World total 73,170 / 28,251

* Countries for which data available

Source: Food and Agriculture Organization of
the United Nations, *Global Forest Resources
Assessment 2005*

Some 42,510 sq km (16,413 sq miles) of
forest was lost in South America each year
between 2000 and 2005, 40,400 sq km
(15,598 sq miles) in Africa and 38,400 sq km
(14,826 sq miles) in Asia. The total global
loss during the period was 439,020 sq km
(169,506 sq miles), an area equivalent to
more than three times that of the UK.

TOP 10 **REFORESTING COUNTRIES***

COUNTRY / ANNUAL FOREST GAIN (2000–05) SQ KM/SQ MILES

1 TREE REPRESENTS APPROX. 1,000 SQ KM (386 SQ MILES)

1 China 40,480 / 15,629

2 Spain 2,960 / 1,142

3 Vietnam 2,410 / 930

4 USA 1,590 / 613

5 Italy 1,060 / 409

6 Chile
570 / 220

7 Cuba
560 / 216

8 Bulgaria
500 / 193

9 France
410 / 158

10 Portugal
400 / 154

UK 100 / 38

* Countries for which data available

Source: Food and Agriculture
Organization of the United Nations,
*Global Forest Resources Assessment
2005*

TOP 10 COUNTRIES WITH THE LARGEST AREAS OF TROPICAL FOREST

	COUNTRY	AREA SQ KM	AREA SQ MILES
1	Brazil	3,012,730	1,163,222
2	Dem. Rep. of Congo	1,350,710	521,512
3	Indonesia	887,440	343,029
4	Peru	756,360	292,032
5	Bolivia	686,380	265,012
6	Venezuela	556,150	214,730
7	Columbia	531,860	205,352
8	Mexico	457,650	176,700
9	India	444,500	171,622
10	Angola	375,640	145,035
	World total	14,076,490	5,434,964

Source: Food and Agriculture Organization of the United Nations, *State of the World's Forests, 2005*

Brazilian rainforest
Despite losing an area the size of Belgium every year, Brazil retains the world's greatest area of rainforest.

TOP 10 COUNTRIES WITH THE LARGEST AREAS OF FOREST

	COUNTRY	SQ KM	% OF TOTAL	SQ MILES
1	Russia	8,087,900	47.9	3,122,756
2	Brazil	4,776,980	57.2	1,844,402
3	Canada	3,101,340	33.6	1,197,434
4	USA	3,030,890	33.1	1,170,233
5	China	1,972,900	21.2	761,741
6	Australia	1,636,780	21.3	631,964
7	Dem. Rep. of Congo	1,336,100	58.9	515,871
8	Indonesia	884,950	48.8	341,681
9	Peru	687,420	53.7	265,414
10	India	677,010	22.8	261,395
	UK	28,450	11.8	10,985
	World total	39,520,250	30.3	15,258,855

Source: Food and Agriculture Organization of the United Nations, *Global Forest Resources Assessment 2005*

TOP 10 MOST COMMON TREES IN THE UK

	TREE / SCIENTIFIC NAME	% OF TOTAL FOREST AREA
1	Sitka spruce (*Picea sitchensis*)	29
2	Scots pine (*Pinus sylvestris*)	10
3	Oak (*Quercus robur*)	9
4	Birch (*Betula pubescens*)	7
5	Lodgepole pine (*Pinus contorta latifolia*)	6
6	= Ash (*Fraxinus excelsior*)	5
	= Japanese/hybrid larch (*Larix kempferi/Larix x eurolepis*)	5
8	Beech (*Fagus sylvatica*)	4
9	= Norway spruce (*Picea abies*)	3
	= Sycamore (*Acer pseudoplatanus*)	3

Source: Forestry Commission

Seven per cent of the UK's forested areas is classified as mixed broadleaves and one per cent as mixed conifers, a large proportion of which grows in forests managed by the Forestry Commission. This body came into existence as a result of the Forestry Act of 1919, planting its first trees at Eggesford Forest, Devon, on 8 December 1919.

THE HUMAN WORLD

3

The Amazing Human Body

TOP 10 MOST COMMON ELEMENTS IN THE HUMAN BODY

	ELEMENT	SYMBOL	AVERAGE ADULT* TOTAL	
			G	OZ
1	Oxygen#	O	48,800	1,721
2	Carbon	C	18,400	649
3	Hydrogen#	H	8,000	282
4	Nitrogen	N	2,080	73
5	Calcium	Ca	1,120	39.5
6	Phosphorus	P	880	31.0
7	= Potassium	K	160	5.6
	= Sulphur	S	160	5.6
9	Sodium	Na	112	4.0
10	Chlorine	Cl	96	3.4

* 80 kg male
\# Mostly combined as water

The Top 10 elements account for more than 99 per cent of the total, the balance comprising minute quantities of metallic elements including iron – enough (4.8 g/0.17 oz) to make a 15-cm (6-in) nail – as well as zinc, tin and aluminium.

TOP 10 LONGEST BONES IN THE HUMAN BODY

	BONE	AVERAGE LENGTH	
		CM	IN
1	Femur (thighbone – upper leg)	50.50	19.88
2	Tibia (shinbone – inner lower leg)	43.03	16.94
3	Fibula (outer lower leg)	40.50	15.94
4	Humerus (upper arm)	36.46	14.35
5	Ulna (inner lower arm)	28.20	11.10
6	Radius (outer lower arm)	26.42	10.40
7	7th rib	24.00	9.45
8	8th rib	23.00	9.06
9	Innominate bone (hipbone – half pelvis)	18.50	7.28
10	Sternum (breastbone)	17.00	6.69

These are average dimensions of the bones of an adult male measured from their extremities (ribs are curved and the pelvis measurement is taken diagonally). The same bones in the female skeleton are usually six to 13 per cent smaller, with the exception of the sternum, which is virtually identical.

TOP 10 LARGEST HUMAN ORGANS

	ORGAN		AVERAGE WEIGHT	
			G	OZ
1	Skin		10,886	384.0
2	Liver		1,560	55.0
3	Brain	male	1,408	49.7
		female	1,263	44.6
4	Lungs	right	580	20.5
		left	510	18.0
		total	1,090	38.5
5	Heart	male	315	11.1
		female	265	9.3
6	Kidneys	right	140	4.9
		left	150	5.3
		total	290	10.2
7	Spleen		170	6.0
8	Pancreas		98	3.5
9	Thyroid		35	1.2
10	Prostate	male only	20	0.7

This list is based on average immediate post-mortem weights, as recorded during a 10-year period. Various instances of organs far in excess of the average have been recorded, including male brains of over 2 kg (4.4 lb). According to some definitions, the skin may be considered an organ, and since it can constitute 16 per cent of a body's total weight, or 10,886 g (384 oz) in a person weighing 68 kg (150 lb), it heads the Top 10.

Great Brain

The brain of Albert Einstein was removed during his autopsy on 18 April 1955 by pathologist Thomas Stoltz Harvey. Far from being larger than the brain of the average male, it was on the small side, at 1,230 g. Harvey cut it into 240 sections, keeping the largest part himself and distributing others to researchers to attempt to uncover the source of Einstein's remarkable brainpower.

THE 10 WORLD'S HEAVIEST PEOPLE

NAME / DATES*	MAX. WEIGHT KG	LBS
1 Carol Yager (1960–94)	726	1,600
2 Jon Brower Minnoch (1941–83)	635	1,400
3 Manuel Uribe Garza (b. 1965), Mexico	560	1,234
4 Rosalie Bradford (1943–2006)	544	1,200
5 Walter Hudson (1944–91)	543	1,197
6 Francis John Lang aka Michael Walker (b. 1934)	538	1,187
7 Johnny Alee (1853–87)	513	1,132
8 Michael Hebranko (b. 1953)	499	1,100
9 Patrick Deuel (b. 1962)	486	1,072
10 Robert Earl Hughes (1926–58)	485	1,069

* All USA unless otherwise stated

Precise weights of certain people were exaggerated for commercial reasons or never verified, while some were so huge that they could not be moved, or broke the scales, but these are the main contenders for the list of 'world's heaviest', based on records of their peak weights. Some later dieted and reduced their weights – in the case of Rosalie Bradford, down from her 1987 peak to 128 kg (283 lb) in 1994.

Robert Earl Hughes
Although relegated by even heavier people, Hughes' chest measurement of 3.15 m (10 ft 4 in) remains an unbroken record.

THE 10 LATEST PEOPLE TO HOLD THE RECORD AS 'WORLD'S OLDEST'

NAME / COUNTRY	AGE YRS	MTHS	DAYS	BORN	DIED
1 Edna (Scott) Parker, USA	114	10	11	20 Apr 1893	*
2 Yone Minagawa, Japan	114	7	10	4 Jan 1893	13 Aug 2007
3 Emma Fanchon (Faust) Tillman, USA	114	2	7	22 Nov 1892	28 Jan 2007
4 Emiliano Mercado Del Toro, Puerto Rico#	115	5	4	21 Aug 1891	24 Jan 2007
5 Elizabeth (Jones) Bolden, USA	116	3	27	15 Aug 1890	11 Dec 2006
6 María Esther (Heredia Lecaro) Capovilla, Ecuador	116	11	14	14 Sep 1889	27 Aug 2006
7 Ramona Trinidad (Iglesias y Jordan de) Soler, Puerto Rico	114	8	29	1 Sep 1889	29 May 2004
8 Mitoyo Kawate, Japan	114	5	30	15 May 1889	13 Nov 2003
9 Kamato Hongo, Japan	116	1	16	16 Sep 1887	31 Oct 2003
10 Maud (Davis) Farris-Luse, USA	115	1	26	21 Jan 1887	18 Mar 2002

* Alive as at 28 March 2008
\# Male – all others female

This list is based on the longevity of the successive holders of the record as 'world's oldest' among people for whom there is undisputed evidence of their birth date. None of those in the past decade has come within five years of the record 122-year 5-month 15-day lifespan of Jeanne Calment (France), who lived from 21 February 1875 to 4 August 1997.

DISEASE	% OF DALYS*
1 HIV/AIDS	7.4
2 Coronary heart disease	6.8
3 Stroke	5.0
4 Depression	4.8
5 Road-traffic injuries	4.3
6 Tuberculosis	4.2
7 Alcohol abuse	3.4
8 Violence	3.3
9 Obstructive pulmonary disease	3.1
10 Hearing loss	2.7

* Among men aged over 15

Source: World Health Organization

DALYs – Disability-adjusted Life Years, expressed here as world averages – are potential healthy years of life that are lost as a result of contracting diseases or through injury or other disability. This is used as a measure of the 'burden of disease' that affects not only the individual sufferer but also has an effect on the cost of the provision of health services and consequent loss to a country's economy.

TOP 10 **COUNTRIES SPENDING THE MOST ON HEALTHCARE**

COUNTRY	HEALTH SPENDING PER CAPITA IN 2004 ($)
1 USA	6,096
2 Luxembourg	5,904
3 Switzerland	5,572
4 Norway	5,405
5 Monaco	5,330
6 Iceland	4,413
7 Denmark	3,897
8 Austria	3,683
9 Sweden	3,532
10 Germany	3,521
UK	*2,900*

Source: World Health Organization, *World Health Statistics 2007*

£ PER CAPITA PER ANNUM (2007)

COUNTRY

	£ PER CAPITA
1 Norway	56.14
2 Japan	54.58
3 Singapore	49.97
4 Taiwan	36.76
5 USA	33.48
6 South Korea	24.25
7 Australia	23.58
8 Belgium	18.70
9 Italy	16.64
10 New Zealand	15.73

UK 11.24

Source: Euromonitor International

THE 10 MOST COMMON PHOBIAS

OBJECT OF PHOBIA	MEDICAL TERM
1 Open spaces	Agoraphobia, cenophobia or kenophobia
2 Driving	No medical term; can be a symptom of agoraphobia
3 Vomiting	Emetophobia or emitophobia
4 Confined spaces	Claustrophobia, cleisiophobia, cleithrophobia or clithrophobia
5 Insects	Entemophobia
6 Illness	Nosemophobia
7 Animals	Zoophobia
8 Flying	Aerophobia or aviatophobia
9 Blushing	Erythrophobia
10 Heights	Acrophobia, altophobia, hypsophobia or hypsiphobia

Source: National Phobics Society

A phobia is a morbid fear that is out of proportion to the object of the fear. Many people would admit to having these phobias to some degree, as well as others, such as snakes (ophiophobia), injections (trypanophobia) or ghosts (phasmophobia), but most do not become obsessive or allow such fears to rule their lives. Perhaps surprisingly, the Top 10 does not remain static and new phobias arise, for example the recently noted 'nonophobia', the fear of being out of mobile-phone contact, as well as certain more unusual or rare ones, such as:

Beards	Pogonophobia
Chins	Geniophobia
Eggshells	No medical term
Everything	Pantophobia, panophobia, panphobia or pamphobia
Going to bed	Clinophobia
Opening one's eyes	Optophobia
Gravity	Barophobia
Hair	Chaetophobia
Mirrors	Eisoptrophobia
Money	Chrometophobia
Satellites plunging to Earth	Keraunothnetophobia
Slime	Blennophobia or myxophobia
String	Linonophobia
Teeth	Odontophobia
The number 13	Terdekaphobia, tridecaphobia, triakaidekaphobia or triskaidekaphobia

Lost in space
Agoraphobia – literally 'fear of the marketplace' – is a phobia where individuals dread having a panic attack and being unable to escape, and so avoid open spaces and public places.

THE 10 MOST COMMON FATAL DISEASES

CAUSE	APPROX. ANNUAL DEATHS
1 Ischaemic heart disease	7,208,000
2 Cancers	7,121,000
3 Cerebrovascular disease	5,509,000
4 Lower respiratory infections	3,884,000
5 HIV/AIDS	2,777,000
6 Chronic obstructive pulmonary disease	2,748,000
7 Perinatal conditions	2,462,000
8 Diarrhoeal diseases	1,798,000
9 Tuberculosis	1,566,000
10 Malaria	1,272,000
Top 10 total	*36,345,000*
World total	*57,029,000*

Source: World Health Organization, *World Health Report 2004*

Living Standards

THE 10 **MOST OBESE COUNTRIES**

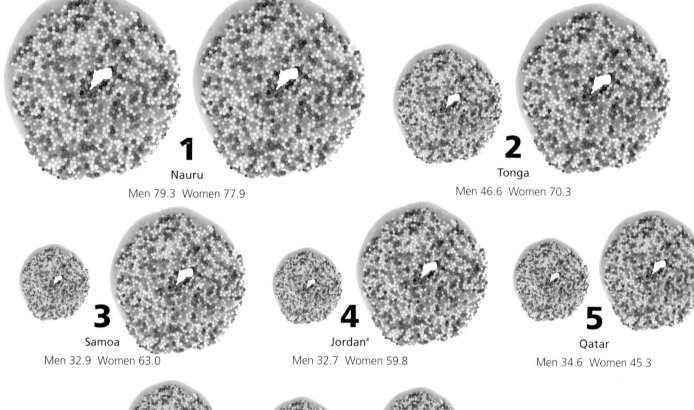

1
Nauru
Men 79.3 Women 77.9

2
Tonga
Men 46.6 Women 70.3

3
Samoa
Men 32.9 Women 63.0

4
Jordan#
Men 32.7 Women 59.8

5
Qatar
Men 34.6 Women 45.3

6
Saudi Arabia
Men 26.4 Women 44.0

7
Lebanon
Men 36.3 Women 38.3

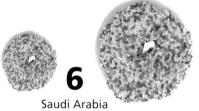

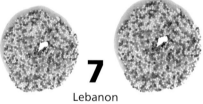

8
Paraguay
Men 22.9 Women 35.7

9
Albania#
Men 22.8 Women 35.6

10
Malta
Men 22.0   Women 35.0

England	*23.1*	*24.3*
Scotland	*22.4*	*26.0*
Wales	*18.0*	*18.0*

* Ranked by percentage of obese women (those with a BMI greater than 30) in those countries and latest year for which data available

Urban population only

Source: International Obesity Task Force (IOTF)

TOP 10 **FAT CONSUMERS**

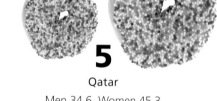

	COUNTRY	AVERAGE DAILY FAT CONSUMPTION PER CAPITA (2002–04)	
		G	OZ
1	France	157	5.53
2	Austria	154	5.43
3	=Belgium	149	5.25
	=Italy	149	5.25
	=Spain	149	5.25
	=Switzerland	149	5.25
7	USA	144	5.07
8	=Canada	141	4.97
	=Hungary	141	4.97
10	=Greece	140	4.93
	=Norway	140	4.93
	UK	*127*	*4.47*

Source: Food and Agriculture Organization of the United Nations

THE 10 LEAST FAT CONSUMERS

	COUNTRY	AVERAGE DAILY FAT CONSUMPTION PER CAPITA (2002–04)	
		G	OZ
1	Burundi	11	0.38
2	Rwanda	16	0.56
3	Ethiopia	21	0.74
4	= Bangladesh	25	0.88
	= Dem. Rep. of Congo	25	0.88
6	= Laos	28	0.98
	= Madagascar	28	0.98
8	Zambia	29	0.98
9	Eritrea	30	1.05
10	Mozambique	31	1.09

Source: Food and Agriculture Organization of the United Nations

THE 10 MOST DEVELOPED COUNTRIES

	COUNTRY	HUMAN DEVELOPMENT INDEX
1	= Iceland	0.968
	= Norway	0.968
3	Australia	0.962
4	Canada	0.961
5	Ireland	0.959
6	Sweden	0.956
7	Switzerland	0.955
8	= Japan	0.953
	= Netherlands	0.953
10	= Finland	0.952
	= France	0.952
	UK	*0.946*

Source: United Nations, *Human Development Report 2007/2008*

HDI rankings are based on a range of factors, including life expectancy, income, education level and living standards. The maximum possible HDI would be 1.00. Although not all member countries are included (some are omitted through lack of reliable data), the figures are widely used by economists, aid organizations and other agencies as a comparative measure of quality of life.

THE 10 LEAST DEVELOPED COUNTRIES

	COUNTRY	HUMAN DEVELOPMENT INDEX
1	Sierra Leone	0.336
2	Burkina Faso	0.370
3	= Niger	0.374
	= Guinea-Bissau	0.374
5	Mali	0.380
6	= Central African Republic	0.384
	= Mozambique	0.384
8	Chad	0.388
9	Ethiopia	0.406
10	Dem. Rep. of Congo	0.411

Source: United Nations, *Human Development Report 2007/2008*

THE 10 COUNTRIES WITH THE MOST DEATHS FROM HEART DISEASE

	COUNTRY	TOTAL DEATHS	AGE-STANDARDIZED DEATH RATE PER 100,000
1	Turkmenistan	11,670	461
2	Moldova	18,558	423
3	Ukraine	335,609	418
4	Azerbaijan	22,301	410
5	Belarus	59,422	396
6	= Uzbekistan	55,692	386
	= Kazakhstan	51,947	386
8	Afghanistan	33,157	354
9	Russia	711,570	343
10	Tajikistan	11,447	339
	UK	*120,530*	*99*

Source: World Health Organization

THE 10 LEAST CALORIE-CONSUMING COUNTRIES

	COUNTRY	AVERAGE DAILY CALORIE CONSUMPTION PER CAPITA (2002–04)
1	Eritrea	1,500
2	Dem. Rep. of Congo	1,590
3	Burundi	1,660
4	Comoros	1,770
5	Ethiopia	1,850
6	Takikistan	1,900
7	Sierra Leone	1,910
8	Liberia	1,930
9	Zambia	1,950
10	= Central African Republic	1,960
	= Tanzania	1,960

Source: Food and Agriculture Organization of the United Nations

TOP 10 PROTEIN CONSUMERS

	COUNTRY	AVERAGE DAILY PROTEIN CONSUMPTION PER CAPITA (2002–04)	
		G	OZ
1	Israel	136	4.79
2	Iceland	134	4.73
3	USA	133	4.69
4	= Ireland	126	4.44
	= Malta	126	4.44
6	= Portugal	125	4.41
	= France	125	4.41
	= Greece	125	4.41
	= Italy	125	4.41
	= Lithuania	125	4.41
	UK	*114*	*4.02*

Source: Food and Agriculture Organization of the United Nations

Births, Marriages & Deaths

TOP 10 **COUNTRIES WITH THE HIGHEST MARRIAGE RATE**

	COUNTRY	MARRIAGES PER 1,000 PER ANNUM*
1	Barbados	13.1
2	Vietnam	12.1
3	Ethiopia	10.2
4	Seychelles	9.9
5	Jordan	9.7
6	Iran	8.9
7 =	Algeria	8.8
=	Mauritius	8.8
9	Jamaica	8.3
10	USA	8.0
	UK	*5.1*

* In 2005 or latest year in those countries for which data available

Source: United Nations

Mass wedding
Jordan, one of the countries with a high marriage rate, offers group weddings, sometimes of hundreds of couples, to enable cost-sharing.

THE 10 **COUNTRIES WITH THE LOWEST MARRIAGE RATE**

	COUNTRY	MARRIAGES PER 1,000 PER ANNUM*
1 =	Colombia	1.7
2 =	Dominican Republic	2.8
=	Saint Lucia	2.8
=	Venezuela	2.8
5 =	Andorra	2.9
=	Peru	2.9
7	United Arab Emirates	3.1
8 =	Argentina	3.2
=	Slovenia	3.2
10	Panama	3.3

* In 2005 or latest year in those countries for which data available

Source: United Nations

Marriage rates are falling worldwide – in 2008 it was reported that the rate in the UK was the lowest since records began in 1862.

THE 10 **COUNTRIES WITH THE LOWEST BIRTH RATE**

	COUNTRY	EST. BIRTH RATE (LIVE BIRTHS PER 1,000, 2009)
1	Japan	7.64
2	Andorra	8.04
3 =	Germany	8.18
=	Italy	8.18
5	Austria	8.65
6	Singapore	8.82
7	Czech Republic	8.83
8	Bosnia and Herzegovina	8.85
9	Slovenia	8.97
10 =	Lithuania	9.11
=	Monaco	9.11
	UK	*10.65*

Source: US Census Bureau, International Data Base

Although not independent countries, several places record similarly low rates, among them Hong Kong (7.42) and Guernsey (8.46).

TOP 10 **COUNTRIES WITH THE HIGHEST BIRTH RATE**

	COUNTRY	EST. BIRTH RATE (LIVE BIRTHS PER 1,000, 2009)
1	Mali	49.15
2	Niger	49.08
3	Uganda	47.84
4	Afghanistan	45.46
5	Sierra Leone	44.71
6	Burkina Faso	44.58
7	Angola	43.69
8	Somalia	43.68
9	Liberia	42.25
10	Yemen	42.14
	World average	*19.80*

Source: US Census Bureau, International Data Base

The countries with the highest birth rates – often also those with the highest fertility rates – are among the poorest in the world.

TOP 10 COUNTRIES WITH THE HIGHEST LIFE EXPECTANCY

2009

	COUNTRY	LIFE EXPECTANCY AT BIRTH
1	Andorra	83.54
2	Japan	82.12
3	Singapore	81.98
4	San Marino	81.97
5	France	80.98
6	Sweden	80.86
7 =	Australia	80.85
=	Switzerland	80.85
9	Iceland	80.67
10	Canada	80.58
	UK	*76.52*

1989

	COUNTRY	LIFE EXPECTANCY AT BIRTH
1	San Marino	79.24
2	Japan	79.00
3	Hong Kong	78.30
4	Iceland	78.17
5	Switzerland	77.89
6	Sweden	77.65
7	Spain	77.30
8	Canada	77.10
9	Greece	77.01
10	Liechtenstein	76.89
	UK	*75.30*

Source: US Census Bureau, International Data Base

THE 10 COUNTRIES WITH THE LOWEST DEATH RATE

	COUNTRY	EST. DEATH RATE (DEATHS PER 1,000, 2009)
1	United Arab Emirates	2.11
2	Kuwait	2.35
3	Saudi Arabia	2.50
4	Jordan	2.75
5	Brunei	3.29
6	Libya	3.45
7	Oman	3.71
8	Solomon Islands	3.78
9	Ecuador	4.21
10 =	Bahrain	4.37
=	Nicaragua	4.37
	UK	*10.02*

Source: US Census Bureau, International Data Base

The crude death rate is derived by dividing the total number of deaths in a given year by the total population and multiplying by 1,000. However, because countries with young populations thus appear to have low death rates and older populations high rates, statisticians also use age-standardized death rates, which factor in the age structure to produce a more accurate assessment.

TOP 10 COUNTRIES WITH THE HIGHEST DEATH RATE

	COUNTRY	EST. DEATH RATE (DEATHS PER 1,000, 2009)
1	Swaziland	30.83
2	Angola	24.08
3	South Africa	22.77
4	Lesotho	22.20
5	Sierra Leone	21.91
6	Zimbabwe	21.64
7	Zambia	21.34
8	Liberia	20.73
9	Mozambique	20.07
10	Niger	19.94
	World average	*8.30*

Source: US Census Bureau, International Data Base

NAME / NO.

1 David Jones
15,763

2 David Smith
14,341

3 John Smith
12,793

4 David Williams
11,392

5 Michael Smith
10,516

6 John Jones
10,021

7 John Williams
8,738

8= Paul Smith
8,348

8= Peter Smith
8,348

10 David Evans
8,103

Source: Office for National Statistics

The most common combinations of first names and surnames – based on those registered with GPs – is entirely male, as there is more variation among female first names. Margaret Smith is the closest qualifier with 7,640 examples, followed by Margaret Jones with 7,068.

TOP 10 **SURNAMES IN ENGLAND AND WALES**

SURNAME / NO.

1	SMITH 652,563	**6**	DAVIES* 279,647
2	JONES 538,874	**7**	EVANS 225,580
3	WILLIAMS 380,379	**8**	THOMAS 202,773
4	TAYLOR 306,296	**9**	WILSON 201,224
5	BROWN 291,872	**10**	JOHNSON 193,260

* There are also 97,349 people bearing the surname Davis

This survey of British surnames is based on an analysis of 54.4 million appearing in the England and Wales electoral rolls – hence enumerating only those aged over 18. Some 12 people out of every 1,000 in the UK are called Smith, compared with 14.55 per 1,000 of names appearing in a sample from the 1851 Census. The decline in part results from the diluting effect of immigrant names.

TOP 10 **SURNAMES IN SCOTLAND**

NAME	FREQUENCY*
1 Smith	4,291
2 Brown	3,030
3 Wilson	2,876
4 Campbell	2,657
5 Stewart	2,626
6 Thomson	2,616
7 Robertson	2,536
8 Anderson	2,297
9 Macdonald	1,844
10 Scott	1,839

* Number recorded in sample of 335,000 births and deaths, 1999–2001

Source: General Register Office for Scotland

NOW & THEN

TOP 10 FIRST NAMES IN ENGLAND & WALES

2007

BOYS		GIRLS
Jack	1	Grace
Thomas	2	Ruby
Oliver	3	Olivia
Joshua	4	Emily
Harry	5	Jessica
Charlie	6	Sophie
Daniel	7	Chloe
William	8	Lily
James	9	Ellie
Alfie	10	Amelia

1987

BOYS		GIRLS
Daniel	1	Rebecca
Christopher	2	Sarah
Michael	3	Emma
James	4	Laura
Matthew	5	Rachel
Andrew	6	Samantha
Adam	7	Charlotte
Thomas	8	Kirsty
David	9	Nicola
Richard	10	Amy

TOP 10 GIRLS' AND BOYS' NAMES IN THE UK 100 YEARS AGO

GIRLS		BOYS
Mary	1	William
Florence	2	John
Doris	3	George
Edith	4	Thomas
Dorothy	5	Arthur
Annie	6	James
Margaret	7	Charles
Alice	8	Frederick
Elizabeth	9	Albert
Elsie	10	Ernest

TOP 10 SURNAMES IN CHINA

1 Li
2 Wáng
3 Zhang
4 Liú
5 Chén
6 Yáng
7 Huáng
8 Zhào
9 Zhou
10 Wú

Source: Chinese
Academy of Sciences

This ranking is based on a 2006 survey of 296 million Chinese inhabitants in 1,110 counties and cities. The survey recorded a total of 4,100 different surnames, but it has been estimated that there are more than 100 million people with the surnames in the first three in the list, with the Top 10 reckoned to be used by much as 40 per cent of the entire Chinese population of 1.3 billion.

Rulers & Royals

TOP 10 **IN LINE TO THE BRITISH THRONE**

HRH The Prince of Wales
(Prince Charles Philip Arthur George)
b. 14 November 1948,
then his elder son:

HRH Prince William of Wales
(Prince William Arthur Philip Louis)
b. 21 June 1982,
then his younger brother:

HRH Prince Henry ('Harry') of Wales
(Prince Henry Charles Albert David)
b. 15 September 1984,
then his uncle:

HRH The Duke of York
(Prince Andrew Albert Christian Edward)
b. 19 February 1960,
then his elder daughter:

HRH Princess Beatrice of York
(Princess Beatrice Elizabeth Mary)
b. 8 August 1988,
then her younger sister:

HRH Princess Eugenie of York
(Princess Eugenie Victoria Helena)
b. 23 March 1990,
then her uncle:

HRH Prince Edward
(Prince Edward Antony Richard Louis)
b. 10 March 1964,
then his son:

Viscount Severn
(James Alexander Philip Theo Windsor)
b. 17 December 2007,
then his sister:

Lady Louise Windsor
(Louise Alice Elizabeth Mary Mountbatten Windsor)
b. 8 November 2003
then her aunt:

HRH The Princess Royal
(Princess Anne Elizabeth Alice Louise)
b. 15 August 1950

Right: Consigned to history
Mohammad Reza Pahlavi ruled as Shah of Iran after his father was deposed in 1941. He was himself deposed and the monarchy abolished on 11 February 1979, as the Iranian Revolution resulted in Ayatollah Khomeini coming to power. The Shah died in exile a year later.

TOP 10 **MONARCHIES WITH THE MOST SUBJECTS** *

	COUNTRY	MONARCH (ACCESSION)	POPULATION (2009)
1	Britain#	Elizabeth II (1952)	130,906,870
2	Japan	Akihito (1989)	127,078,679
3	Thailand	Bhumibol Adulyadej (1946)	65,905,410
4	Spain	Juan Carlos I (1975)	40,525,002
5	Morocco	Mohammed VI (1999)	34,787,968
6	Nepal	Gyanendra Bir Bikram Shah Dev (2001)	30,138,172
7	Saudi Arabia	Abdullah (2005)	28,701,335
8	Malaysia	Mizan Zainal Abidin (2006)	25,700,294
9	Netherlands	Beatrix (1980)	16,715,999
10	Cambodia	Norodom Sihamoni (1999)	14,494,293

* By population
# Total of British Commonwealth realms with monarch as head of state

Source: US Census Bureau

A total of 45 countries (including 16 belonging to the British Commonwealth) have monarchies, the Top 10 alone with some 515 million subjects. With a population of 32,920, Monaco is the world's smallest monarchy.

THE 10 **LATEST COUNTRIES TO ABOLISH MONARCHIES**

COUNTRY / MONARCHY ABOLISHED
1 Iran 1979
2 Laos 1975
3 Ethiopia* 1974
4 Afghanistan 1973
5 Greece# 1973
6 Cambodia† 1970
7 Libya 1969
8 Maldives 1968
9 Burundi 1966
10 Zanzibar§ 1964

* Emperor deposed 1974
# King exiled 1967
† Restored 1993
§ Joined with Tanganyika to form Tanzania

This list excludes countries that detached from British rule and became republics.

Revolving monarchy
The 2006 coronation of Mizan Zainal Abidin, the 13th Malaysian ruler since the country's independence in 1957, with Sultanah Nur Zahirah. Malaysia has a revolving monarchy, with a new Yang di-Pertuan, often translated as 'king', serving a five-year term.

THE 10 LATEST MONARCHS TO ASCEND THE THRONE

TITLE / NAME	COUNTRY	ACCESSION
1 King Jigme Khesar Namgyal Wangchuck	Bhutan	15 Dec 2006
2 Sultan Mizan Zainal Abidin	Malaysia	13 Dec 2006
3 Emir Sabah al-Ahmad al-Saba	Kuwait	29 Jan 2006
4 King George Tupou V	Tonga	11 Sep 2006
5 Emir Sabah Al-Ahmad Al-Jaber Al-Sabah	Kuwait	29 Jan 2006
6 Emir Mohammed bin Rashid Al Maktoum	Dubai	4 Jan 2006
7 King Abdullah	Saudi Arabia	1 Aug 2005
8 Prince Albert II	Monaco	6 Apr 2005
9 Emir Khalifa bin Zayed Al Nahayan	Abu Dhabi	3 Nov 2004
10 King Norodom Sihamoni	Cambodia	14 Oct 2004

TOP 10 LONGEST-SERVING PRESIDENTS TODAY

PRESIDENT	COUNTRY	TOOK OFFICE
1 El Hadj Omar Bongo	Gabon	2 Dec 1967
2 Colonel Mu'ammar Gaddafi*	Libya	1 Sep 1969
3 Ali Abdullah Saleh	Yemen	17 Jul 1978
4 Maumoon Abdul Gayoom	Maldives	11 Nov 1978
5 Teodoro Obiang Nguema Mbasogo	Equatorial Guinea	3 Aug 1979
6 José Eduardo dos Santos	Angola	21 Sep 1979
7 Hosni Mubarak	Egypt	6 Oct 1981
8 Paul Biya	Cameroon	7 Nov 1982
9 Lansana Conté	Guinea	3 Apr 1984
10 Yoweri Museveni	Uganda	29 Jan 1986

* Since a reorganization in 1979, Colonel Gaddafi has held no formal position, but continues to rule under the ceremonial title of 'Leader and Guide of the Revolution'

All the presidents in this list have been in power for more than 22 – some for more than 40 – years. Fidel Castro became prime minister of Cuba in 1959, president in 1976 and retired on 24 February 2008.

Mr President

TOP 10 LONGEST-LIVED US PRESIDENTS

	PRESIDENT	BORN	DIED	YRS	MTHS	DAYS
1	Gerald Ford	14 Jul 1913	26 Dec 2006	93	5	13
2	Ronald Reagan	6 Feb 1911	5 Jun 2004	93	4	0
3	John Adams	30 Oct 1735	4 Jul 1826	90	8	5
4	Herbert Hoover	10 Aug 1874	20 Oct 1964	90	2	11
5	Harry S. Truman	8 May 1884	26 Dec 1972	88	7	19
6	James Madison	16 Mar 1751	28 Jun 1836	85	3	13
7	Thomas Jefferson	13 Apr 1743	4 Jul 1826	83	2	22
8	George H. W. Bush	12 Jun 1924	*	82	6	21
9	Jimmy Carter	1 Oct 1924	*	82	3	1
10	Richard Nixon	9 Jan 1913	22 Apr 1994	81	3	14

* Still alive, age at 1 January 2008

Political stature
Lyndon B. Johnson was only fractionally shorter than Lincoln – whose height has been claimed to have resulted from his suffering from an endocrine deficiency.

THE 10 LAST US PRESIDENTS AND VICE-PRESIDENTS TO DIE IN OFFICE

NAME / PRESIDENT/VICE-PRESIDENT / DEATH DATE

1 **John F. Kennedy** * (P)
22 Nov 1963

2 **Franklin D. Roosevelt** (P)
12 Apr 1945

3 **Warren G. Harding** (P)
2 Aug 1923

4 **James S. Sherman** (V-P)
30 Oct 1912

5 **William McKinley** * (P)
14 Sep 1901

6 **Garret A. Hobart** (V-P)
21 Nov 1899

7 **Thomas A. Hendricks** (V-P)
25 Nov 1885

8 **James A. Garfield** * (P)
19 Sep 1881

9 **Henry Wilson** (V-P)
10 Nov 1875

10 **Abraham Lincoln** * (P)
15 Apr 1865

* Assassinated

John Fitzgerald Kennedy was the 15th and last US president or vice-president to die in office, and the fourth to die by an assassin's bullet. Prior to Lincoln, two presidents and three vice-presidents had died in office.

TOP 10 TALLEST US PRESIDENTS

	PRESIDENT	M	FT	IN
1	Abraham Lincoln	1.92	6	3.75
2	Lyndon B. Johnson	1.91	6	3.5
3	Thomas Jefferson	1.89	6	2.5
4	= Chester A. Arthur	1.88	6	2
	= George H. W. Bush	1.88	6	2
	= Franklin D. Roosevelt	1.88	6	2
7	= Bill Clinton	1.87	6	1.5
	= George Washington	1.87	6	1.5
9	= Andrew Jackson	1.85	6	1
	= Ronald Reagan	1.85	6	1

It is often claimed that the taller candidate has always won US presidential elections, but statistically this is only marginally true.

TOP 10 **MOST POPULAR US PRESIDENTS**

	PRESIDENT	SURVEY DATE	HIGHEST APPROVAL RATING (%)*
1	George W. Bush	21–22 Sep 2001	90
2	George H. W. Bush	28 Feb 1991	89
3	Harry S. Truman	May/Jun 1945	87
4	Franklin D. Roosevelt	Jan 1942	84
5	John F. Kennedy	28 Apr 1961	83
6	Dwight D. Eisenhower	14 Dec 1956	79
7	Lyndon B. Johnson	5 Dec 1963	78
8	Jimmy Carter	18 Mar 1977	75
9	Gerald Ford	16 Aug 1974	71
10	Bill Clinton	30 Jan–1 Feb 1998	69

* Identical or inferior ratings recorded on other occasions during presidency

Source: The Gallup Organization

The Gallup Organization began surveying approval ratings of US presidents in October 1938. Since then, the only president not to make the Top 10 is Richard Nixon, whose highest approval rating was 67 per cent. George W. Bush's highest ratings were achieved shortly after the events of 9/11. In response to the continuing presence of US troops in Iraq and Afghanistan, the state of the US economy and other factors, he has recorded the biggest ever differential between approval ratings, a total of 73 percentage points. The one president to not make the least popular list is John F. Kennedy, whose highest disapproval was 30 per cent in September 1963, the survey compiled two months before his assassination.

THE 10 **LEAST POPULAR US PRESIDENTS**

	PRESIDENT	SURVEY DATE	LOWEST APPROVAL RATING (%)*
1	George W. Bush	15–19 Feb 2008	19
2	Harry S. Truman	9–14 Sep 1952	22
3	Richard Nixon	12–15 Jul 1974	24
4	Jimmy Carter	29 Jun–2 Jul 1979	28
5	George H. W. Bush	31 Jul–2 Aug 1992	29
6	= Ronald W. Reagan	1 Jan 1983	35
	= Lyndon B. Johnson	7 Aug 1968	35
8	= Gerald Ford	31 Mar 1975	37
	= Bill Clinton	27 May 1994	37
10	Dwight D. Eisenhower	Jul 1960	49

* Identical or better ratings recorded on other occasions during presidency

Source: The Gallup Organization

Rise and fall
George W. Bush's approval rating has swung between two extremes, reflecting the highs and lows of his two terms in office.

To the Ends of the Earth

THE 10 **FIRST EXPLORERS TO LAND IN THE AMERICAS**

	EXPLORER* / COUNTRY	TERRITORY	LANDED
1	Christopher Columbus, Italy	West Indies	12 Oct 1492
2	John Cabot, Italy/England	Nova Scotia/ Newfoundland	24 Jun 1497
3	Alonso de Ojeda, Spain	Brazil	1499
4	Vicente Yáñez Pinzón, Spain	Amazon	26 Jan 1500
5	Pedro Alvarez Cabral, Portugal	Brazil	23 Apr 1500
6	Gaspar Corte-Real, Portugal	Labrador	late 1500
7	Rodrigo de Bastidas, Spain	Central America	Mar 1501
8	Vasco Nuñez de Balboa, Spain	Panama	25 Sep 1513
9	Juan Ponce de León, Spain	Florida	8 Apr 1513
10	Juan Díaz de Solís, Spain	Río de la Plata	1 Jan 1516

* Expedition leader only listed

After his pioneering voyage of 1492, Columbus made three subsequent journeys to the West Indies and South America. Although Ojeda (or Hojeda) was the leader of the 1499 expedition, Amerigo Vespucci, after whom America is named, was also on the voyage.

THE 10 **FIRST MOUNTAINEERS TO CLIMB EVEREST**

	MOUNTAINEER / COUNTRY	DATE
1	Edmund Hillary, New Zealand	29 May 1953
2	Tenzing Norgay, Nepal	29 May 1953
3	Jürg Marmet, Switzerland	23 May 1956
4	Ernst Schmied, Switzerland	23 May 1956
5	Hans-Rudolf von Gunten, Switzerland	24 May 1956
6	Adolf Reist, Switzerland	24 May 1956
7	Wang Fu-chou, China	25 May 1960
8	Chu Ying-hua, China	25 May 1960
9	Konbu, China	25 May 1960
10 =	Nawang Gombu, India	1 May 1963
=	James Whittaker, USA	1 May 1963

Nawang Gombu and James Whittaker are 10th equal because, neither wishing to deny the other the privilege of being first, they ascended the last steps to the summit side by side. Up to the end of 2007 there were 3,679 successful ascents of Everest – 40 of them on a single day, 10 May 1993 – but some 210 have died in the attempt, the bodies of many remaining on the mountain.

TOP 10 **FASTEST CROSS-CHANNEL SWIMS**

SWIMMER / COUNTRY / YEAR / TIME (HR:MIN)

1
Petar Stoychev,
Bulgaria
24 Aug 2007 / 6:58

2
Christof Wandratsch,
Germany
1 Aug 2005 / 7:04

3
Yuri Kudinov,
Russia
24 Aug 2007 / 7:06

4
Chad Hundeby,
USA
27 Sep 1994 / 7:17

5
Christof Wandratsch,
Germany
20 Aug 2003 / 7:20

Right: Polar pugilists
The dispute as to which – if either – of rival Arctic explorers *Robert Peary* and *Frederick Cook* reached the North Pole first was satirized in this caricature in the French magazine Le Petit Journal, *published in 1909, the year after their claimed conquests.*

THE 10 **FIRST PEOPLE TO REACH THE SOUTH POLE**

NAME / COUNTRY	DATE
1 = Roald Amundsen* (Norway; 1872–1928)	14 Dec 1911
= Olav Olavson Bjaaland (Norway; 1873–1961)	14 Dec 1911
= Helmer Julius Hanssen (Norway; 1870–1956)	14 Dec 1911
= Sverre Helge Hassel (Norway; 1876–1928)	14 Dec 1911
= Oscar Wisting (Norway; 1871–1936)	14 Dec 1911
6 = Robert Falcon Scott* (Britain; 1868–1912)	17 Jan 1912
= Henry Robinson Bowers (Britain; 1883–1912)	17 Jan 1912
= Edgar Evans (Britain; 1876–1912)	17 Jan 1912
= Lawrence Edward Grace Oates (Britain; 1880–1912)	17 Jan 1912
= Edward Adrian Wilson (Britain; 1872–1912)	17 Jan 1912

* Expedition leader

Just 33 days separate the first two expeditions to reach the South Pole. Scott's British Antarctic Expedition was organized with its avowed goal 'to reach the South Pole and to secure for the British Empire the honour of this achievement'. Meanwhile, Norwegian explorer Roald Amundsen also set out on an expedition to the Pole. When Scott eventually reached his goal, he discovered that the Norwegians had beaten him. Demoralized, Scott's team began the arduous return journey, but plagued by illness, hunger, bad weather and exhaustion, the entire expedition died just as Amundsen's triumph was being reported to the world.

THE 10 **FIRST PEOPLE CLAIMED TO HAVE REACHED THE NORTH POLE**

NAME / COUNTRY	DATE
1 = Frederick Albert Cook, USA	21 Apr 1908
= Ahwelah, Inuit	21 Apr 1908
= Etukishook, Inuit	21 Apr 1908
4 = Robert Edwin Peary, USA	6 Apr 1909
= Matthew Alexander Henson, USA	6 Apr 1909
= Ooqueah, Inuit	6 Apr 1909
= Ootah, Inuit	6 Apr 1909
= Egingwah, Inuit	6 Apr 1909
= Seegloo, Inuit	6 Apr 1909
10 = Pavel Afanaseyevich Geordiyenko, USSR	23 Apr 1948
= Mikhail Yemel'yenovich Ostrekin, USSR	23 Apr 1948
= Pavel Kononovich Sen'ko, USSR	23 Apr 1948
= Mikhail Mikhaylovich Somov, USSR	23 Apr 1948

Cook's claim to have reached the North Pole is not generally accepted. Doubts also remain as to the validity of Peary's team's claim, which has never been officially corroborated. The first undisputed 'conquest', that of the 1948 Soviet team, was achieved by landing in an aircraft, rather than overland.

* Fastest woman swimmer

6 Petar Stoychev, Bulgaria
22 Aug 2006 / 7:21

7 David Meca, Spain
29 Aug 2005 / 7:22

8 Yvetta Hlavácová*, Czech Republic
5 Aug 2006 / 7:25

9 Penny Lee Dean, USA
29 Jul 1978 / 7:40

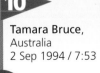
10 Tamara Bruce, Australia
2 Sep 1994 / 7:53

Nobel Prizes

THE 10 **LATEST WINNERS OF THE NOBEL PEACE PRIZE**

YEAR / WINNER / COUNTRY

Intergovernmental Panel on Climate Change and Al Gore Jr
USA

Muhammad Yunus and Grameen Bank
Bangladesh

International Atomic Energy Agency and Mohamed El Baradei
Egypt

Wangari Maathai
Kenya

Shirin Ebadi
Iran

Jimmy Carter
USA

United Nations and Kofi Annan, Ghana

Kim Dae-jung
South Korea

Médecins Sans Frontières

John Hume and David Trimble, UK

TOP 10 **YOUNGEST NOBEL PRIZE WINNERS**

WINNER / COUNTRY / DATE OF BIRTH	AWARD	YRS	AGE* MTHS	DAYS
1 William Lawrence Bragg (UK) 31 Mar 1890	Physics 1915	25	8	10
2 Werner Karl Heisenberg (Germany) 5 Dec 1901	Physics 1932	31	0	5
3 Tsung-dao Lee (China) 24 Nov 1926	Physics 1957	31	0	16
4 Carl David Anderson (USA) 3 Sept 1905	Physics 1936	31	3	7
5 Paul Adrien Maurice Dirac (UK) 8 Aug 1902	Physics 1933	31	4	2
6 Frederick Grant Banting (Canada) 14 Nov 1891	Medicine 1923	32	0	26
7 Rudolf Ludwig Mössbauer (West Germany) 31 Jan 1929	Physics 1961	32	10	10
8 Maidread Corrigan (UK) 27 Jan 1944	Peace 1976	32	10	13
9 Joshua Lederberg (USA) 23 May 1925	Medicine 1958	33	6	17
10 Betty Williams (UK) 22 May 1943	Peace 1976	33	6	18

* At date of award ceremony; prizes are awarded annually on 10 December, Alfred Nobel's birthday

TOP 10 **OLDEST NOBEL PRIZE WINNERS**

WINNER / COUNTRY / DATE OF BIRTH	AWARD	YRS	AGE* MTHS	DAYS
1 Leonid Hurwicz (USA) 21 Aug 1917	Economics 2007	90	3	28
2 Raymond Davis Jr (USA) 14 Oct 1914	Physics 2002	88	1	26
3 Doris Lessing (UK) 22 Oct 1919	Literature 2007	88	1	18
4 Vitaly L. Ginzburg (Russia) 4 Oct 1916	Physics 2003	87	2	6
5 Peyton Rous (USA) 5 Oct 1879	Medicine 1966	87	2	5
6 Joseph Rotblat (UK) 4 Nov 1908	Peace 1995	87	1	6
7 Karl von Frisch (Germany) 20 Nov 1886	Medicine 1973	87	0	20
8 Ferdinand Buisson (France) 20 Dec 1841	Peace 1927	85	11	20
9 John B. Fenn (USA) 15 Jun 1917	Chemistry 2002	85	5	25
10 Thomas S. Schelling (USA) 14 Apr 1921	Economics 2005	84	7	26

* At date of award ceremony; prizes are awarded annually on 10 December, Alfred Nobel's birthday

THE 10 **LATEST WINNERS OF THE NOBEL PRIZE FOR LITERATURE**

YEAR / WINNER / COUNTRY

2007 Doris Lessing, UK

2006 Orhan Pamuk, Turkey

2005 Harold Pinter, UK

2004 Elfriede Jelinek, Austria

2003 J. M. Coetzee, South Africa

2002 Imre Kertész, Hungary

2001 Sir V. S. Naipaul, UK

2000 Gao Xingjian, China

1999 Günter Grass, Germany

1998 José Saramago, Portugal

Doris Lessing
British writer Doris Lessing is the most recent of the 11 women to be awarded the Nobel Prize for Literature, and the oldest of all 34 female Nobel laureates.

TOP 10 **LANGUAGES OF NOBEL PRIZE FOR LITERATURE WINNERS**

	LANGUAGE	% OF TOTAL*	NO.
1	English	25.47	27
2	French	12.26	13
3	German	11.32	12
4	Spanish	9.43	10
5	= Italian	5.67	6
	= Swedish	5.67	6
7	Russian	4.72	5
8	Polish	3.77	4
9	= Danish	2.83	3
	= Norwegian	2.83	3

* Of 106 Nobel Prizes awarded 1901–2007

THE 10 **LATEST WOMEN TO WIN A NOBEL PRIZE**

	WINNER	COUNTRY	PRIZE	YEAR
1	Doris Lessing (b. 1919)	UK	Literature	2007
2	= Linda B. Buck (b. 1947)	USA	Medicine	2004
	= Elfriede Jelinek (b. 1946)	Austria	Literature	2004
	= Wangari Maathai (b. 1940)	Kenya	Peace	2004
5	Shirin Ebadi (b. 1947)	Iran	Peace	2003
6	Jody Williams (b. 1950)	USA	Peace	1997
7	Wislawa Szymborska (b. 1923)	Poland	Literature	1996
8	Christiane Nüsslein-Volhard (b. 1942)	Germany	Medicine	1995
9	Toni Morrison (b. 1931)	USA	Literature	1993
10	Rigoberta Menchú Tum (b. 1959)	Guatemala	Peace	1992

A total of 34 women have won Nobel Prizes since 1901, 12 of them for Peace, 11 for Literature, three for Physiology or Medicine, three for Chemistry and two for Physics. The total includes Marie Curie, who won twice: for Physics (1903) and Chemistry (1911). No woman has ever won the Nobel Prize for Economics.

Criminal Records

THE 10 **COUNTRIES WITH THE HIGHEST REPORTED CRIME RATES**

COUNTRY / REPORTED CRIMES PER 100,000 POPULATION

Iceland
21,211.97

Sweden
13,836.67

UK
11,014.38

Finland
10,005.65

Belgium
9,421.74

Denmark
9,137.07

Netherlands
8,813.57

Austria
6,863.95

South Africa
5,918.73

Luxembourg
5,866.22

Source: United Nations Office on Drugs and Crime, *Eighth United Nations Survey of Crime Trends and Operations of Criminal Justice Systems*, 2006

An appearance in this list does not necessarily confirm these as the most crime-ridden countries, since the rate of reporting relates closely to such factors as confidence in local law-enforcement authorities. However, a rate of approximately 1,000 per 100,000 may be considered average, so those in the Top 10 are well above it.

THE 10 **MOST COMMON MOTORING OFFENCES IN ENGLAND AND WALES**

OFFENCE	NO. (2004)
1 Obstruction, waiting and parking offences	8,553,900
2 Speed-limit offences	2,104,800
3 Vehicle licence, insurance and record-keeping offences	1,387,200
4 Vehicle test offences	353,900
5 Neglect of traffic signs, directions and pedestrian rights	267,300
6 Vehicle or part in dangerous or defective condition	139,300
7 Careless driving	138,300
8 Driving after consuming alcohol or taking drugs	107,200
9 Lighting and noise offences	42,300
10 Unauthorized taking or theft of a motor vehicle	40,400
Total (including offences not in Top 10)	*13,539,000*

Source: Home Office

THE 10 **MOST COMMON CRIMES IN ENGLAND AND WALES**

CRIME	NO. RECORDED (2006–07)
1 Theft and handling stolen goods (excl. car theft)	1,181,047
2 Criminal damage	1,185,111
3 Violence against the person	1,046,437
4 Car theft (incl. theft from vehicles)	765,056
5 Burglary (excl. domestic)	329,759
6 Domestic burglary	292,285
7 Fraud and forgery	199,778
8 Drug offences	194,302
9 Robbery	101,370
10 Sexual offences	57,542
Top 10 total	*5,352,687*
Total (including those not in Top 10)	*5,428,273*

Source: Home Office, *Crime in England and Wales 2005/06*

WANTED

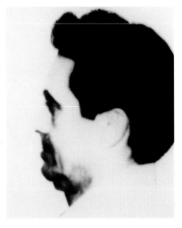

Donald Eugene Webb

After the killing of a police officer in 1980, Donald Eugene Webb (born 14 July 1931) became the 375th person and longest resident on the FBI's 'Most Wanted' list.

THE 10 CRIMINALS LONGEST ON THE FBI'S '10 MOST WANTED' LIST

FUGITIVE (FBI NO.) / CRIME	ADDED TO LIST	REMOVED FROM LIST	PERIOD ON LIST		
			YRS	MTHS	DAYS
1 Donald Eugene Webb (375) Alleged cop killer	4 May 1981	31 Mar 2007	25	10	27
2 Victor Manuel Gerena (386) Armed robbery	14 May 1984	*	23	10	25
3 Charles Lee Heron (265) Murder	9 Feb 1968	18 Jun 1986	18	4	9
4 Frederick J. Tenuto (14) Murder	24 May 1950	9 Mar 1964	13	9	14
5 Katherine Ann Power (315) Bank robbery	17 Oct 1970	15 Jun 1984	13	7	29
6 Glen Stewart Godwin (447) Murder	7 Dec 1996	*	11	4	1
7 Arthur Lee Washington Jr (427) Attempted murder	18 Oct 1989	27 Dec 2000	11	2	19
8 David Daniel Keegan (78) Murder, robbery	21 Jun 1954	13 Dec 1963	9	5	22
9 James Eddie Diggs (36) Alleged murder	27 Aug 1952	14 Dec 1961	9	3	17
10 Eugene Francis Newman (97) Car theft, burglary	28 May 1956	11 Jun 1965	9	0	14

* Still at large, periods as at 8 April 2008

The United States' Federal Bureau of Investigation officially launched its celebrated '10 Most Wanted' list on 14 March 1950. Since then almost 500 criminals have figured on it, the most notable in recent years being No. 456, Osama Bin Laden, who has been included since 7 June 1999. Names appear until individuals are captured, die or charges are dropped. On 8 January 1969 bank robber and double cop murderer Billie Austin Bryant appeared on the list for the record shortest time – just two hours – before he was arrested.

Murder Most Foul

THE 10 **COUNTRIES WITH THE HIGHEST MURDER RATES**

COUNTRY / MURDERS PER 100,000 POPULATION*

1 Venezuela 42.0

2 South Africa 39.5

3 Colombia 39.3

4 Jamaica 31.6

5 El Salvador 31.5

6 Brazil 27.0

7 Guatemala 25.5

8 Russia 19.8

9 Ecuador 18.3

10 Kazakhstan 16.3

* In latest year for which figures available

THE 10 **MOST COMMON MURDER WEAPONS AND METHODS IN ENGLAND AND WALES**

WEAPON/METHOD	VICTIMS (2006–07)		
	MEN	WOMEN	TOTAL
1 Sharp instrument	185	73	25
2 Hitting and kicking	126	14	140
3 Unknown	51	19	70
4 Shooting	53	6	59
5 Strangulation	15	41	56
6 Other	28	15	43
7 Blunt instrument	33	8	41
8 Burning	13	15	28
9 Poison or drugs	24	1	25
10 Drowning	7	1	8

Source: Home Office

THE 10 **WORST YEARS FOR MURDER IN ENGLAND AND WALES***

YEAR#	MURDER RATE PER MILLION POPULATION	TOTAL
1 **2003**	18.2	952
2 **2002**	15.4	803
3 **2005**	15.5	793
4 **2004**	15.0	788
5 **2001**	14.9	771
6 **2007**	13.7	757
7 **2006**	14.0	746
8 **2000**	13.0	675
9 **1995**	13.0	662
10 **1994**	12.4	632

* Since 1946; some offences initially recorded as homicide are later reclassified, so figures may reduce over time

Prior to 1997, data relate to calendar year, from 1997 to financial year

Source: Home Office

Murders in England and Wales were in the low hundreds throughout the nineteenth century. They topped 400 in 1952, 500 in 1974 and 600 in 1987. Since the 1960s, the number of murders per million population has more than doubled.

PERPETRATOR / LOCATION / DATE / CIRCUMSTANCES   NO. KILLED

57

1 Woo Bum Kong, SangNamdo, South Korea, 28 Apr 1982
Off-duty policeman Woo Bum Kong (or Wou BomKon), 27, went on a drunken rampage with rifles and hand grenades, killing 57 and injuring 38 before blowing himself up with a grenade.

35

2 Martin Bryant, Port Arthur, Tasmania, Australia, 28 Apr 1996
Bryant, a 28-year-old Hobart resident, used a rifle in a horrific spree that began in a restaurant and ended with a siege in a guesthouse, in which he held hostages. He set it on fire before being captured by police.

32

3 Seung-Hui Cho, Virginia Tech, Blacksburg, Virginia, USA, 16 Apr 2007
South Korean-born Cho used handguns to kill 27 fellow students and five faculty members of Virginia Tech before turning a gun on himself in America's worst school shooting.

29

4= Baruch Kappel Goldstein, Hebron, occupied West Bank, Israel, 25 February 1994
Goldstein, a 42-year-old US immigrant doctor, carried out a gun massacre of Palestinians at prayer at the Tomb of the Patriarchs before being beaten to death by the crowd.

= Matsuo Toi, Tsuyama, Japan, 21 May 1938 29
Twenty-one-year old Toi used a rifle and swords to kill 29 of his neighbours before committing suicide.

28

6 Campo Elias Delgado, Bogota, Colombia, 4 Dec 1986
Delgado, a Vietnamese war veteran and electronics engineer, stabbed two and shot a further 26 people before being killed by police.

22

7= George Jo Hennard, Killeen, Texas, USA, 16 Oct 1991
Hennard drove his pickup truck through the window of Luby's Cafeteria and, in 11 minutes, killed 22 with semiautomatic pistols before shooting himself.

7= James Oliver Huberty, San Ysidro, California, USA, 18 Jul 1984
Huberty, aged 41, opened fire in a McDonald's restaurant, killing 21 before being shot dead by a SWAT marksman. A further 19 were wounded, including a victim who died the following day.

17

9= Thomas Hamilton, Dunblane, Stirling, UK, 13 Mar 1996
Hamilton, 43, shot 16 children and a teacher in Dunblane Primary School before killing himself in the UK's worst shooting incident – as a result of which firearm laws were tightened in the UK.

9= Robert Steinhäuser, Erfurt, Germany, 26 Apr 2000
Former student Steinhäuser returned to Johann Gutenberg Secondary School and killed 14 teachers, two students and a police officer with a handgun before shooting himself.

* By individuals, excluding terrorist and military actions; totals exclude perpetrator

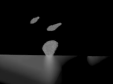

Punishment

THE 10 LAST WOMEN TO BE HANGED IN THE UK

VICTIM (AGE) / CRIME	DATE
1 Ruth Ellis (28) Shooting murder of David Blakely.	13 Jul 1955
2 Styllou Christofi (53) Murder of daughter-in-law Hella Christofi.	15 Dec 1954
3 Louisa Merrifield (46) Poisoning of her employer, Sarah Rickets.	18 Sep 1953
4 Margaret Allen (43) Murder of Ellen Chadwick.	12 Jan 1949
5 Charlotte Bryant (34) Poisoning of husband Frederick.	15 Jul 1936
6 Dorothea Waddingham (36) Poisoning of Louisa Baguley and daughter, Ada Baguley.	16 Apr 1936
7 Ethel Lillie Major (42) Poisoning of husband Arthur.	19 Dec 1934
8 Louie Calvert (33) Murder of Lily Waterhouse.	24 Jun 1926
9 Susan Newell (30) Murder of paperboy John Johnston (13).	10 Oct 1923
10 Edith Jessie Thompson (28) Murder of husband Percy.	9 Jan 1923

Between 1868 – when public hanging ended and executions were carried out within prisons – and 1955, a total of 40 women were hanged in the UK. The last hangings in the UK, of Peter Allen at Liverpool and John Welby at Manchester for the murder of John West, took place on the same day, 13 August 1964. Capital punishment was abolished in the UK on 9 November 1965.

THE 10 FIRST COUNTRIES TO ABOLISH CAPITAL PUNISHMENT

COUNTRY / ABOLISHED
1 Russia 1826
2 Venezuela 1863
3 San Marino 1865
4 Portugal 1867
5 Costa Rica 1877
6 Brazil 1889
7 Panama 1903
8 Norway 1905
9 Ecuador 1906
10 Uruguay 1907
UK 1965

Some countries abolished capital punishment in peacetime only, or for all crimes except treason, later extending it totally. Some countries officially retain capital punishment, but have effectively abolished it: the last execution in Liechtenstein, for example, took place in 1785. Among countries to abolish the death penalty recently are the Philippines in 2006, Albania and Rwanda in 2007, and Uzbekistan in 2008.

THE 10 LAST PEOPLE TO BE BEHEADED IN ENGLAND

VICTIM	DATE
1 Simon Fraser, Lord Lovat, (b. c.1667)	9 Apr 1747
2 Charles Radclyffe (b. 1693)	8 Dec 1746
3 = William Boyd, Lord Kilmarnock (b. 1704)	18 Aug 1746
= Arthur Elphinstone, Lord Balmerino (b. 1688)	18 Aug 1746
5 = William, Viscount Kenmure (birthdate unknown)	24 Feb 1716
6 = Sir James Radclyffe, Earl of Derwentwater (b. 1689)	24 Feb 1716
7 Alice Lisle (b. c.1614)	2 Sep 1685
8 James, Duke of Monmouth (b. 1649)	15 Jul 1685
9 William Russell (b. 1639)	21 Jul 1683
10 William Howard, Viscount Stafford (b. 1614)	29 Dec 1680

The 80-year-old peer, beheaded for treason at Tower Hill, London, was the last person to be beheaded in Britain. Beheading was introduced in England by William the Conqueror. Waltheof, Earl of Northumberland, was the first to be executed, at Winchester on 31 May 1076. It was thereafter the most common method for people of high rank. Beheading was the most common method used in cases of treason during the reigns of King Henry VIII and queens Elizabeth and Mary. Earl Ferrers, the last peer to be executed (for murder), requested beheading, but it was denied and he was hanged instead on 5 May 1760, at Tyburn, using a new trapdoor-like apparatus, and wearing his white wedding suit – but not, as popular legend has it, with a silk rope.

THE 10 **COUNTRIES WITH THE HIGHEST PRISON POPULATIONS**

COUNTRY	PRISONERS PER 100,000 OF POPULATION	TOTAL PRISONERS*
1 USA	751	2,258,983
2 China	119	1,565,771
3 Russia	632	892,330
4 Brazil	219	419,551
5 India	32	358,368
6 Mexico	198	217,436
7 South Africa	348	165,987
8 Thailand	253	165,316
9 Iran	222	158,351
10 Ukraine	325	149.690

* As at date of most recent data

Source: International Centre for Prison Studies

THE 10 **LARGEST PRISONS IN THE UK**

PRISON	CAPACITY*
1 Wandsworth, London	1,481
2 Winson Green, Birmingham	1,466
3 Walton, Liverpool	1,381
4 Altcourse, Liverpool	1,314
5 Wormwood Scrubs, London	1,264
6 Strangeways, Manchester	1,219
7 Parc, Bridgend	1,162
8 Doncaster	1,149
9 Pentonville, London	1,138
10 Forest Bank, Pendlebury	1,119

* As at February 2008

Source: HM Prison Service

Prison numbers
Top: Inmates at a Russian correctional labour settlement. Russia has the world's third largest prison population, but is second only to the United States for its incarceration rate as a percentage of the population.

Inset: A female chain gang in the USA: women represent over nine per cent of the total prison population – 12.9 per cent of local jail inmates and 7.2 of state and federal prisoners.

World Wars

THE 10 **LARGEST ARMED FORCES OF WORLD WAR I**

1 SOLDIER = 1,000,000 / COUNTRY   PERSONNEL*

#	Country	Personnel*
1	Russia	12,000,000
2	Germany	11,000,000
3	British Empire	8,904,467
4	France	8,410,000
5	Austria-Hungary	7,800,000
6	Italy	5,615,000
7	USA	4,355,000
8	Turkey	2,850,000
9	Bulgaria	1,200,000
10	Japan	800,000

* Total at peak strength

Russia's armed forces were relatively small in relation to the country's population – some six per cent, compared with 17 per cent in Germany. Several other European nations had forces that were similarly substantial in relation to their populations: Serbia's army was equivalent to 14 per cent of its population. In total, more than 65,000,000 combatants were involved in fighting some of the costliest battles – in terms of numbers killed – that the world has ever known.

THE 10 **LARGEST ARMED FORCES OF WORLD WAR II**

1 SOLDIER = 1,000,000 / COUNTRY   PERSONNEL*

#	Country	Personnel*
1	USSR	12,500,000
2	USA	12,364,000
3	Germany	10,000,000
4	Japan	6,095,000
5	France	5,700,000
6	UK	4,683,000
7	Italy	4,500,000
8	China	3,800,000
9	India	2,150,000
10	Poland	1,000,000

* Total at peak strength

Allowing for deaths and casualties, the total forces mobilized during the course of the war is, of course, greater than the peak strength figures: that of the USSR, for example, has been put as high as 20,000,000, the USA 16,354,000, Germany 17,900,000 million, Japan 9,100,000 million and the UK 5,896,000. In contrast, the forces of a number of Central and South American countries that did not declare war until a late stage were numbered in the low thousands.

THE 10 **COUNTRIES SUFFERING THE GREATEST MILITARY LOSSES IN WORLD WAR I**

#	COUNTRY	KILLED
1	Germany	1,773,700
2	Russia	1,700,000
3	France	1,357,800
4	Austria-Hungary	1,200,000
5	British Empire*	908,371
6	Italy	650,000
7	Romania	335,706
8	Turkey	325,000
9	USA	116,516
10	Bulgaria	87,500

* Including Australia, Canada, India, New Zealand, South Africa, etc.

THE 10 **COUNTRIES SUFFERING THE GREATEST MILITARY LOSSES IN WORLD WAR II**

#	COUNTRY	KILLED
1	USSR	13,600,000*
2	Germany	3,300,000
3	China	1,324,516
4	Japan	1,140,429
5	British Empire# (UK 264,000)	357,116
6	Romania	350,000
7	Poland	320,000
8	Yugoslavia	305,000
9	USA	292,131
10	Italy	279,800
	Total	21,268,992

* Total, of which 7.8 million battlefield deaths
# Including Australia, Canada, India, New

TOP 10 BRITISH AND COMMONWEALTH AIR ACES OF WORLD WAR II

PILOT	COUNTRY	KILLS CLAIMED
1 Sqd Ldr Marmaduke Thomas St John Pattle	South Africa	50.67
2 Gp Capt James Edgar 'Johnny' Johnson	UK	36.92
3 Wng Cdr Brendan Eamonn Fergus 'Paddy' Finucane	Ireland	32.00
4 William 'Cherry' Vale	UK	31.50
5 Flt Lt George Frederick Beurling	Canada	31.33
6 Gp Capt Adolph Gysbert 'Sailor' Malan	South Africa	29.50
7 Wng Cdr John Randall Daniel 'Bob' Braham	UK	29.00
8 Wng Cdr Clive Robert Caldwell	Australia	28.50
9 Sqd Ldr James Harry 'Ginger' Lacey	UK	28.00
10 Wng Cdr Colin Falkland Gray	New Zealand	27.70

TOP 10 LUFTWAFFE ACES OF WORLD WAR II

PILOT	KILLS CLAIMED
1 Major Eric Hartmann	352
2 Major Gerhard Barkhorn	301
3 Major Günther Rall	275
4 Oberleutnant Otto Kittel	267
5 Major Walther Nowotny	258
6 Major Wilhelm Batz	237
7 Major Erich Rudorffer	222
8 Oberst. Heinz Bär	220
9 Oberst. Hermann Graf	212
10 Major Heinrich Ehrler	209

Kills that are expressed as fractions refer to those that were shared with others, the number of fighters involved and the extent of each pilot's participation determining the proportion allocated to him. 'Probable' victories are excluded.

Scramble!
British and Commonwealth fighter pilots take to the skies. Many air aces' combat victories were achieved in the Battle of Britain, during the summer of 1940.

Right: Eric Hartmann
Although the Luftwaffe's apparently high claims have been dismissed by some military historians as inflated for propaganda purposes, few have questioned the so-called 'Blond Knight' Eric Hartmann's achievement, however, and his victories over Soviet aircraft so outraged the USSR that after the war he was arrested and sentenced to 25 years in a Russian labour camp. He was released in 1955, returned to serve in the West German air force, and died on 20 September 1993.

The Military Balance

TOP 10 LARGEST ARMED FORCES

COUNTRY	ARMY	ESTIMATED ACTIVE FORCES NAVY	AIR	TOTAL
1 China	1,600,000	255,000	250,000	2,105,000
2 USA	593,327	341,588	336,081	1,498,157*
3 India	1,100,000	55,000	125,000	1,288,000#
4 North Korea	950,000	46,000	110,000	1,106,000
5 Russia	360,000	142,000	195,000	1,027,000†
6 South Korea	560,000	63,000	64,000	687,000
7 Pakistan	550,000	24,000	45,000	619,000
8 Iran	350,000	18,000	52,000	545,000§
9 Turkey	402,000	48,600	60,000	510,600
10 Egypt	340,000	18,500	30,000	468,500‡
UK	*99,707*	*38,900*	*41,920*	*180,527*

* Includes 186,661 Marine Corps and 40,500 Coast Guard
\# Includes 8,000 Coast Guard
† Includes 80,000 Strategic Deterrent Forces and 250,000 Command and Support
§ Includes 125,000 Islamic Revolutionary Guard Corps
‡ Includes 80,000 Air Defence Command

Source: The International Institute for Strategic Studies, *The Military Balance 2008*

Several countries also have substantial reserves on standby: South Korea's has been estimated at some 4.5 million plus 3.5 Paramilitary, Vietnam's at five million and China's 800,000. North Korea has the highest number of troops in relation to its population – 47.85 per 1,000.

Korean People's Army
Despite its precarious economy, North Korea is the world's most militarized country, with one in five of its adult population in the armed forces, the highest military/civilian ratio.

TOP 10 COUNTRIES WITH THE MOST SUBMARINES

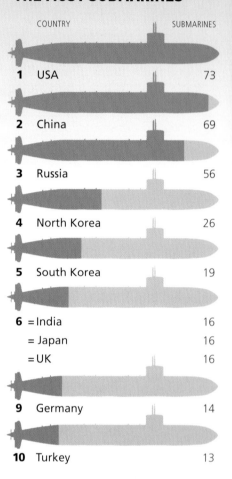

COUNTRY	SUBMARINES
1 USA	73
2 China	69
3 Russia	56
4 North Korea	26
5 South Korea	19
6 = India	16
= Japan	16
= UK	16
9 Germany	14
10 Turkey	13

TOP 10 **ARMS IMPORTERS**

COUNTRY (1 CRATE = $1 MILLION)   IMPORTS 2006 ($)

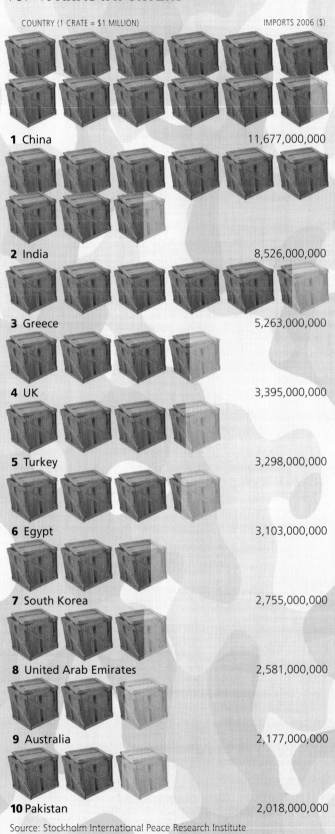

1 China   11,677,000,000

2 India   8,526,000,000

3 Greece   5,263,000,000

4 UK   3,395,000,000

5 Turkey   3,298,000,000

6 Egypt   3,103,000,000

7 South Korea   2,755,000,000

8 United Arab Emirates   2,581,000,000

9 Australia   2,177,000,000

10 Pakistan   2,018,000,000

Source: Stockholm International Peace Research Institute

TOP 10 **ARMS MANUFACTURERS**

COMPANY / COUNTRY	SALES 2006 ($)
1 Boeing (USA)	28,050,000,000
2 Northrop Grumman (USA)	27,590,000,000
3 Lockheed Martin (USA)	26,460,000,000
4 BAE Systems (UK)	23,230,000,000
5 Raytheon (USA)	19,800,000,000
6 General Dynamics (USA)	16,570,000,000
7 Finmeccanica (Italy)	9,800,000,000
8 EADS (Europe)	9,580,000,000
9 L-3 Communications (USA)	8,970,000,000
10 Thales (France)	8,940,000,000

TOP 10 **MILITARY EXPENDITURE COUNTRIES**

COUNTRY	MILITARY EXPENDITURE 2006 ($) PER CAPITA	TOTAL
1 USA	1,756	528,700,000,000
2 UK	990	59,200,000,000
3 France	875	53,100,000,000
4 China	37	49,500,000,000
5 Japan	341	43,700,000,000
6 Germany	447	37,000,000,000
7 Russia	244	34,700,000,000
8 Italy	514	29,900,000,000
9 Saudi Arabia	1,152	29,000,000,000
10 India	21	23,900,000,000
Top 10	–	*888,700,000,000*
World total	–	*1,158,000,000,000*

Source: SIPRI

World Religions

TOP 10 RELIGIOUS BELIEFS

	RELIGION	FOLLOWERS
1	Christianity	2,159,141,594
2	Islam	1,345,175,832
3	Hinduism	859,893,462
4	Buddhism	380,567,154
5	Chinese folk-religions	380,486,297
6	Ethnic religions	258,307,065
7	New religions	104,923,020
8	Sikhism	22,199,953
9	Judaism	14,678,791
10	Spiritists	13,176,576

Source: World Christian Database

These authoritative estimates imply that almost one-third of the world's population are nominally (self-declared), if not practising, Christians, and one-fifth followers of Islam. Mainstream religions have seen a decline in formal attendance, while it is reckoned that more than 14 per cent of the world population profess no religious beliefs of any kind.

TOP 10 LARGEST CHRISTIAN POPULATIONS

	COUNTRY	CHRISTIANS
1	USA	244,520,177
2	Brazil	170,208,945
3	Russia	113,269,039
4	China	109,815,781
5	Mexico	102,594,161
6	Philippines	74,170,629
7	India	64,514,845
8	Nigeria	59,960,048
9	Germany	59,382,852
10	Dem. Rep. of Congo	54,882,976
	UK	*48,357,974*
	World	*2,159,141,594*

Source: World Christian Database

TOP 10 LARGEST MUSLIM POPULATIONS

	COUNTRY	MUSLIMS
1	Pakistan	151,428,138
2	India	150,951,110
3	Bangladesh	125,614,365
4	Indonesia	124,903,322
5	Turkey	71,285,299
6	Iran	68,339,642
7	Egypt	62,948,005
8	Nigeria	58,053,739
9	Algeria	31,831,159
10	Morocco	30,965,312
	UK	*1,524,990*
	World	*1,345,175,832*

Source: World Christian Database

TOP 10 COUNTRIES WITH MOST ATHEISTS AND NON-RELIGIOUS PEOPLE

	COUNTRY	ATHEISTS	NON-RELIGIOUS	TOTAL
1	China	106,975,051	540,062,607	647,037,658
2	USA	1,160,293	33,742,215	34,902,508
3	Germany	1,971,964	17,162,813	19,134,777
4	Japan	3,675,370	13,032,785	16,708,155
5	Vietnam	5,781,497	10,653,043	16,434,540
6	North Korea	3,503,650	12,523,632	16,027,282
7	India	1,771,096	13,729,435	15,500,531
8	Russia	2,197,538	10,375,595	12,573,133
9	France	2,387,472	9,617,460	12,004,932
10	Italy	2,083,530	7,404,434	9,487,964
	UK	*839,047*	*7,232,994*	*8,072,041*
	World	*148,028,092*	*764,002,046*	*912,030,138*

Source: World Christian Database

Time for prayer
A Bedouin Arab in the Negev Desert, Israel, faces Mecca to perform salah – the ritual of prayer that Muslims practise five times daily.

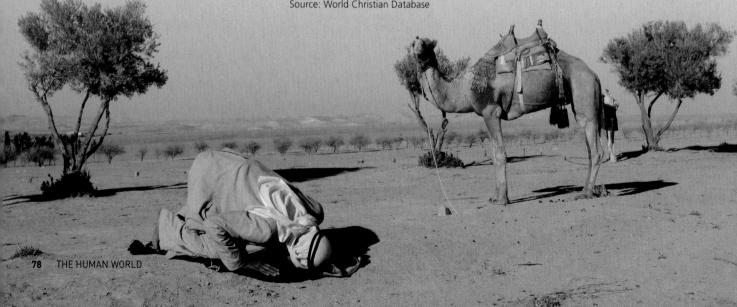

TOP 10 **LARGEST JEWISH POPULATIONS**

	COUNTRY	JEWS
1	USA	5,729,147
2	Israel	4,867,198
3	France	604,955
4	Argentina	512,671
5	Canada	418,285
6	Brazil	383,837
7	UK	279,602
8	Germany	225,063
9	Russia	186,935
10	Ukraine	*180,726*
	World	*14,678,791*

Source: World Christian Database

Almost every country in the world has Jewish communities. While not an independent country, the Gaza Strip and West Bank are reckoned to contain 437,638 Jews.

TOP 10 **LARGEST HINDU POPULATIONS**

	COUNTRY	HINDUS
1	India	803,533,560
2	Nepal	19,329,934
3	Bangladesh	13,661,586
4	Indonesia	7,112,335
5	Sri Lanka	2,342,834
6	Pakistan	2,055,274
7	Malaysia	1,588,790
8	USA	1,330,446
9	South Africa	1,128,942
10	Myanmar	861,787
	UK	*615,354*
	World	*859,893,462*

Source: World Christian Database

Hindus comprise 73 per cent of the population of India and 71 per cent of Nepal, but only 10 per cent of that of Bangladesh.

TOP 10 **LARGEST BUDDHIST POPULATIONS**

	COUNTRY	BUDDHISTS
1	China	117,016,597
2	Japan	71,533,450
3	Thailand	53,394,844
4	Vietnam	40,821,035
5	Myanmar	37,419,764
6	Sri Lanka	14,302,328
7	Cambodia	11,999,857
8	India	7,576,063
9	South Korea	7,225,875
10	Malaysia	5,970,800
	UK	*189,887*
	World	*380,567,154*

Source: World Christian Database

Indian religion
The elephant deity Ganesh is at the centre of a Hindu festival in Mumbai, India.

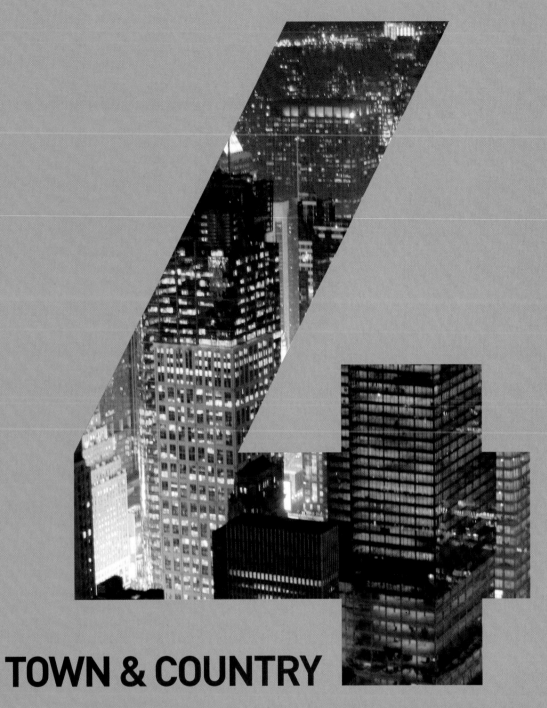

TOWN & COUNTRY

Countries Large & Small

TOP 10 **LARGEST LANDLOCKED COUNTRIES**

COUNTRY / NEIGHBOURS	AREA SQ KM	SQ MILES
1 Kazakhstan China, Kyrgyzstan, Russia, Turkmenistan, Uzbekistan	2,717,300	1,049,156
2 Mongolia China, Russia	1,564,116	603,908
3 Niger Algeria, Benin, Burkina Faso, Chad, Libya, Mali, Nigeria	1,266,699	489,075
4 Chad Cameroon, Central African Republic, Libya, Niger, Nigeria, Sudan	1,259,201	486,180
5 Mali Algeria, Burkina Faso, Côte d'Ivoire, Guinea, Mauritania, Niger, Senegal	1,219,999	471,044
6 Ethiopia Djibouti, Eritrea, Kenya, Somalia, Sudan	1,127,127	435,186
7 Bolivia Argentina, Brazil, Chile, Paraguay, Peru	1,098,580	424,164
8 Zambia Angola, Dem. Rep. of Congo, Malawi, Mozambique, Namibia, Tanzania, Zimbabwe	752,614	290,585
9 Afghanistan China, Iran, Pakistan, Tajikistan, Turkmenistan, Uzbekistan	647,500	250,001
10 Central African Republic Cameroon, Chad, Congo, Dem. Rep. of Congo, Sudan	622,984	240,535

There are 43 landlocked countries in the world. Kazakhstan and Turkmenistan both have coasts on the Caspian Sea – which is itself landlocked.

One steppe beyond
Mongolia, the world's least densely populated country, is second in size only to Kazakhstan among the world's landlocked countries. The economies of such territories often suffer through their lack of coastal access for trade.

TOP 10 **LARGEST COUNTRIES**

COUNTRY	AREA SQ KM	SQ MILES	% OF WORLD TOTAL
1 Russia	17,075,200	6,592,772	11.5
2 Canada	9,984,670	3,855,103	6.7
3 USA	9,631,420	3,718,712	6.5
4 China	9,596,960	3,705,407	6.4
5 Brazil	8,511,965	3,286,488	5.7
6 Australia	7,686,850	2,967,910	5.2
7 India	3,287,590	1,269,346	2.2
8 Argentina	2,766,890	1,068,302	2.1
9 Kazakhstan	2,717,300	1,049,156	1.9
10 Sudan	2,505,810	967,499	1.7
UK	*244,820*	*94,526*	*0.2*
World total	*148,940,000*	*57,506,062*	*100.0*

Source: CIA, *The World Factbook 2008*

This list is based on the total area of a country within its borders, including offshore islands, inland water such as lakes and rivers and reservoirs. It may thus differ from versions in which these are excluded. Antarctica has an approximate area of 13,200,000 sq km (5,096,549 sq miles), but is discounted as it is not considered a country. The countries in the Top 10 collectively comprise 50 per cent of the total Earth's surface.

Landlocked Doubles
Two countries in the world are doubly landlocked – completely surrounded by other landlocked countries: Uzbekistan (surrounded by Afghanistan, Kazakhstan, Kyrgyzstan, Tajikistan and Turkmenistan) and Liechtenstein (Austria and Switzerland), the third smallest landlocked country after Vatican City (0.44 sq km/0.17 sq miles) and San Marino (61.20 sq km/23.63 sq miles), both of which are surrounded by Italy.

TOP 10 **COUNTRIES WITH THE LONGEST SINGLE COUNTRY BORDER**

	COUNTRY / BORDERED BY	BORDER KM	MILES
1	Canada (USA)	8,893	5,530
2	Portugal (Spain)	1,214	754
3	Lesotho (South Africa)	909	565
4	The Gambia (Senegal)	740	460
5	Brunei (Malaysia)	381	237
6 =	Dominican Republic (Haiti)	360	220
=	Ireland (UK: Northern Ireland)	360	220
8	South Korea (North Korea)	238	148
9	East Timor (Indonesia)	228	142
10	Denmark (Germany)	68	42

Canada coastline
Including all its islands, the coastline of Canada is more than six times as long as the distance round the Earth at the Equator.

TOP 10 **COUNTRIES WITH THE LONGEST COASTLINES**

	COUNTRY	TOTAL COASTLINE LENGTH KM	MILES
1	Canada	202,080	125,566
2	Indonesia	54,716	33,999
3	Russia	37,653	23,396
4	Philippines	36,289	22,559
5	Japan	29,751	18,486
6	Australia	25,760	16,007
7	Norway	25,148	15,626
8	USA	19,924	12,380
9	New Zealand	15,134	9,404
10	China	14,500	9,010

Source: CIA, *The World Factbook 2008*

THE 10 **SMALLEST COUNTRIES**

	COUNTRY	AREA SQ KM	SQ MILES
1	Vatican City	0.44	0.17
2	Monaco	1.95	0.75
3	Nauru	21.20	8.18
4	Tuvalu	25.63	9.89
5	San Marino	61.20	23.63
6	Liechtenstein	160.00	61.77
7	Marshall Islands	181.43	70.05
8	Saint Kitts and Nevis	269.40	104.01
9	Maldives	298.00	115.05
10	Malta	315.10	121.66

There are some 25 'microstates' – independent countries with a land area of less than 1,000 sq km (386 sq miles).

Countries – Population

TOP 10 **MOST DENSELY POPULATED COUNTRIES**

	COUNTRY	AREA (SQ KM)	POPULATION (2009 EST.)	POPULATION PER SQ KM
1	Monaco	1.95	32,920	16,460.0
2	Singapore	683	4,657,542	6,819.2
3	Vatican City	0.44	932	2,118.2
4	Maldives	300	389,434	1,298.1
5	Malta	316	405,165	1,282.2
6	Bangladesh	133,910	156,654,645	1,169.9
7	Bahrain	665	727,785	1,094.4
8	Nauru	21	14,014	667.3
9	Barbados	431	282,967	656.5
10	Mauritius	2,030	1,284,264	632.6
	UK	*241,590*	*61,113,205*	*253.0*
	World	*130,772,591*	*6,757,062,760*	*51.7*

Source: US Census Bureau, International Data Base

Crowded islands
Although some of its islands are virtually uninhabited, the Maldives has one of the world's highest birth rates and average population densities.

TOP 10 **LEAST DENSELY POPULATED COUNTRIES**

	COUNTRY	AREA (SQ KM)	POPULATION (2009 EST.)	POPULATION PER SQ KM
1	Mongolia	1,564,116	3,041,142	1.94
2	Namibia	825,418	2,071,015	2.50
3	Australia	7,617,930	20,764,417	2.73
4	Suriname	161,470	481,267	2.98
5	Iceland	100,250	306,694	3.06
6	Botswana	585,370	1,868,330	3.19
7	Mauritania	1,030,400	3,462,063	3.36
8	Libya	1,759,540	6,310,434	3.59
9	Canada	9,093,507	33,966,667	3.74
10	Guyana	196,850	772,298	3.92

Source: US Census Bureau, International Data Base

In contrast to those countries that have population densities in the hundreds (and, in some instances, thousands) per sq km, these sparsely populated countries of the world generally present environmental disadvantages that make human habitation challenging, with large tracts of mountain, desert or dense forest, or extreme climates. Although not a country, Greenland, with an area of 2,166,086 sq km and a population of 56,307, has a density of just 0.03 people per sq km.

TOP 10 **LEAST POPULATED COUNTRIES**

COUNTRY	POPULATION (2009 EST.)
1 Vatican City	557
2 Tuvalu	12,378
3 Nauru	14,014
4 Palau	21,331
5 San Marino	30,324
6 Monaco	32,920
7 Liechtenstein	34,741
8 Saint Kitts and Nevis	39,941
9 Marshall Islands	64,522
10 Antigua and Barbuda	70,194

Source: US Census Bureau, International Data Base

The most recent and unusually precise official census statistics, published by Vatican City in 2007, revealed that the resident population comprised the pope and 57 cardinals, 293 clergy members of pontifical representations, 62 other clergy, 101 members of the Swiss Guard and 43 lay persons with unspecified functions.

TOP 10 **MOST POPULATED COUNTRIES**

COUNTRY	POPULATION (2009 EST.)
1 China	1,338,612,968
2 India	1,166,079,217
3 USA	306,499,395
4 Indonesia	240,271,522
5 Brazil	193,767,441
6 Pakistan	170,790,583
7 Bangladesh	156,654,645
8 Nigeria	141,617,030
9 Russia	140,041,247
10 Japan	127,078,679
UK	*61,113,205*
World	*6,757,062,760*

Source: US Census Bureau, International Data Base

In 2009, the population of Nigeria will overtake that of Russia, which has experienced progressive decline. Mexico (111,211,789), is the only other country with a population of more than 100 million.

Youngest country
Precisely half the population of Uganda is aged under 15, imposing a considerable economic and social burden on the country.

TOP 10 **COUNTRIES WITH THE YOUNGEST POPULATIONS**

COUNTRY	% UNDER 15 (2009 EST.)
1 Uganda	50.0
2 Mali	48.3
3 Dem. Rep. of Congo	47.3
4 Niger	46.9
5 São Tomé and Príncipe	46.8
6 Chad	46.7
7 Burkina Faso	46.4
8 = Burundi	46.2
= Yemen	46.2
10 Congo	46.0
UK	*16.7*
World average	*26.9*

TOP 10 **COUNTRIES WITH THE OLDEST POPULATIONS**

COUNTRY	% OVER 65 (2009 EST.)
1 Monaco	22.9
2 Japan	22.2
3 = Germany	20.3
= Italy	20.3
5 Greece	19.2
6 Sweden	18.8
7 Spain	18.1
8 Bulgaria	17.7
9 = Belgium	17.6
= Portugal	17.6
UK	*16.2*
World	*7.7*

Source: US Census Bureau, International Data Base

With lower death rates and a higher life expectancy than elsewhere, nine of these 10 countries are in Europe. On average, 18 per cent of people in Western Europe are over 65 and five per cent over 80.

Population Projections

The only way is up
Its dense population has compelled Singapore to build upward: it has 38 skyscrapers higher than 152 m (500 ft).

THE 10 **LEAST DENSELY POPULATED COUNTRIES IN 2050**

	COUNTRY	AREA (SQ KM)	EST. POPULATION (2050)	EST. POPULATION PER SQ KM
1	Namibia	825,418	1,795,852	2.2
2	Mongolia	1,564,116	4,340,496	2.8
3	Guyana	196,850	597,806	3.0
4	Australia	7,617,930	24,175,783	3.2
5	Iceland	100,250	350,922	3.5
6	Suriname	161,470	617,249	3.8
7	Botswana	585,370	2,385,685	4.1
8	Canada	9,093,507	41,429,579	4.6
9	Kazakhstan	2,669,800	15,099,700	5.7
10	Libya	1,759,540	10,817,176	6.1

Source: US Census Bureau, International Data Base

Russia, with a vast area (16,995,800 sq km) and projected 2050 population of 109,187,353, falls just short of the Top 10. While not an independent country, Greenland (410,449 sq km; projected 2050 population 56,644) will have just 0.14 people per sq km.

TOP 10 **MOST DENSELY POPULATED COUNTRIES IN 2050**

	COUNTRY	AREA (SQ KM)	EST. POPULATION (2050)	EST. POPULATION PER SQ KM
1	Monaco	1.95	32,964	16,482.0
2	Singapore	683	4,635,110	6,786.4
3	Maldives	300	815,031	2,716.8
4	Bangladesh	133,910	279,955,405	2,090.6
5	Bahrain	665	973,412	1,463.8
6	Malta	316	395,639	1,344.7
7	Nauru	21	22,696	1,252.0
8	Rwanda	24,948	25,128,735	1,007.2
9	Burundi	25,650	22,852,556	890.9
10	Comoros	2,170	1,837,671	846.9
	UK	*241,590*	*63,977,435*	*264.8*
	World	*130,772,591*	*9,401,550,854*	*71.9*

Source: US Census Bureau, International Data Base

TOP 10 **FASTEST-GROWING COUNTRIES**

COUNTRY / POPULATION INCREASE 2006–2050   RED FIGURES REPRESENT % GROWTH

Source: Population Reference Bureau, *2006 World Population Data Sheet*

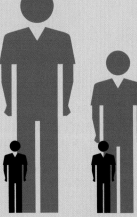

1 Uganda 371   **2=** Niger 248 = Malawi 248   **4** Burundi 229   **5** Guinea-Bissau 225

6 East Timor 224   **7** Liberia 217   **8=** Yemen 214 = Chad 214   **10** Mali 202

World 41

TOP 10 **MOST POPULATED COUNTRIES IN 2025**

	COUNTRY	EST. POPULATION (2025)
1	China	1,453,123,817
2	India	1,448,821,234
3	USA	349,666,199
4	Indonesia	278,502,882
5	Pakistan	218,495,756
6	Brazil	217,825,222
7	Nigeria	206,165,946
8	Bangladesh	204,538,715
9	Mexico	130,198,692
10	Russia	128,180,396
	Top 10 total	*4,635,518,859*
	UK	*63,818,586*
	World	*7,958,508,362*

Source: US Census Bureau, International Data Base

In a single generation, from 2000 to 2025, Nigeria's population is forecast to increase by almost 75 per cent, elevating it from tenth to sixth place in this list, while Mexico makes leaps into the Top 10, ousting Japan.

TOP 10 **MOST POPULATED COUNTRIES IN 2050**

	COUNTRY	EST. POPULATION (2050)
1	India	1,807,878,574
2	China	1,424,161,948
3	USA	420,080,587
4	Nigeria	356,523,597
5	Indonesia	313,020,847
6	Bangladesh	279,955,405
7	Pakistan	277,554,980
8	Brazil	228,426,737
9	Dem. Rep. of Congo	203,039,557
10	Mexico	47,907,650
	Top 10 total	*5,358,549,882*
	UK	*63,977,435*
	World	*9,401,505,490*

Source: US Census Bureau, International Data Base

Estimates of national populations in 2050 present a striking change as long-time world leader China is markedly eclipsed by India, a reversal that is projected to take place around the year 2026.

Slowing the tide
Since the introduction 30 years ago of a one-child policy, China's runaway population growth has been curbed and is projected to decline as India's goes into overdrive and overtakes it to become the world's most populous country.

THE 10 **LEAST POPULATED COUNTRIES IN 2050**

	COUNTRY	EST. POPULATION (2050)
1	Tuvalu	20,018
2	Nauru	22,696
3	Palau	26,300
4	Monaco	32,964
5	San Marino	35,335
6	Liechtenstein	35,776
7	Saint Kitts and Nevis	52,348
8	Dominica	64,772
9	Andorra	69,129
10	Antigua and Barbuda	69,259

Source: US Census Bureau, International Data Base

Cities

TOP 10 **MOST URBANIZED COUNTRIES**

COUNTRY	% OF POPULATION LIVING IN URBAN AREAS (2005)
1 = Singapore	100.0
= Monaco	100.0
= Nauru	100.0
= Vatican	100.0
5 Kuwait	98.3
6 Belgium	97.2
7 Bahrain	96.5
8 Qatar	95.4
9 Malta	95.3
10 Venezuela	93.4
UK	*89.7*
World	*48.6*

Source: United Nations, *Human Development Report 2007–2008*

THE 10 **LEAST URBANIZED COUNTRIES**

COUNTRY	% OF POPULATION LIVING IN URBAN AREAS (2005)
1 Burundi	10.0
2 Bhutan	11.1
3 Trinidad & Tobago	12.2
4 Papua New Guinea	13.4
5 Uganda	14.5
6 Sri Lanka	15.1
7 Nepal	15.8
8 Ethiopia	16.0
9 Niger	16.8
10 Solomon Islands	17.0

Source: United Nations, *Human Development Report 2007–2008*

NOW & THEN

2007   **1987**

TOP 10 **LARGEST CITIES**

2007

CITY / COUNTRY	POPULATION
1 Tokyo, Japan	33,600,000
2 Seoul, South Korea	23,400,000
3 Mexico City, Mexico	22,400,000
4 New York, USA	21,900,000
5 Mumbai (Bombay), India	21,600,000
6 Delhi, India	21,500,000
7 São Paulo, Brazil	20,600,000
8 Los Angeles, USA	18,000,000
9 Shanghai, China	17,500,000
10 Osaka, Japan	16,700,000

1987

CITY / COUNTRY	POPULATION
1 Tokyo, Japan	23,322,000
2 New York, USA	15,827,000
3 Mexico City, Mexico	14,474,000
4 São Paulo, Brazil	13,427,000
5 Shanghai, China	12,396,000
6 Los Angeles, USA	10,445,000
7 Osaka, Japan	10,351,000
8 Buenos Aires, Argentina	10,269,000
9 Bombay, India	9,898,000
10 Calcutta, India	9,882,000

Source: Th. Brinkhoff: The Principal Agglomerations of the World, http://www.citypopulation.de, 2007-09-30

The populations listed are those of the urban agglomerations – the central cities and surrounding continuous built-up suburban areas, regardless of administrative boundaries. Specific definitions of agglomerations usually identify them as those with a density of over 400 people per sq km (1,000 per sq mile). In the 20 years from 1987 to 2007, the total population of the cities in each Top 10 went up from 130,291,000 to 217,200,000.

Megacity
Tokyo's population grew by 44 per cent between 1987 and 2007 and is now greater than that of Canada.

TOP 10 **LARGEST CAPITAL CITIES**

CITY / COUNTRY	EST. POPULATION (2007)
1 Tokyo (including Yokohama and Kawasaki), Japan	33,600,000
2 Seoul (including Bucheon, Goyang, Incheon, Seongnam and Suweon), South Korea	23,400,000
3 Mexico City (including Nezahualcóyotl, Ecatepec and Naucalpan), Mexico	22,400,000
4 Delhi (including Faridabad and Ghaziabad), India	21,500,000
5 Cairo (including Al-Jizah and Shubra al-Khaymah), Egypt	16,100,000
6 Manila (including Kalookan and Quezon City), Philippines	15,600,000
7 Jakarta (including Bekasi, Bogor, Depok and Tangerang), Indonesia	15,100,000
8 Buenos Aires (including San Justo and La Plata), Argentina	13,600,000
9 Moscow, Russia	13,500,000
10 Beijing, China	12,800,000

Source: Th. Brinkhoff: The Principal Agglomerations of the World, http://www.citypopulation.de, 2007-09-30

On top of the world
Founded as a silver-mining town, the elevated city of Potosi, Bolivia, dates to the mid-sixteenth century. It was once home to the country's National Mint and is a UNESCO World Heritage Site.

TOP 10 **HIGHEST TOWNS AND CITIES**

CITY / COUNTRY	HEIGHT M	FT
1 La Rinconada, Peru	5,100	16,732
2 Wenzhuan, Tibet, China	5,099	16,730
3 El Alto*, Bolivia	4,150	13,615
4 Potosí, Bolivia	4,090	13,419
5 Oruro, Bolivia	3,702	12,146
6 Lhasa#, Tibet, China	3,684	12,087
7 Apartaderos, Venezuela	3,505	11,502
8 Cusco, Peru	3,360	11,024
9 Huancayo, Peru	3,271	10,732
10 Alma, Colorado, USA	3,158	10,361

* A suburb of La Paz; the main city – the world's highest capital – is at 3,632 m (11,916 ft)
# Former capital of independent Tibet

Place Names

TOP 10 LARGEST COUNTRIES THAT CHANGED THEIR NAMES IN THE PAST 100 YEARS

	FORMER NAME	CURRENT NAME	YEAR CHANGED	AREA SQ KM	AREA SQ MILES
1	Zaïre	Dem. Rep. of Congo	1997	2,345,410	905,567
2	Dutch East Indies	Indonesia	1945	1,919,440	741,100
3	Persia	Iran	1935	1,648,000	636,296
4	Tanganyika/Zanzibar	Tanzania	1964	945,087	364,900
5	South West Africa	Namibia	1990	825,418	318,695
6	Northern Rhodesia	Zambia	1964	752,614	290,586
7	Burma	Myanmar	1989	678,500	261,970
8	Ubanghi Shari	Central African Republic	1960	622,984	240,535
9	Bechuanaland	Botswana	1966	600,370	231,804
10	Siam	Thailand	1939	514,000	198,457

Source: CIA, *The World Factbook 2008*

Although not a country, Greenland (2,166,086 sq km/836,331 sq miles) has been officially known as Kalaallit Nunaat since 1979.

TOP 10 MOST COMMON STREET NAMES IN THE UK

1 High Street
2 Station Road
3 Main Street
4 Park Road
5 Church Road
6 Church Street
7 London Road
8 Victoria Road
9 Green Lane
10 Manor Road

Source: HBOS

TOP 10 MOST COMMON PLACE NAMES IN GREAT BRITAIN

NAME	NO. OF OCCURRENCES
1 NEWTON	150
2 BLACKHILL/BLACK HILL	136
3 CASTLEHILL/CASTLE HILL	128
4 MOUNTPLEASANT/MOUNT PLEASANT	126
5 WOODSIDE/WOOD SIDE	112
6 NEWTOWN/NEW TOWN	110
7 BURNSIDE	107
8 GREENHILL/GREEN HILL	105
9 WOODEND/WOOD END	101
10 BEACON HILL	95

Source: *Ordnance Survey*

These entries include the names of towns, villages and other inhabited settlements, as well as woods, hills and named locations, but exclude combinations of these names with others (Newton Abbot and Newton-le-Willows, for example, are not counted with the Newtons).

Greetings from...
The place with the world's longest name, otherwise known as Bangkok (left), and a railway station in North Wales (below), which was specially named to make it third longest in the world.

GORSAFAWDDACHAIDRAIGDDANHEDDOGLEDDOLLÔNPENRHYNAREURDRAETHCEREDIGION

TOP 10 **LONGEST PLACE NAMES** *

NAME   LETTERS

1 Krung Thep Mahanakhon Amon Rattanakosin Mahinthara Ayuthaya Mahadilok Phop Noppharat Ratchathani Burirom Udomratchaniwet Mahasathan Amon Piman Awatan Sathit Sakkathattiya Witsanukam Prasit   168

It means 'The city of angels, the great city, the eternal jewel city, the impregnable city of God Indra, the grand capital of the world endowed with nine precious gems, the happy city, abounding in an enormous Royal Palace that resembles the heavenly abode where reigns the reincarnated god, a city given by Indra and built by Vishnukarn'. When the poetic name of Bangkok, capital of Thailand, is used, it is usually abbreviated

to 'Krung Thep' (city of angels).

2 Taumatawhakatangihangakoauauotamateaturipukakapiki-maungahoronukupokaiwhenuakitanatahu   85

This is the longer version (the other has a mere 83 letters) of the Maori name of a hill in New Zealand. It translates as 'The place where Tamatea, the man with the big knees, who slid, climbed and swallowed mountains, known as land-eater, played on the flute to his loved one'.

3 Gorsafawddachaidraigddanheddogleddollônpenrhyn-areurdraethceredigion   67

A name contrived by the Fairbourne Steam Railway, Gwynedd, North Wales, for publicity purposes and in order to outdo its rival, No. 4. It means 'The Mawddach station and its dragon teeth at the Northern Penrhyn Road on the golden beach of Cardigan Bay'.

4 Llanfairpwllgwyngyllgogerychwyrndrobwllllantysilio-gogogoch   58

It means 'St Mary's Church in the hollow of the white hazel near to the rapid whirlpool of the church of St Tysilo near the Red Cave'. Questions have been raised about its authenticity, since its official name comprises only the first 20 letters, and the full name appears to have been invented as a hoax.

5 El Pueblo de Nuestra Señora la Reina de los Ángeles de la Porciúncula   57

The site of a Franciscan mission and the full Spanish name of Los Angeles; it means 'The town of Our Lady the Queen of the Angels of the Little Portion'. Nowadays it is customarily known by its initial letters, 'LA', making it also one of the shortest-named cities in the world.

6 Chargoggagoggmanchaugagoggchaubunagungamaug   43

America's longest place name, a lake near Webster, Massachusetts. Its Indian name, loosely translated, is claimed to mean 'You fish on your side, I'll fish on mine, and no one fishes in the middle'. It is said to be pronounced 'Char-gogg-a-gogg (pause) man-chaugg-a-gog (pause) chau-bun-a-gung-amaug'. It is, however, an invented extension of its real name (Chabunagungamaug, or 'boundary fishing place'), devised in the 1920s by Larry Daly, the editor of the *Webster Times*.

7 = Lower North Branch Little Southwest Miramichi   40

Canada's longest place name – a short river in New Brunswick.

= Villa Real de la Santa Fé de San Francisco de Asis   40

The full Spanish name of Santa Fe, New Mexico, translates as, 'Royal city of the holy faith of St Francis of Assisi'.

9 Te Whakatakanga-o-te-ngarehu-o-te-ahi-a-Tamatea   38

The Maori name of Hammer Springs, New Zealand; like the second name in this list, it refers to a legend of Tamatea, explaining how the springs were warmed by 'the falling of the cinders of the fire of Tamatea'.

10 Meallan Liath Coire Mhic Dhubhghaill   32

The longest multiple name in Scotland, a place near Aultanrynie, Highland, alternatively spelled Meallan Liath Coire Mhic Dhughaill (30 letters).

* Including single-word, hyphenated and multiple names

United States

THE 10 **FIRST US STATES**

	STATE	ENTERED UNION
1	Delaware	7 Dec 1787
2	Pennsylvania	12 Dec 1787
3	New Jersey	18 Dec 1787
4	Georgia	2 Jan 1788
5	Connecticut	9 Jan 1788
6	Massachusetts	6 Feb 1788
7	Maryland	28 Apr 1788
8	South Carolina	23 May 1788
9	New Hampshire	21 Jun 1788
10	Virginia	25 Jun 1788

THE 10 **LAST US STATES**

	STATE	ENTERED UNION
1	Hawaii	21 Aug 1959
2	Alaska	3 Jan 1959
3	Arizona	14 Feb 1912
4	New Mexico	6 Jan 1912
5	Oklahoma	16 Nov 1907
6	Utah	4 Jan 1896
7	Wyoming	10 Jul 1890
8	Idaho	3 Jul 1890
9	Washington	11 Nov 1889
10	Montana	8 Nov 1889

THE 10 **LEAST POPULATED STATES**

	STATE	POPULATION (2006)
1	Wyoming	515,004
2	Vermont	623,908
3	North Dakota	635,867
4	Alaska	670,053
5	South Dakota	781,919
6	Delaware	853,476
7	Montana	944,632
8	Rhode Island	1,067,610
9	Hawaii	1,285,498
10	New Hampshire	1,314,895

Source: US Census Bureau

THE 10 **MOST POPULATED STATES**

	STATE	POPULATION (2006)
1	California	36,457,549
2	Texas	23,507,783
3	New York	19,306,183
4	Florida	18,089,888
5	Illinois	12,831,970
6	Pennsylvania	12,440,621
7	Ohio	11,478,006
8	Michigan	10,095,643
9	Georgia	9,363,941
10	North Carolina	8,856,505

THE 10 **LEAST DENSELY POPULATED US STATES**

	STATE	POPULATION DENSITY (2005)	
		SQ KM	SQ MILES
1	Alaska	0.46	1.2
2	Wyoming	2.00	5.2
3	Montana	2.47	6.4
4	North Dakota	3.55	9.2
5	South Dakota	3.93	10.2
6	New Mexico	6.13	15.9
7	Idaho	6.67	17.3
8	Nevada	8.49	22.0
9	Nebraska	8.84	22.9
10	Utah	11.62	30.1

Source: US Census Bureau

THE 10 **MOST DENSELY POPULATED US STATES**

	STATE	POPULATION DENSITY (2005)	
		SQ KM	SQ MILES
1	New Jersey	453.79	1,175.3
2	Rhode Island	396.74	1,029.9
3	Massachusetts	315.13	816.2
4	Connecticut	279.73	724.5
5	Maryland	221.23	573.0
6	Delaware	166.71	431.8
7	New York	157.45	407.8
8	Florida	127.37	329.9
9	Ohio	108.10	280.0
10	Pennsylvania	107.06	277.3
	US average	*32.35*	*83.8*

Source: US Census Bureau

American extremes
Alaska, the penultimate state to join the Union, is also the largest, comprising more than 16 per cent of the entire area of the USA. In total contrast, Rhode Island measures just 60 km (37 miles) by 77 km (48 miles), but has a tidal shoreline totalling 618 km (384 miles).

THE 10 **LARGEST US STATES**

STATE	LAND AREA*	
	SQ KM	SQ MILES
1 Alaska	1,481,347	571,951
2 Texas	678,051	261,797
3 California	403,933	155,959
4 Montana	376,979	145,552
5 New Mexico	314,309	121,356
6 Arizona	294,312	113,635
7 Nevada	284,448	109,826
8 Colorado	268,627	103,718
9 Wyoming	251,489	97,100
10 Oregon	248,631	95,997
Total (all states)	*9,161,923*	*3,537,438*

* Excluding water

The total land area of the United States has grown progressively: in 1800 it was 2,248,058 sq km (867,980 sq miles), and by 1900 it had grown to 7,703,036 sq km (2,974,159 sq miles).

THE 10 **SMALLEST US STATES**

STATE	LAND AREA*	
	SQ KM	SQ MILES
1 Rhode Island	2,706	1,045
2 Delaware	5,063	1,955
3 Connecticut	12,548	4,845
4 Hawaii	16,635	6,423
5 New Jersey	19,215	7,419
6 Massachusetts	20,300	7,838
7 New Hampshire	23,229	8,969
8 Vermont	23,955	9,249
9 Maryland	25,317	9,775
10 West Virginia	62,385	24,087

* Excluding water

Smallest state Rhode Island has the longest official name, 'State of Rhode Island and Providence Plantations'. A total of 547 Rhode Islands – which also includes some 1,295 sq km (500 sq miles) of inland water – could be fitted into the land area of Alaska.

Reaching for the Sky

TOP 10 CITIES WITH MOST SKYSCRAPERS*

	CITY / LOCATION	SKYSCRAPERS
1	Hong Kong, China	199
2	New York City, USA	190
3	Chicago, USA	90
4	Shanghai, China	71
5	Tokyo, Japan	69
6	Singapore City, Singapore	38
7	Dubai, UAR	35
8	Shenzen, China	31
9	Houston, USA	29
10	Seoul, South Korea	27
	London	9

* Completed habitable buildings of more than 152 m (500 ft)

Inspired by spires
Its recent surge in high-rise building has resulted in Hong Kong, with more skyscrapers and the greatest density of tall buildings in the world, seizing New York's longstanding world lead.

TOP 10 TALLEST HABITABLE BUILDINGS IN THE UK*

	BUILDING / LOCATION	YEAR COMPLETED	STOREYS	ROOF HEIGHT M	FT
1	One Canada Square, Canary Wharf, London	1991	50	235.1	771
2	=8 Canada Square (HSBC Tower), Canary Wharf, London	2002	45	199.5	655
	=25 Canada Square, Canary Wharf, London	2001	45	199.5	655
4	Tower 42 (formerly National Westminster Tower), London	1980	47	183.0	600
5	30 St Mary Axe ('The Gherkin'), London	2004	41	179.8	590
6	Broadgate Tower, London	2008	36	164.3	539
7	Beetham Tower, Manchester	2006	50	157.0	515
8	1 Churchill Place, London	2004	32	156.4	513
9	=25 Bank Street, London	2003	33	153.0	502
	=40 Bank Street, London	2003	33	153.0	502

* Excluding communications masts and towers, chimneys and church spires

TOP 10 TALLEST CHURCHES

	CHURCH / LOCATION / YEAR COMPLETED	HEIGHT* M	FT
1	Sagrada Família, Barcelona, Spain, 2026#	170.0	558
2	Ulm Cathedral, Ulm, Germany, 1890	161.5	530
3	Our Lady of Peace Basilica, Yamoussoukro, Côte d'Ivoire, 1990	158.0	518
4	Cologne Cathedral, Cologne, Germany, 1880	157.4	516
5	Notre-Dame Cathedral, Rouen, France, 1876	151.0	495
6	St Nicholas, Hamburg, Germany, 1847	147.3	483
7	Notre Dame Cathedral, Strasbourg, France, 1439	144.0	472
8	St Peter's, Rome, Italy, 1626	138.0	454
9	St Stephen's Cathedral, Vienna, Austria, 1570	137.0	449
10	Neuer Dom, Linz, Austria, 1924	134.1	440

* To tip of spire
\# Under construction – scheduled completion date

At 123 m (404 ft), Salisbury Cathedral (1315) is the UK's tallest church and the world's tallest fourteenth-century building.

TOP 10 **TALLEST HABITABLE BUILDINGS**

2009

BUILDING / LOCATION / YEAR COMPLETED	STOREYS	ROOF HEIGHT M	FT
1 Burj Dubai, Dubai, UAR, 2008*	162	643.2	2,110
2 Shanghai World Financial Center, Shanghai, China, 2008*	101	492.0	1,614
3 Abraj Al Bait Hotel Tower, Mecca, Saudi Arabia, 2008*	76	485.0	1,591
4 Greenland Square Zifeng Tower, Nanjing, China, 2008*	69	450.0	1,476
5 Taipei 101, Taipei, Taiwan, 2004	101	449.2	1,474
6 Sears Tower, Chicago, USA, 1973	110	442.3	1,451
7 Guangzhou Twin Towers, Guangzhou, China, 2009*	103	437.5	1,435
8 Jin Mao Tower, Shanghai, China, 1998	88	420.5	1,380
9 Princess Tower, Dubai, UAE, 2009*	107	414.0	1,358
10 Al Hamra Tower, Kuwait, 2008*	77	412.0	1,352

* Under construction – scheduled completion date

1989

BUILDING / LOCATION / YEAR COMPLETED	STOREYS	ROOF HEIGHT M	FT
1 Sears Tower, Chicago, USA, 1973	110	442.3	1,451
2 1 World Trade Center, New York, USA*, 1972	110	417.0	1,368
3 2 World Trade Center, New York, USA*, 1973	110	415.4	1,363
4 Empire State Building, New York, USA, 1931	102	381.0	1,250
5 Aon Center, Chicago, USA, 1973	83	346.3	1,136
6 John Hancock Center, Chicago, USA, 1969	100	343.5	1,127
7 US Bank Tower, Los Angeles, 1989	73	310.3	1,018
8 J. P. Morgan Chase Tower, Houston, USA, 1982	75	305.0	1,002
9 Wells Fargo Plaza, Houston, USA, 1983	71	302.4	992
10 First Canadian Place, Toronto, Canada, 1975	72	298.1	978

* Destroyed in 9/11 terrorist attacks

Below: Top tower
Completed in 2008, the Burj Dubai (Dubai Tower) is the world's tallest structure of any kind ever built.

Right: High wire
The Sears Tower, Chicago, during construction. Once the world's tallest building, it has since been overtaken by Middle- and Far-Eastern skyscrapers.

Bridges

TOP 10 **LONGEST BRIDGES IN THE UK**

BRIDGE / LOCATION	TYPE*	YEAR COMPLETED	LENGTH OF MAIN SPAN M	FT
1 Humber Estuary, Hessle–Barton-on-Humber	S	1980	1,410	4,626
2 Forth Road, North Queensferry–South Queenferry	S	1964	1,006	3,300
3 Severn Bridge, Bristol	S	1966	988	3,240
4 Firth of Forth, North Queensferry–South Queenferry	CT	1890	521	1,710
5 Second Severn Crossing, Bristol	CSG	1996	456	1,496
6 Queen Elizabeth II, Dartford	CSG	1991	450	1,476
7 Tamar, Saltash–Plymouth	S	1961	335	1,100
8 Runcorn–Widnes	SA	1961	330	1,082
9 Erskine, Glasgow	CSG	1971	305	1,000
10 Skye, Kyleakin-Kyle of Lochalsh	PCG	1995	250	820

* S = Suspension; CT = Cantilever truss; CSG = Cable-stayed steel girder and truss; SA = Steel arch; PCG = Pre-stressed concrete girder

The Humber Estuary bridge is not only the longest single-span suspension bridge in the UK, but was also the longest bridge in the world until the completion in 1997 of the East Bridge section of Denmark's Great Belt Fixed Link. Each of its twin concrete anchorages weighs 400,000 tonnes and the suspension cables were spun from 66,000 km (41,000 miles) of wire.

TOP 10 **LONGEST CANTILEVER BRIDGES**

BRIDGE / LOCATION	YEAR COMPLETED	LONGEST SPAN M	FT
1 Pont de Québec, Canada	1917	549	1,800
2 Firth of Forth, Scotland	1890	521	1,710
3 Minato Ohashi, Osaka, Japan	1974	510	1,673
4 Commodore John Barry, New Jersey/Pennsylvania, USA	1974	494	1,622
5 =Greater New Orleans 1*, Louisiana, USA	1958	480	1,575
=Greater New Orleans 2*, Louisiana, USA	1988	480	1,575
7 Howrah, Calcutta, India	1943	457	1,500
8 Veterans Memorial, Gramercy, Louisiana, USA	1995	445	1,460
9 Transbay, San Francisco, USA	1936	427	1,400
10 Horace Wilkinson, Baton Rouge, Louisiana, USA	1969	376	1,235

* Jointly known as Crescent City Connection

TOP 10 **LONGEST CABLE-STAYED BRIDGES**

BRIDGE / LOCATION

1 Sutong, Changshu-Nantong, China

2 Stonecutters, Hong Kong

3 Tatara, Onomichi-Imabari, Japan

4 Pont de Normandie, Le Havre, France

5 Incheon-Yeongjong, South Korea

6 Third Nanjing Yangtze Bridge, Nanjing, China

7 Suramdu, Madura Strait, Indonesia

8 Second Nanjing Yangtze Bridge, Nanjing, China

9 Baishazhou, Wuhan, China

10 Minjiang, Qinghzhou China

TOP 10 **LONGEST STEEL ARCH BRIDGES**

	BRIDGE / LOCATION	YEAR COMPLETED	LONGEST SPAN M	FT
1	Chaotianmen, Chongqing, China	2008	552	1,811
2	New River Gorge, Fayetteville, West Virginia, USA	1977	518	1,699
3	Kill van Kull, Bayonne, New Jersey/ Staten Island, New York, USA	1931	504	1,654
4	Sydney Harbour, Australia	1932	503	1,650
5	Caiyuanba, Chongqing, China	2007	420	1,378
6	Fremont, Portland, Oregon, USA	1973	382	1,253
7	Port Mann, Vancouver, Canada	1964	366	1,201
8 =	Cold Spring Canyon, Santa Barbara, California, USA	1963	350	1,148
=	Nanning Yonghe, Nanning, China	2004	350	1,148
10	Bridge of the Americas, Balboa, Panama	1962	344	1,129

This list includes only exclusively steel structures. The Lupu Bridge, Shanghai, China, completed in 2003, and at 550 m (1,804 ft) then the world's longest arch construction, combines steel and concrete.

Bridge of size
The longest exclusively steel arch bridge in the world, the Chaotianmen Bridge features a six-lane highway on its upper deck, a four-lane road and light railway on the lower, and pedestrian walkways on both.

YEAR COMPLETED	LENGTH OF MAIN SPAN M	FT
2008	1,088	3,570
2008	1,018	3,339
1999	890	2,920
1994	856	2,808
2009	800	2,625
2005	648	2,126
2008	630	2,067
2001	628	2,060
2000	618	2,027
1999	605	1,985

TOP 10 **LONGEST SUSPENSION BRIDGES**

	BRIDGE / LOCATION	YEAR COMPLETED	LENGTH OF MAIN SPAN M	FT
1	Akashi-Kaikyo, Kobe-Naruto, Japan	1998	1,991	6,532
2	Xihoumen, China	2007	1,650	5,413
3	Great Belt, Denmark	1997	1,624	5,328
4	Ryungyang, China	2005	1,490	4,888
5	Humber Estuary, UK	1980	1,410	4,625
6	Jiangyin, China	1998	1,385	4,543
7	Tsing Ma, Hong Kong, China	1997	1,377	4,518
8	Verrazano Narrows, New York, USA	1964	1,298	4,260
9 =	Golden Gate, San Francisco, USA	1937	1,280	4,200
=	Yangluo, China	2007	1,280	4,200

The planned Messina Strait Bridge between Sicily and Calabria, Italy, would have had the longest centre span of any bridge at 3,300 m (10,827 ft), but the project was cancelled on 11 October 2006.

Tunnels

TOP 10 LONGEST CANAL TUNNELS

TUNNEL / CANAL / LOCATION	YEAR COMPLETED	LENGTH M	LENGTH FT
1 Le Rôve, Canal de Marseille au Rhône, France	1927	7,120	23,359
2 Bony ('Le Grand Souterrain'), Canal de St Quentin, France	1810	5,677	18,625
3 Standedge, Huddersfield Narrow, UK	1811	5,210	17,093
4 Mauvages, Canal de la Marne et Rhin, France	1853	4,970	16,305
5 Balesmes, Canal Marne à la Saône, France	1883	4,820	15,813
6 Ruyaulcourt, Canal du Nord, France	1923	4,500	14,763
7 Strood*, Thames and Medway, UK	1924	3,608	11,837
8 Lapal, Birmingham, UK	1798	3,570	11,712
9 Sapperton, Thames and Severn, UK	1789	3,488	11,443
10 Pouilly-en-Auxois, Canal de Bourgogne, France	1832	3,333	10,935

* Later converted to a rail tunnel

Begun in 1911, work on the Rôve tunnel, cut through through the Chaîne de l'Estaque, was put on hold during the First World War and finally completed in 1927. Although out of service since 16 June 1963, it remains the longest and largest canal tunnel in the world, once capable of accommodating ocean-going ships. It is 22 m (72 ft) wide and 15.4 m (50.5 ft) high, with a bore area of 320 sq m (3,444 sq ft), or about six times the size of a double-track rail tunnel. A total volume of 2,500,000 cu m (88,286,674 cu ft) of rock was extracted.

TOP 10 LONGEST SUBSEA TUNNELS

TUNNEL / LOCATION	YEAR COMPLETED	LENGTH M	LENGTH FT
1 Seikan, Japan	1988	53,850	176,673
2 Channel Tunnel, France/England	1994	50,450	165,518
3 Shin-Kanmon, Japan	1975	18,680	61,286
4 Tokyo Bay Aqualine Expressway*, Japan	1997	9,583	31,440
5 Great Belt Fixed Link (Eastern Tunnel), Denmark	1997	8,024	26,325
6 Bømlafjord*, Norway	2000	7,931	26,020
7 Eiksund*, Norway	2008	7,797	25,581
8 Oslofjord*, Norway	2000	7,390	24,245
9 Severn, UK	1886	7,008	22,992
10 Magerøysund*, Norway	1999	6,875	22,556

* Road; others rail

The need to connect the Japanese islands of Honshu, Kyushu and Hokkaido has resulted in a wave of undersea tunnel building in recent years, with the Seikan the most ambitious project of all. Connecting Honshu and Hokkaido, 23.3 km (14.4 miles) of the tunnel is 100 m (328 ft) below the sea bed. The Channel Tunnel was first proposed in 1802 and test borings undertaken in 1876, but it was over 100 years before technology made it feasible. Its overall length is shorter than the Seikan Tunnel, but the undersea portion is longer, at 38.0 km (23.6 miles).

TOP 10 LONGEST WATER-SUPPLY TUNNELS

TUNNEL / LOCATION	YEAR COMPLETED	LENGTH KM	LENGTH MILES
1 Delaware Aqueduct, New York, USA	1945	169.0	105.0
2 Päijänne, Finland	1982	120.0	74.6
3 Orange-Fish, South Africa	1975	82.8	51.4
4 Bolmen, Sweden	1987	82.0	51.0
5 Thames Water Ring Main, London, UK	1994	80.0	49.7
6 West Delaware, New York, USA	1960	70.8	44.0
7 Zelivka, Czech Republic	1972	51.9	32.2
8 Central outfall, Mexico City	1975	50.0	31.1
9 Thames Lee, UK	1960	30.3	18.8
10 Shandaken, USA	1923	29.1	18.1

TOP 10 **LONGEST ROAD TUNNELS**

TUNNEL / LOCATION	YEAR COMPLETED	LENGTH M	FT
1 Lærdal, Norway	2000	24,510	80,413
2 Zhongnanshan, China	2007	18,040	59,186
3 St Gotthard, Switzerland	1980	16,918	55,505
4 Arlberg, Austria	1978	13,972	45,850
5 Hsuehshan, Taiwan	2006	12,900	42,323
6 Fréjus, France/Italy	1980	12,895	42,306
7 Mont-Blanc, France/Italy	1965	11,611	38,094
8 Gudvangen, Norway	1991	11,428	37,493
9 Folgefonn, Norway	2001	11,100	36,417
10 Kan-Etsu II (southbound), Japan	1991	11,010	36,122

Nos. 1, 3, 4 and 7 have all held the record as 'world's longest road tunnel'. Previous record-holders include the 5,854-m (19,206-ft) Grand San Bernardo (Italy-Switzerland; 1964); the 5,133-m (16,841-ft) Alfonos XIII or Viella (Spain; 1948); and the 3,237-m (10,620-ft) Queensway (Mersey) Tunnel (connecting Liverpool and Birkenhead, UK; 1934). The 4,200-m (13,780-ft) Ted Williams/Interstate 190 Extension tunnel, Boston, Massachusetts (1995–2003) is the USA's longest road tunnel, while the 4,184-m (13,727-ft) Anton Anderson Memorial Tunnel, Alaska, is America's longest combined rail and road tunnel. The Eisenhower-Johnson Memorial Tunnel, Colorado, is, at 3,401 m (11,158 ft), the highest road tunnel in the world.

Breakthrough!
Workers celebrate as two sections of the world-beating Gotthard AlpTransit are connected in 2006 – with 12 more years of work ahead of them.

TOP 10 **LONGEST RAIL TUNNELS**

TUNNEL / LOCATION	YEAR COMPLETED	LENGTH M	FT
1 Gotthard AlpTransit, Switzerland	2018*	57,072	187,244
2 Seikan, Japan	1988	53,850	176,673
3 Channel Tunnel, France/England	1994	50,450	165,518
4 Moscow Metro (Serpukhovsko-Timiryazevskaya line), Russia	1983	38,900	127,625
5 Lötschberg Base, Switzerland	2007	34,577	113,442
6 Guadarrama, Spain	2007	28,377	97,100
7 London Underground (East Finchley/Morden, Northern Line), UK	1939	27,840	91,339
8 Hakkoda, Japan	2010*	26,455	86,795
9 Iwate-Ichinohe, Japan	2002	25,810	84,678
10 Pajares Base, Spain	2011*	24,667	80,928

* Under construction – scheduled completion date

The world's longest rail tunnel, the Gotthard AlpTransit, Switzerland, was proposed as early as 1947 and given the go-ahead in 1998 after a referendum of the Swiss electorate. When completed, trains will travel through it at 250 km/h (155 mph).

5

CULTURE & LEARNING

Language

TOP 10 **LONGEST WORDS IN THE OXFORD ENGLISH DICTIONARY**

	WORD (EARLIEST RECORDED USE) / MEANING	LETTERS
1	**Supercalifragilisticexpialidocious** (1964) Wonderful, from song of this title in the film *Mary Poppins*.	34
2	**Floccinaucinihilipilification** (1741) The action or habit of estimating as worthless	29
3	**Honorificabilitudinitatibus** (1599) Honourableness	27
4	**Antidisestablishmentarians** (1900) Those opposed to the disestablishment of the Church of England	26
5	**Overintellectualization** (1922) Excessive intellectualization	23
6 =	**Incircumscriptibleness** (1550) Incapable of being circumscribed	22
=	**Omnirepresentativeness** (1842) The quality of being representative of all forms or kinds	22
=	**Reinstitutionalization** (1978) Institutionalize again	22
9	**Undercharacterization** (1968) To depict or play with insufficient characterization or subtlety	21
10	**Lithochromatographic*** (1843) Colour printing technique using stone	20

* One of several examples of 20-letter words

These are strictly non-medical terms or names of chemical compounds, which can achieve colossal lengths. It thus excludes words such as the 45-letter pneumonoultramicroscopicsilico-volcanoconiosis (1935), which the OED admits occurs 'only as an instance of a very long word', along with others invented by writers with inclusion in reference books in mind.

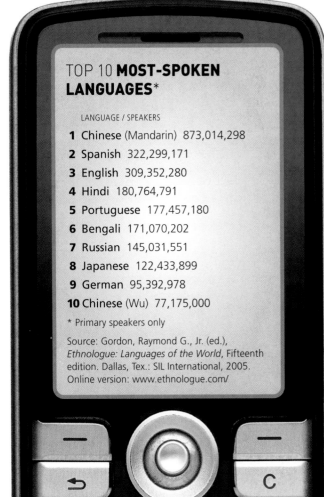

TOP 10 **ONLINE LANGUAGES**

	LANGUAGE	% OF ALL INTERNET USERS	INTERNET USERS*
▶ 1	English	30.1	379,529,347
▶ 2	Chinese (Mandarin)	14.7	184,901,513
▶ 3	Spanish	9.0	113,463,158
▶ 4	Japanese	6.9	87,540,000
▶ 5	French	5.1	63,761,141
▶ 6	German	4.9	61,912,361
▶ 7	Portuguese	4.0	50,828,760
▶ 8	Arabic	3.7	46,359,140
▶ 9	Korean	2.7	34,430,000
▶ 10	Italian	2.6	33,143,152
	Top 10 languages	83.7	1,055,868,572
	Rest of world languages	16.3	206,164,125
	World total	100.0	1,262,032,697

* As at 30 November 2007

Source: www.internetworldstats.com

TOP 10 **MOST-SPOKEN LANGUAGES***

LANGUAGE / SPEAKERS

1 Chinese (Mandarin) 873,014,298

2 Spanish 322,299,171

3 English 309,352,280

4 Hindi 180,764,791

5 Portuguese 177,457,180

6 Bengali 171,070,202

7 Russian 145,031,551

8 Japanese 122,433,899

9 German 95,392,978

10 Chinese (Wu) 77,175,000

* Primary speakers only

Source: Gordon, Raymond G., Jr. (ed.), *Ethnologue: Languages of the World*, Fifteenth edition. Dallas, Tex.: SIL International, 2005. Online version: www.ethnologue.com/

Chinese whispers
Mandarin is the most commonly spoken language across China, but another five languages in China have more than 20 million speakers, in addition to numerous minor languages and mutually unintelligible dialects.

The Ultimate Polyglot

New Zealand-born Harold Williams (1876–1928) is considered one of the greatest linguists of all time. He was able to speak 58 different languages and many dialects, ranging from Ancient Greek and Swahili to Basque and various Polynesian tongues. As the foreign editor of the *London Times*, he was the only person capable of addressing all the members of the League of Nations (the forerunner of the United Nations) in their own language.

TOP 10 COUNTRIES WITH THE MOST ENGLISH-LANGUAGE SPEAKERS

	COUNTRY	APPROX. NO. OF SPEAKERS*
1	USA	215,423,557
2	UK	58,190,000
3	Canada	20,000,000
4	Australia	14,987,000
5	Ireland	3,750,000
6	= New Zealand	3,700,000
	= South Africa	3,700,000
8	Jamaica#	2,600,000
9	Trinidad and Tobago#	1,145,000
10	Guyana#	650,000

* People for whom English is their mother tongue
\# Includes English Creole

The Top 10 represents the countries with the greatest numbers of inhabitants who speak English as their mother tongue.

TOP 10 COUNTRIES WITH THE MOST SPANISH-LANGUAGE SPEAKERS

	COUNTRY	APPROX. NO. OF NATIVE SPEAKERS
1	Mexico	106,255,000
2	Colombia	45,600,000
3	Spain	44,400,000
4	Argentina	41,248,000
5	USA	31,000,000
6	Venezuela	26,021,000
7	Peru	23,191,000
8	Chile	15,795,000
9	Cuba	11,285,000
10	Ecuador	10,946,000

As a result of colonization in parts of Africa, the Americas and Asia, a total of 21 countries speak Spanish as their principal language, making it the second most spoken after Mandarin Chinese and the third most used language on the Internet.

Education

Primary colours
An art class in Indonesia. After India and China, the country
has more children in primary school than any other.

TOP 10 **LARGEST UNIVERSITIES**

UNIVERSITY / LOCATION	APPROX. ENROLMENT
1 Allama Iqbal Open University, Islamabad, Pakistan	1,806,214
2 Indira Gandhi National Open University, New Delhi, India	1,500,000
3 Islamic Azad University, Tehran, Iran	1,300,000
4 Anadolu University, Eski ehir, Turkey	884,081
5 Bangladesh Open University, Gazipur, Bangladesh	600,000
6 Dr Babasaheb Ambedkar Open University, Andhra Pradesh, India	450,000
7 State University of New York, New York, USA	418,000
8 California State University, California, USA	417,000
9 Universitas Terbuka, Jakarta, Indonesia	350,000
10 Universidad de Buenos Aires, Buenos Aires, Argentina	316,050

TOP 10 **COUNTRIES WITH MOST PRIMARY SCHOOL PUPILS**

COUNTRY	PRIMARY SCHOOL PUPILS (2005)
1 India	140,012,901
2 China	112,739,964
3 Indonesia	29,149,746
4 USA	24,454,602
5 Nigeria	22,267,407
6 Brazil	18,968,584
7 Bangladesh	17,953,300
8 Pakistan	17,257,947
9 Mexico	14,700,005
10 Philippines	13,083,744
Top 10 total	*410,588,200*
UK	*4,634,991*
World total	*688,784,276*

Source: UNESCO, *Global Education Digest 2007*

TOP 10 COUNTRIES WITH MOST SECONDARY SCHOOL PUPILS

COUNTRY (% FEMALE) / SECONDARY SCHOOL PUPILS

1 China (48)
100,631,925

2 India (43)
89,461,794

3 Brazil (52)
25,127,503

4 USA (49)
24,431,934

5 Indonesia (49)
15,993,187

6 Russia (49)
12,433,155

7 Mexico (51)
10,564,404

8 Bangladesh (50)
10,354,760

9 Iran (47)
9,942,201

10 Vietnam (49)
9,939,319

Top 10 total (av. 49) 308,880,182
UK (49) 5,747,422
World total (47) 512,553,149

Source: UNESCO, *Global Education Digest 2007*

TOP 10 COUNTRIES WITH THE HIGHEST PERCENTAGE OF ADULTS IN FURTHER EDUCATION

	COUNTRY	% SCHOOL LEAVERS OF BOTH SEXES IN FURTHER EDUCATION
1	Finland	92
2	South Korea	91
3	Greece	89
4	USA	83
5 =	New Zealand	82
=	Sweden	82
7	Slovenia	81
8 =	Denmark	80
=	Norway	80
10	Lithuania	73
	UK	*60*
	World average	*24*

Source: UNESCO, *Global Education Digest 2007*

TOP 10 OLDEST UNIVERSITIES IN THE UK

	UNIVERSITY	FOUNDED
1	Oxford	1117
2	Cambridge	1209
3	St Andrews	1411
4	Glasgow	1451
5	Aberdeen	1495
6	Edinburgh	1583
7	Dublin*	1592
8	Durham#	1832
9	London†	1836
10	Manchester	1851

* Ireland then part of England
\# A short-lived Cromwellian establishment was set up in 1657
† Constituent colleges founded earlier: University College 1826, King's College 1828

Although its constituent colleges were founded earlier – Lampeter 1822, Aberystwyth 1872, Cardiff 1883, Bangor 1884 – the University of Wales dates from 1893.

Books

TOP 10 MOST TRANSLATED AUTHORS

AUTHOR / COUNTRY / DATES	TRANSLATIONS
1 Agatha Christie (UK, 1890–1976)	6,362
2 Jules Verne (France, 1828–1905)	4,021
3 V. I. Lenin (Russia, 1870–1924)	3,497
4 William Shakespeare (England, 1564–1616)	3,435
5 Enid Blyton (UK, 1897–1968)	3,433
6 Barbara Cartland (UK, 1901–2000)	3,315
7 Danielle Steel (USA, b. 1947)	2,767
8 Hans Christian Andersen (Denmark, 1805–75)	2,624
9 Stephen King (USA, b. 1947)	2,591
10 Jakob Grimm (Germany, 1785–1863)	2,382

According to UNESCO's *Index Translationum*, the total number of translations of books in the period 1979–2005 places British crime writer Agatha Christie as the world's most translated novelist by a substantial margin. Just outside the Top 10 are such popular authors as Mark Twain and Arthur Conan Doyle. Although not an 'author' as such, by virtue of the total translations of Walt Disney Productions titles, which number 8,677, the company leads the field.

Queen of crime
Agatha Christie (1890–1976) is one of the bestselling authors of all time, and, according to UNESCO, the most translated.

THE 10 FIRST POCKET BOOKS

AUTHOR / TITLE

1 James Hilton, Lost Horizon
2 Dorothea Brande, Wake Up and Live!
3 William Shakespeare, Five Great Tragedies
4 Thorne Smith, Topper
5 Agatha Christie, The Murder of Roger Ackroyd
6 Dorothy Parker, Enough Rope
7 Emily Brontë, Wuthering Heights
8 Samuel Butler, The Way of All Flesh
9 Thornton Wilder, The Bridge of San Luis Rey
10 Felix Saltern, Bambi

All 10 Pocket Books were published in the USA in 1939 (a single title, Pearl S. Buck's Nobel Prize-winning *The Good Earth*, had been test-marketed the previous year, but only in New York). Unlike their British counterparts, Penguin Books, Pocket Books titles all had pictorial covers: the first 10 were created by Isador N. Steinberg and Frank J. Lieberman (who also drew the Pocket Books logo, a kangaroo that he named Gertrude, after his mother-in-law). When a survey of sales was conducted 18 years later, it was discovered that of the first 10, Shakespeare was the bestselling title with over 2,000,000 copies in print, followed by James Hilton's *Lost Horizon* (1,750,000), Thorne Smith's *Topper* (1,500,000) and Emily Brontë's *Wuthering Heights* (more than 1,000,000).

TOP 10 BESTSELLING BOOKS OF ALL TIME

AUTHOR / BOOK / DATE	EST. SALES
1 The Bible, c. 1456–	6,000,000,000
2 Quotations from the Works of Mao Tse-tung, 1966	900,000,000
3 Qur'an (Koran)	800,000,000
4 Miguel de Cervantes, Don Quixote, 1605	500,000,000
5 Xinhua Zidian (Chinese dictionary), 1953–	400,000,000
6 Thomas Cranmer, Book of Common Prayer, 1549	300,000,000
7 John Bunyan, The Pilgrim's Progress, 1678	250,000,000
8 John Foxe, Foxe's Book of Martyrs, 1563	150,000,000
9 J. K. Rowling, Harry Potter and the Philosopher's Stone, 1997	117,000,000
10 Agatha Christie, And Then There Were None, 1939	110,000,000

The publication of multiple editions, translations, and pirated copies – and often exaggerated sales claims – make it notoriously problematic to establish precise sales of recently published books.

THE 10 **LATEST MAN BOOKER PRIZE WINNERS**

YEAR   AUTHOR / TITLE

2007 Anne Enright, The Gathering

2006 Kiran Desai, The Inheritance of Loss

2005 John Banville, The Sea

2004 Alan Hollinghurst, The Line of Beauty

2003 D. B. C. Pierre, Vernon God Little

2002 Yann Martel, Life of Pi

2001 Peter Carey, True History of the Kelly Gang

2000 Margaret Atwood, The Blind Assassin

1999 J. M. Coetzee, Disgrace

1998 Ian McEwan, Amsterdam

THE 10 **FIRST PENGUIN PAPERBACKS**

AUTHOR / TITLE

1 André Maurois, Ariel

2 Ernest Hemingway, A Farewell to Arms

3 Eric Linklater, Poet's Pub

4 Susan Ertz, Madame Claire

5 Dorothy L. Sayers, The Unpleasantness at the Bellona Club

6 Agatha Christie, The Mysterious Affair at Styles

7 Beverley Nichols, Twenty-five

8 E. H. Young, William

9 Mary Webb, Gone to Earth

10 Compton Mackenzie, Carnival

Paperbacks have a much longer history than most people realize. In 1837 the German publishing company Tauchnitz began to issue paperback novels in English. Curiously, for copyright and other reasons, they were available everywhere except Great Britain, but through healthy sales to English-speaking Europeans and British and American travellers, the company was able to add a new title virtually every week for the next 100 years. A rival to Tauchnitz, the Albatross Modern Continental Library, began publishing in 1932 – but sales of their English-language paperbacks were similarly restricted to the Continent. Although some books had appeared in paperback in England during this period, they were generally of poor quality. It was the British publisher Allen Lane (1902–70; knighted 1952) who, remarking 'I would be the first to admit that there is no fortune in this series for anyone concerned', launched his first Penguin titles in Great Britain on 30 July 1935. Originally Penguins were paperback reprints of books that had been previously published as hardbacks; their quality, range of subjects and low price established them as the pioneering books in the 'paperback revolution'.

The importance of being Ernest
American author Ernest Hemingway's A Farewell to Arms was one of the first Penguin paperbacks. By the time it was published in 1939, the novel (first issued in 1929) had been made into an Oscar-nominated film.

Libraries & Loans

TOP 10 **MOST-BORROWED ADULT FICTION AUTHORS IN THE UK**

AUTHOR

1 James Patterson
2 Josephine Cox
3 Nora Roberts
4 Danielle Steel
5 Ian Rankin
6 Bernard Cornwell
7 Katie Flynn
8 Michael Connelly
9 Agatha Christie
10 Anna Jacobs

Source: Public Lending Right, 2006–07

Page-turner Patterson
Author James Patterson has sold over 150 million books worldwide and has established the PageTurner Awards to encourage reading.

TOP 10 **MOST-BORROWED ADULT FICTION TITLES IN THE UK**

AUTHOR / TITLE

1 Patricia Cornwell, At Risk
2 Victoria Hislop, The Island
3 James Patterson and Andrew Gross, Judge and Jury
4 Dan Brown, The Da Vinci Code
5 James Patterson, Mary, Mary
6 Josephine Cox, Journey's End
7 Dorothy Koomson, My Best Friend's Girl
8 James Patterson and Maxine Paetro, The 5th Horseman
9 Lee Child, The Hard Way
10 Elizabeth Kostova, The Historian

Source: Public Lending Right, 2006–07

TOP 10 **LARGEST LIBRARIES**

LIBRARY	LOCATION	FOUNDED	BOOKS
1 Library of Congress	Washington DC, USA	1800	32,124,001
2 British Library*	London, UK	1753	29,000,000
3 Deutsche Bibliothek#	Frankfurt, Germany	1990	22,200,000
4 Library of the Russian Academy of Sciences	St Petersburg, Russia	1714	20,500,000
5 National Library of Canada	Ottawa, Canada	1953	19,500,000
6 Russian State Library†	Moscow, Russia	1862	17,000,000
7 Harvard University Library	Cambridge, Massachusetts, USA	1638	15,826,570
8 Boston Public Library	Boston, Massachusetts, USA	1895	15,686,902
9 Vernadsky National Scientific Library of Ukraine	Kiev, Ukraine	1919	15,000,000
10 National Library of Russia	St Petersburg	1795	14,799,267

* Founded as part of the British Museum, 1753; became an independent body in 1973
# Formed in 1990 through the unification of the Deutsche Bibliothek, Frankfurt (founded 1947) and the Deutsche Bucherei, Leipzig
† Founded 1862 as Rumyantsev Library, formerly State V. I. Lenin Library

Comparisons between libraries based on their holdings vary according to what is included. The figure for the Library of Congress is for printed books only, but it also has more than 100 million catalogued items, including manuscripts, maps and photographs.

TOP 10 **MOST-BORROWED CHILDREN'S FICTION TITLES IN THE UK**

AUTHOR / TITLE

1 J. K. Rowling, Harry Potter and the Half-Blood Prince
2 Jacqueline Wilson*, Candyfloss
3 Francesca Simon#, Horrid Henry and the Football Field
4 Francesca Simon#, Horrid Henry's Underpants
5 Francesca Simon#, Horrid Henry and the Mega-Mean Time Machine
6 Francesca Simon#, Horrid Henry Meets the Queen
7 Jacqueline Wilson*, Sleepovers
8 Francesca Simon#, Horrid Henry and the Bogey Babysitter
9 Jacqueline Wilson*, Starring Tracy Beaker
10 Julia Donaldson†, The Gruffalo's Child

* Illustrated by Nick Sharratt
# Illustrated by Tony Ross
† Illustrated by Axel Scheffler

Source: Public Lending Right, 2006–07

TOP 10 **OLDEST NATIONAL LIBRARIES**

LIBRARY / LOCATION	FOUNDED
1 Národní Knihovna Ceské Republiky National Library of the Czech Republic, Prague, Czech Republic	1366
2 Österreichische Nationalbibliothek National Library of Austria, Vienna, Austria	1368
3 Biblioteca Nazionale Marciana, Venice, Italy	1468
4 Bibliothèque Nationale de France National Library of France, Paris, France	1480
5 National Library of Malta, Valletta, Malta	1555
6 Bayericsche Staatsbibliothek, Munich, Germany	1558
7 Bibliothèque Royale Albert 1er National Library of Belgium, Brussels, Belgium	1559
8 Nacionalna i Sveucilicna Knjisnica Zagreb National and University Library, Zagreb, Croatia	1606
9 Helsingin Yliopisto Kirjasto National Library of Finland, Helsinki, Finland	1640
10 Det Kongeligie Bibliotek National Library of Denmark, Copenhagen, Denmark	1653

What may claim to be the world's first national library was that in Alexandria, Egypt, founded in about 307 BC by King Ptolemy I Soter. It assembled the world's largest collection of scrolls, which were partly destroyed during Julius Caesar's invasion of 48 BC, and totally by Arab invaders under Amr ibn al'Aas in AD 642, an event that is considered one of the greatest losses to world scholarship.

TOP 10 **MOST BORROWED CLASSIC ADULT TITLES IN THE UK**

AUTHOR / TITLE

1 J. D. Salinger, Catcher in the Rye

2 Daphne du Maurier, Rebecca

3 Charlotte Brontë, Jane Eyre

4 Harper Lee, To Kill a Mockingbird (Arrow, 2000)

5 Jane Austen, Persuasion

6 Emily Brontë, Wuthering Heights

7 Harper Lee, To Kill a Mockingbird (Minerva, 1991)

8 Daphne du Maurier, Jamaica Inn

9 Agatha Christie, The Hollow

10 Daphne du Maurier, Frenchman's Creek

Source: Public Lending Right, 2006–07

Austrian National Library
The imperial library founded by Austrian Duke Albrecht III (1349–95) has grown into an institution with a collection of some 7.5 million books.

The Press

TOP 10 DAILY NEWSPAPERS IN THE UK

NEWSPAPER	AVERAGE NET CIRCULATION*
1 The Sun	3,077,060
2 The Daily Mail	2,294,880
3 The Mirror	1,894,732
4 The Daily Telegraph	866,693
5 Daily Express	736,634
6 Daily Star	723,905
7 The Times	613,068
8 Financial Times	448,342
9 Daily Record (Scotland)	394,189
10 The Guardian	355,634

* As at 7 April 2008

Source: Audit Bureau of Circulations Ltd

TOP 10 MAGAZINES IN THE UK

TITLE	AVERAGE NET CIRCULATION*
1 Asda Magazine	2,910,280
2 Tesco Magazine	2,436,491
3 Sainsbury's Fresh Ideas	1,500,218
4 TV Choice	1,403,512
5 What's on TV	1,385,840
6 The Somerfield Magazine	1,197,371
7 Radio Times	1,051,746
8 Take a Break	988,056
9 OK! Magazine	608,638
10 Reader's Digest	657,458

* July–December 2007

Source: Audit Bureau of Circulations Ltd

TOP 10 MAGAZINES

MAGAZINE*	AVERAGE CIRCULATION
1 Reader's Digest	12,078,000
2 Better Homes and Gardens	7,605,000
3 Family Circle	4,634,000
4 Woman's Day	4,205,000
5 Time	4,112,000
6 Ladies' Home Journal	4,101,000
7 Kampioen (Netherlands)	3,756,000
8 People	3,625,000
9 Playboy	3,215,000
10 Newsweek	3,183,000

* All US unless otherwise stated

Source: International Federation of Audit Bureaux of Circulations

TOP 10 DAILY NEWSPAPERS

NEWSPAPER	COUNTRY	AVERAGE DAILY CIRCULATION*, 2006
1 Yomiuri Shimbun	Japan	14,246,000
2 Asahi Shimbun	Japan	12,326,000
3 Mainichi Shimbun	Japan	5,635,000
4 Nihon Keizai Shimbun	Japan	4,737,000
5 Chunichi Shimbun	Japan	4,571,000
6 Bild	Germany	4,220,000
7 The Sun	UK	3,461,000
8 Sankei Shimbun	Japan	2,665,000
9 USA Today	USA	2,603,000
10 Canako Xiaoxi (Beijing)	China	2,530,000

* Averaged over a whole year rather than a period

Source: International Federation of Audit Bureaux of Circulations

Yomiuri Shimbun was founded in Japan 1874. In 1998 it became the country's and the world's bestselling daily newspaper, achieving a record average sale of 14,532,694 copies a day.

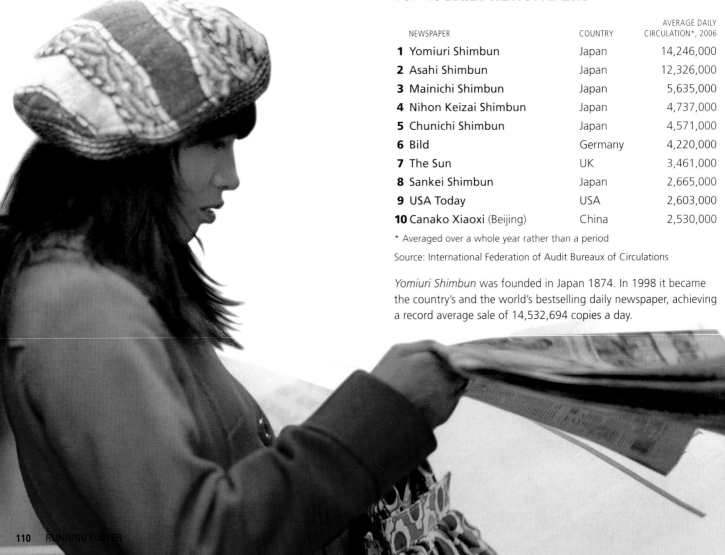

TOP 10 OLDEST NATIONAL NEWSPAPERS PUBLISHED IN THE UK

NEWSPAPER	FIRST PUBLISHED
1 The London Gazette	16 Nov 1665

Originally published in Oxford as the *Oxford Gazette*, while the royal court resided there during an outbreak of the plague. After 23 issues, it moved to London with the court and changed its name.

2 Lloyd's List	Apr 1734

Providing shipping news, originally on a weekly basis (as *Lloyd's News*), but since 1 July 1837 Britain's oldest daily.

3 The Times	1 Jan 1785

First published as the *Daily Universal Register*, it changed its name to *The Times* on 1 March 1788.

4 The Observer	4 Dec 1791

Britain's first Sunday newspaper was *Johnson's British Gazette and Sunday Monitor*, first published on 2 March 1780. It survived only until 1829, thus making *The Observer* the longest-running Sunday paper.

5 Morning Advertiser	8 Feb 1794

Britain's oldest trade newspaper (a daily established by the Licensed Victuallers Association to earn income for its charity), and the first national paper on Fleet Street, the *Morning Advertiser* changed its name to *The Licensee* and became a twice-weekly news magazine in 1994, at the time of its 200th anniversary, reverting to its original name in 2000.

6 The Scotsman	25 Jan 1817

Originally published weekly, the *Daily Scotsman* was published from July 1855 to December 1859 and retitled *The Scotsman* in January 1860.

7 The Sunday Times	18 Feb 1821

Issued as the *New Observer* until March 1821 and the *Independent Observer* from April 1821 until 22 October 1822, when it changed its name to the *Sunday Times*. On 4 February 1962 it became the first British newspaper to issue a colour supplement.

8 The Guardian	5 May 1821

A weekly until 1855 (and called *The Manchester Guardian* until 1959).

9 News of the World	1 Oct 1843

The first issue of the national Sunday newspaper declared its aim as being 'To give to the poorer classes of society a paper that would suit their means, and to the middle, as well as the rich, a journal which, from its immense circulation, should command their attention'. This aspiration was achieved in April 1951, when sales peaked at 8,480,878 copies, the highest-ever circulation of any British newspaper.

10 The Daily Telegraph	29 Jun 1855

The first issues were published as the *Daily Telegraph and Courier*, but from 20 August 1855, *Courier* was dropped from the title.

TOP 10 OLDEST NEWSPAPERS

NEWSPAPER	COUNTRY	FOUNDED
1 Haarlems Dagblad	Netherlands	1656
2 Gazzetta di Mantova	Italy	1664
3 The London Gazette	UK	1665
4 Wiener Zeitung	Austria	1703
5 Hildesheimer Allgemeine Zeitung	Germany	1705
6 Berrow's Worcester Journal	UK	1709
7 Newcastle Journal	UK	1711
8 Stamford Mercury	UK	1712
9 Northampton Mercury	UK	1720
10 Hanauer Anzeiger	Germany	1725

This list includes only newspapers that have been published continuously since their founding, under the same name – or at least containing the name, as in the case of the *Worcester Journal*, which was founded in 1690 as *Worcester Post Man*, published irregularly until it became the *Worcester Journal* in 1709, and adopted the name of its proprietor, Harvey Berrow, to become *Berrow's Worcester Journal* in 1753. The former No. 1 on this list, the Swedish *Post-och Inrikes Tidningar*, founded in 1645, ceased publication on paper on 1 January 2007, and is now available only online.

Art

TOP 10 **BEST-ATTENDED ART EXHIBITIONS, 2007**

	EXHIBITION	VENUE / CITY / DATES	DAILY AVERAGE	ATTENDANCE* TOTAL#
1	Tutankhamun and the Golden Age of the Pharaohs	Franklin Institute, Philadelphia, USA, 3 Feb–30 Sep 2007	5,375	1,290,000
2	Manet to Picasso	National Gallery, London, UK, 22 Sep 2006–23 May 2007	4,635	1,110,044
3	Ways of Seeing: John Baldessari Explores	Hirshhorn Museum, Washington DC, USA, 26 Jul 2006–23 Sep 2007	2,062	874,203
4	The Mind of Leonardo	National Museum, Tokyo, Japan, 20 Mar–17 Jun 2007	10,071	796,004
5	Richard Serra Sculpture: 40 Years	Museum of Modern Art, New York. USA, 3 Jun–10 Sep 2007	8,585	737,074
6	Monet's Art and its Posterity	National Art Center, Tokyo, Japan, 7 Apr–2 Jul 2007	9,273	704,420
7	Masterpieces of French Painting	Neue Nationalgalerie, Berlin, Germany, 1 Jun–7 Oct 2007	6,115	677,000
8	Anselm Kiefer	Museo Guggenheim, Bilbao, Spain, 28 Mar–9 Sep 2007	3,707	576,214
9	Masterpieces of French Painting from the Met	Museum of Fine Arts, Houston, Texas, USA, 4 Feb–6 May 2007	7,268	574,207
10	Heaven or Hell	Royal Ontario Museum, Toronto, Canada, 25 Nov 2006–8 Oct 2007	1,645	519,747

* With longest part of run in 2007
\# Approximate totals provided by museums

Source: *The Art Newspaper*

TOP 10 **ART GALLERIES AND MUSEUMS IN THE UK**

	ATTRACTION / LOCATION	VISITORS (2006)
1	Tate Modern, London	4,915,000
2	British Museum, London	4,837,878
3	National Gallery, London	4,562,471
4	Natural History Museum, London	3,754,496
5	Science Museum, London	2,421,440
6	Victoria & Albert Museum, London	2,372,919
7	National Portrait Gallery, London	1,601,448
8	Tate Britain, London	1,597,000
9	National Maritime Museum, London	1,572,310
10	National Gallery of Scotland, Edinburgh	942,788

Tutankhamun on show
Treasures from the tomb of Tutankhamun formed the centrepiece of a popular exhibition shown in five locations in the USA and in London.

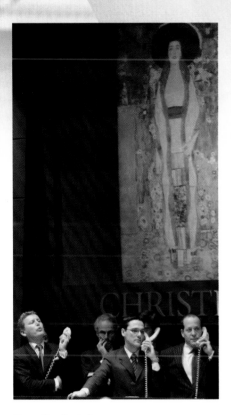

Portraits of a lady
After lengthy litigation to establish their
ownership, Gustav Klimt's two portraits of Adele
Bloch-Bauer were sold in 2006, the first for an
estimated $135 million, setting a world record
for a private transaction, while the second
fetched almost $88 million at auction.

The Prince of Prints

While paintings are the most
expensive works of art sold at auction,
in recent years many photographs
have sold for increasingly high prices.
In 2005 American photographer
Richard Prince became the first whose
prints sold for more than $1 million
when his large *Untitled (Cowboy)*
realized $1,248,000 (£715,268) at
Christie's New York. Since then, three
more prints of the same image have
sold for in excess of $1 million.

TOP 10 **MOST EXPENSIVE PAINTINGS SOLD AT AUCTION**

2008

PAINTING / ARTIST		SALE	PRICE ($)
1	**Garçon à la pipe**, Pablo Picasso (Spanish; 1881–1973)	Sotheby's New York, 5 May 2004	104,168,000
2	**Dora Maar au chat,** Pablo Picasso	Sotheby's New York, 3 May 2006	95,216,000
3	**Portrait of Adele Bloch-Bauer II**, Gustav Klimt (Austrian; 1862–1918)	Christie's New York, 8 Nov 2006	87,936,000
4	**Portrait du Dr Gachet,** Vincent van Gogh (Dutch; 1853–90)	Christie's New York, 15 May 1990	82,500,000
5	**Bal au Moulin de la Galette,** Montmartre Pierre-Auguste Renoir (French; 1841–1919)	Sotheby's New York, 17 May 1990	78,100,000
6	**The Massacre of the Innocents,** Sir Peter Paul Rubens (Flemish; 1577-1640)	Sotheby's London, 10 Jul 2002	75,930,440 (£49,506,648)
7	**White Center (Yellow, pink and lavender on rose)** Mark Rothko (American; 1903–70)	Sotheby's New York, 15 May 2007	72,840,000
8	**Green Car Crash – Green Burning Car I,** Andy Warhol (American 1928–87)	Christie's New York, 16 May 2007	71,720,000
9	**Portrait de l'Artiste Sans Barbe,** Vincent van Gogh	Christie's New York, 19 Nov 1998	71,502,496
10	**Rideau, Cruchon et Compôtier,** Paul Cézanne (French; 1839–1906)	Sotheby's New York, 10 May 1999	60,502,500

1988

PAINTING / ARTIST		SALE	PRICE ($)
1	**Irises**, Vincent van Gogh, (Dutch; 1853–90)	Sotheby's New York, 11 Nov 1987	53,900,000
2	**Sunflowers**, Vincent Van Gogh	Christie's London, 30 Mar 1987	39,404,600 (£24,750,000)
3	**Acrobate et Jeune Arlequin,** Pablo Picasso, (Spanish; 1881–1973)	Christie's London, 28 Nov 1988	38,138,700 (£20,900,000)
4	**Dans la Prairie**, Claude Monet (French; 1840–1926)	Sotheby's London, 28 Jun 1988	25,417,700 (£14,300,000)
5	**Maternité**, Pablo Picasso	Christie's New York, 14 Jun 1988	24,750,000
6	**Le Pont de Trinquetaille,** Vincent van Gogh	Christie's London, 29 Jun 1987	20,622,800 (£12,650,000)
7	**False Start**, Jasper Johns (American; b.1930)	Sotheby's New York, 10 Nov 1988	17,050,000
8	**La Cage d'Oiseaux**, Pablo Picasso	Sotheby's New York, 10 Nov 1988	15,400,000
9	**Adoration of the Magi**, Andrea Mantegna (Italian; 1431–1506)	Christie's London, 18 Apr 1985	10,317,780 (£8,100,000)
10	**Paysage au Soleil Levant,** Vincent Van Gogh	Sotheby's New York, 24 Apr 1985	9,900,000

Monumental Achievements

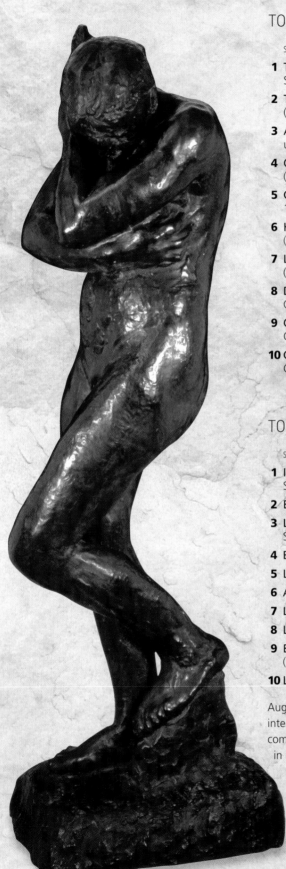

TOP 10 **MOST EXPENSIVE SCULPTURES SOLD AT AUCTION**

SCULPTURE / ARTIST / SALE	PRICE ($)
1 The Guennol Lioness (c. 3000 BC), unknown artist, Sotheby's New York, 5 Dec 2007	57,161,000
2 Tête de femme (Dora Maar) (1941), Pablo Picasso (Spanish; 1881–1973), Sotheby's New York, 7 Nov 2007	29,161,000
3 Artemis and the stag (1st C BC–1st C AD), unknown artist, Sotheby's New York, 10 Jun 2007	28,600,000
4 Oiseau dans l'espace (1922–23), Constantin Brancusi (Romanian; 1876–1957), Christie's New York, 4 May 2005	27,456,000
5 Cubi XXVIII (1965), David Smith (American; 1906–65), Sotheby's New York, 5 Nov 2005	23,816,000
6 Hanging heart (Magenta/Gold) (1994–2006), Jeff Koons (American; b.1955), Sotheby's New York, 14 Nov 2007	23,561,000
7 L'homme qui chavire (1947), Alberto Giacometti (Swiss/Italian; 1901–66), Christie's New York, 9 May 2007	18,520,000
8 Danaïde (1913), Constantin Brancusi (Romanian; 1876–1956), Christie's New York, 7 May 2002	18,159,000
9 Grande Femme Debout I (1960), Alberto Giacometti, Christie's New York, 8 Nov 2000	14,306,000
10 Grande Tete de Diego (1954), Alberto Giacometti, Sotheby's New York, 8 May 2002	13,759,500

TOP 10 **MOST EXPENSIVE SCULPTURES BY AUGUSTE RODIN**

SCULPTURE / SALE	PRICE ($)
1 Iris, messagère des dieux (1890–91), Sotheby's London, 19 Jun, 2007	9,114,624 (£4,612,000)
2 Eve (1880–81), Christie's New York, 8 Nov 1999	4,842,500
3 Les Bourgeois de Calais, Grandmodele, Sotheby's New York, 17 May 1990	4,290,000
4 Balzac, Sotheby's New York, 13 May 1998	3,522,500
5 Le penseur (The Thinker) (1880), Sotheby's New York, 7 Nov 2007	3,065,000
6 Andromède (1886), Christie's New York, 8 Nov 2006	3,040,000
7 L'Enfant prodigue (1884), Sotheby's New York, 3 May 2006	2,928,000
8 Le baiser (The Kiss) (1886), Christie's New York, 8 May 2000	2,756,000
9 Eve au rocher, petit modèle – modèle aux pieds détaillés (1883), Christie's New York, 9 May 2007	2,616,000
10 Le baiser (The Kiss) (1886), Sotheby's New York, 7 Nov 2001	2,425,750

Auguste Rodin (1840–1917) was the foremost French sculptor of his day. He achieved international fame through such creations as his *The Thinker* and *The Kiss*, which was commissioned by an American connoisseur Edward Perry Warren, and kept at his house in Lewes, England, until it was sold to the Tate Gallery, London. Bronze casts of Rodin's works mean that multiple copies exist of a number of them, including *The Burghers of Calais*, one of his most celebrated sculptures, a version of which is in third place in this list, but can also be seen in Calais and in Victoria Tower Gardens in London.

Record Rodin
Rodin's life-sized Eve set a twentieth-century record for the sculptor when it made $4.8 million at auction. The original sculpture, dating from 1880–81, was cast in bronze in 1897.

TOP 10 **TALLEST FREE-STANDING STATUES**

Mighty project
The model of the memorial to Native American warrior Crazy Horse (c.1842–77) is just ¹/₃₄th the size of the actual statue, in progress for 60 years.

STATUE / LOCATION	HEIGHT M	FT

1 Crazy Horse Memorial,
Thunderhead Mountain, South Dakota, USA — 172 — 563
Started in 1948 by Polish-American sculptor Korczak Ziolkowski and continued after his death in 1982 by his widow and eight of his children, this gigantic equestrian statue, even longer than it is high (195 m/641 ft), is not expected to be completed for several years.

2 Foshan Jinfo (Vairocana Buddha),
Lushan, Henan, China — 128 — 420
Completed in 2001, the Buddha sits on a 20-m (66-ft) throne atop a 25-m (82 ft) pedestal.

3 Ushiku Amida Buddha,
Joodo Teien Garden, Japan — 120 — 394
This Japan-Taiwanese project, unveiled in 1993, took seven years to complete and weighs 1,000 tonnes.

4 Nanshan Haishang Guanyin (Avalokitesvara),
Sanya, Hainan, China — 108 — 354
Depicting the bodhisattva Guan Yin, the statue was completed in 2005 after six years' construction.

5 Emperors Yan and Huang,
Zhengzhou, Henan, China — 106 — 348
Completed in 2007.

6 The Indian Rope Trick,
Riddersberg Säteri, Jönköping, Sweden — 103 — 337
Sculptor Calle Örnemark's 144-tonne wooden sculpture depicts a long strand of "rope" held by a fakir, while another figure ascends.

7 Sendai Daikannon (Avalokitesvara)
Sendai, Japan — 100 — 328
Built by a construction company during the late twentieth-century economic boom in Japan.

8 Peter the Great, Moscow, Russia — 96 — 315
Georgian sculptor Zurab Tsereteli's statue of the Russian ruler on a galleon was moved from St Petersburg in 1997.

9 = Grand Buddha at Ling Shan
(Gautama Buddha), Wuxi, China — 88 — 289
This gigantic bronze statue was completed in 1996.

=Dai Kannon of Kita no Miyako park
(Avalokitesvara) Ashibetsu, Hokkaido, Japan — 88 — 289
Completed in 1989.

MUSIC

Singles

TOP 10 **SINGLES THAT STAYED LONGEST IN THE UK CHARTS**

	TITLE / ARTIST	FIRST CHART ENTRY	WEEKS IN CHART
1	'My Way', Frank Sinatra (42)	1969	124
2	'Amazing Grace', Judy Collins (32)	1970	66
3	'Relax', Frankie Goes to Hollywood (48)	1983	59
4 =	'Rock Around the Clock', Bill Haley & His Comets (17)	1955	57
=	'Release Me', Engelbert Humperdinck (56)	1967	57
6	'Stranger on the Shore', Mr. Acker Bilk (55)	1961	55
7	'Blue Monday', New Order (17)	1983	53
8	'Chasing Cars', Snow Patrol (65)	2006	48
9	'I Love You Because', Jim Reeves (39)	1964	47
10	'Let's Twist Again', Chubby Checker (27)	1961	44

Source: Music Information Database

These include reissues and remixes. Numbers in parentheses denote the longest consecutive run on the charts. 'My Way' charted for 122 weeks in 1969–71 and two in 1994.

Left: Sweet success
Stefani's Sweet Escape *album generated a world tour and a single that reached No. 2 on the UK singles chart and achieved a Top 10 slot as a download.*

Right: Timbaland
Taken from his album Shock Value, *Timbaland's 'The Way I Are' hit No. 1 in the UK singles chart, where it stayed for 23 weeks.*

TOP 10 **SINGLES OF ALL TIME IN THE UK**

	TITLE / ARTIST / YEAR OF ENTRY	EST. UK SALES
1	'Candle In The Wind (1997)'/'Something About the Way You Look Tonight', Elton John, 1997	4,875,000
2	'Do They Know It's Christmas?', Band Aid, 1984	3,550,000
3	'Bohemian Rhapsody', Queen, 1975/91	2,130,000
4	'Mull of Kintyre', Wings, 1977	2,050,000
5	'Rivers of Babylon'/'Brown Girl in the Ring, Boney M, 1978	1,985,000
6	'You're the One that I Want', John Travolta and Olivia Newton-John, 1978	1,975,000
7	'Relax', Frankie Goes to Hollywood, 1984	1,910,000
8	'She Loves You', The Beatles, 1963	1,890,000
9	'Unchained Melody', Robson Green and Jerome Flynn, 1995	1,843,700
10	'Mary's Boy Child'/'Oh My Lord', Boney M, 1978	1,790,000

Source: The Official UK Charts Company

TOP 10 **BESTSELLING SINGLES OF THE PAST DECADE IN THE UK**

	TITLE	ARTIST	YEAR
1	'Anything is Possible'/ 'Evergreen'	Will Young	2002
2	'Believe'	Cher	1998
3	'Baby One More Time'	Britney Spears	1999
4	'Unchained Melody'	Gareth Gates	2002
5	'My Heart Will Go On'	Celine Dion	1998
6	'Never Ever'	All Saints	1998
7	'It Wasn't Me'	Shaggy feat. Rik Rok	2001
8	'Heartbeat'/'Tragedy'	Steps	1999
9	'It's Like That'	Run DMC vs. Jason Nevins	1998
10	'Can We Fix It?'	Bob the Builder	2000

Source: Music Information Database

Sales of Will Young's bestseller are in excess of 1.78 million copies. The market has changed so much that in the past five years not one single has sold enough to make this list.

TOP 10 **ARTISTS WITH THE MOST NO. 1 SINGLES IN THE UK**

ARTIST / TOTAL CHART HITS	NO. 1 SINGLES*
1 Elvis Presley (173)	21
2 The Beatles (54)	17
3 = Cliff Richard (132)	14
= Westlife (22)	14
5 Madonna (63)	12
6 Take That (20)	10
7 = Abba (27)	9
= Spice Girls (11)	9
9 = Rolling Stones (55)	8
= Oasis (24)	8

* Including subsequent re-releases

Source: Music Information Database

Presley's No. 1 UK singles span 50 years, from 'All Shook Up' (1957) to the re-release of 'It's Now or Never' (2007).

TOP 10 **SINGLES IN THE UK, 2007**

	TITLE	ARTIST
1	'Bleeding Love'	Leona Lewis
2	'Umbrella'	Rihanna feat. Jay-Z
3	'Grace Kelly'	Mika
4	'When You Believe'	Leon Jackson
5	'Rule the World'	Take That
6	'About You Now'	Sugababes
7	'The Way I Are'	Timbaland feat. D.O.E./Keri Hilson
8	'(I'm Gonna Be) 500 Miles'	Proclaimers, Brian Potter and Andy Pipkin
9	'Valerie'	Mark Ronson feat. Amy Winehouse
10	'Ruby'	Kaiser Chiefs

Source: The Official UK Charts Company

Leona Lewis, Rhianna and Take That also managed to make the 2006 list.

TOP 10 **DOWNLOADED SINGLES IN THE UK, 2007**

	SINGLE	ARTIST
1	'Bleeding Love'	Leona Lewis
2	'Umbrella'	Rihanna feat. Jay-Z
3	'Grace Kelly'	Mika
4	'How to Save a Life'	Fray
5	'About You Now'	Sugarbabes
6	'Ruby'	Kaiser Chiefs
7	'The Way I Are'	Timbaland feat. D.O.E./Keri Hilson
8	'Hey There Delilah'	Plain White Ts
9	'Rule the World'	Take That
10	'Valerie'	Mark Ronson feat. Amy Winehouse

Source: The Official UK Charts Company

Albums

TOP 10 ALBUMS IN THE UK, 2007

TITLE / ARTIST

1 Back to Black
Amy Winehouse

2 Spirit
Leona Lewis

3 Life in Cartoon Motion
Mika

4 Beautiful World
Take That

5 Back Home
Westlife

6 Long Road Out of Eden
Eagles

7 Yours Truly Angry Mob
Kaiser Chiefs

8 Favourite Worst Nightmare
Arctic Monkeys

9 Shock Value
Timbaland

10 Good Girl Gone Bad
Rihanna

Source: The Official UK Charts Company

Bob dazzles
Bob Dylan performing at the inaugural Farm Aid concert (1985). His UK album career spans 44 years, during which he has achieved 49 chart hits.

TOP 10 SOLO ARTISTS WITH THE MOST CHART ALBUMS IN THE UK*

	ARTIST	CHART ALBUMS
1	Elvis Presley	110
2	James Last	60
3	Cliff Richard	57
4	Frank Sinatra	54
5	Bob Dylan	49#
6	David Bowie	40
7	Elton John	39
8	Diana Ross	38†
9	Shirley Bassey	37
10	Neil Diamond	35

* To December 2007
# Including one album with the Grateful Dead
† Including one album with Marvin Gaye and one with Michael Jackson

Source: Music Information Database

TOP 10 ALBUMS IN THE UK IN THE PAST 10 YEARS

TITLE / ARTIST

2007 Back to Black
Amy Winehouse

2006 Eyes Open
Snow Patrol

2005 Back to Bedlam
James Blunt

2004 Scissor Sisters
Scissor Sisters

2003 Life For Rent
Dido

2002 Escapology
Robbie Williams

2001 No Angel
Dido

2000 1
The Beatles

1999 Come on Over
Shania Twain

1998 Talk on Corners
The Corrs

Source: The Official UK Charts Company

TOP 10 ALBUMS THAT STAYED LONGEST AT NO. 1 IN THE UK

	TITLE / ARTIST	WEEKS AT NO. 1
1	South Pacific, Soundtrack	115
2	The Sound of Music, Soundtrack	70
3	Bridge Over Troubled Water, Simon & Garfunkel	41
4	Please Please Me, The Beatles	30*
5	Sgt. Pepper's Lonely Hearts Club Band, The Beatles	27
6	G.I. Blues, Elvis Presley/Soundtrack	22
7	=With The Beatles, The Beatles	21*
	=A Hard Day's Night, The Beatles/Soundtrack	21*
9	=Blue Hawaii, Elvis Presley/Soundtrack	18
	=Saturday Night Fever, Soundtrack	18*

* Continuous run

Source: Music Information Database

Long players
Simon & Garfunkel at the time of the release of their 1972 Greatest Hits. Cumulatively, two of their albums have amassed a total UK chart residence of 590 weeks.

TOP 10 **ALBUMS THAT STAYED LONGEST IN THE UK CHARTS**

TITLE / ARTIST / LONGEST CONSECUTIVE RUN	FIRST CHART ENTRY	WEEKS IN CHART
1 Rumours, Fleetwood Mac (120)	1977	478
2 Bat Out of Hell, Meat Loaf (329)	1978	473
3 Greatest Hits, Queen (222)	1981	452
4 The Sound of Music, Soundtrack (318)	1965	382
5 The Dark Side of the Moon, Pink Floyd (135)	1973	366
6 Gold – Greatest Hits, Abba (101)	1992	357
7 South Pacific, Soundtrack (153)	1960	319
8 Bridge Over Troubled Water, Simon & Garfunkel (244)	1970	307
9 Greatest Hits, Simon & Garfunkel (195)	1972	283
10 Tubular Bells, Mike Oldfield (128)	1973	276

Source: Music Information Database

TOP 10 **ALBUMS OF ALL TIME IN THE UK**

TITLE / ARTIST / YEAR	SALES
1 Greatest Hits, Queen (1981)	5,580,000
2 Sgt. Pepper's Lonely Hearts Club Band, The Beatles (1967)	4,500,000
3 (What's the Story) Morning Glory, Oasis (1995)	4,365,000
4 Gold – Greatest Hits, Abba (1990)	4,100,000
5 Brothers in Arms, Dire Straits (1985)	4,030,000
6 The Dark Side of the Moon, Pink Floyd (1973)	3,925,000
7 Greatest Hits II, Queen (1991)	3,710,000
8 Thriller, Michael Jackson (1982)	3,615,000
9 Bad, Michael Jackson (1987)	3,570,000
10 The Immaculate Collection, Madonna (1990)	3,560,000

Source: The Official UK Charts Company

A survey of Britain's bestselling albums conducted at the end of 2006 placed Queen's *Greatest Hits* at the top of the list. It has been estimated that it has sold over 43 million copies worldwide.

Record Firsts

THE 10 FIRST FEMALE SINGERS TO HAVE A NO. 1 HIT IN THE UK

	ARTIST	TITLE	DATE AT NO. 1
1	Jo Stafford	'You Belong to Me'	17 Jan 1953
2	Kay Starr	'Comes A-Long A-Love'	24 Jan 1953
3	Lita Roza	'(How Much is That) Doggie In The Window?'	18 Apr 1953
4	Doris Day	'Secret Love'	17 Apr 1954
5	Kitty Kallen	'Little Things Mean a Lot'	11 Sep 1954
6	Vera Lynn	'My Son, My Son'	6 Nov 1954
7	Rosemary Clooney	'This Ole House'	27 Nov 1954
8	Ruby Murray	'Softly Softly'	19 Feb 1955
9	Alma Cogan	'Dreamboat'	16 Jul 1955
10	Anne Shelton	'Lay Down Your Arms'	22 Sep 1956

Source: Music Information Database

The first UK singles chart was published on 15 November 1952. Al Martino's inaugural No. 1 was followed by Jo Stafford and Kay Starr. Lita Roza, covering a US No. 1 by Patti Page, was the first British female artist to reach the summit, six months into the life of the chart. Winifred Atwell topped the chart on 4 December 1954 with 'Let's Have Another Party', but she was an instrumentalist, and therefore ineligible for this list.

THE 10 FIRST UK MALE ARTISTS TO TOP THE US SINGLES CHART

	TITLE / ARTIST	DATE AT NO. 1
1	'He's Got the Whole World (In His Hands)', Laurie London	19 Apr 1958
2	'Stranger on the Shore', Mr. Acker Bilk	26 May 1962
3	'The Stripper', David Rose	7 Jul 1962
4	'Sunshine Superman', Donovan	3 Sep 1966
5	'My Sweet Lord'/'Isn't it a Pity', George Harrison	26 Dec 1970
6	'Maggie May'/'Reason to Believe', Rod Stewart	2 Oct 1971
7	'Crocodile Rock', Elton John	3 Feb 1973
8	'Photograph', Ringo Starr	26 Jan 1974
9	'I Shot the Sheriff', Eric Clapton	14 Sep 1974
10	'Whatever Gets You Thru the Night', John Lennon	16 Nov 1974

Source: Music Information Database

THE 10 **FIRST NATIONALITIES TO TOP THE UK SINGLES CHART***

NATIONALITY / ARTIST / TITLE	DATE AT NO. 1
1 Italian, Mantovani 'Moulin Rouge'	15 Aug 1953
2 Trinidadian, Winifred Atwell 'Let's Have Another Party'	4 Dec 1954
3 Cuban, Perez 'Prez Prado' 'Cherry Pink and Apple Blossom White'	30 Apr 1955
4 Canadian, Paul Anka 'Diana'	31 Aug 1957
5 St Lucian, Emile Ford & the Checkmates 'What Do You Want to Make Those Eyes At Me For'	19 Dec 1959
6 South African, Danny Williams 'Moon River'	30 Dec 1961
7 Australian, The Seekers 'The Carnival is Over'	27 Nov 1965
8 Palestinian, Esther and Abi Ofarim 'Cinderella Rockefella'	2 Mar 1968
9 Jamaican, Desmond Dekker and the Aces 'The Israelites'	19 Apr 1969
10 Irish, Dana 'All Kinds of Everything'	18 Apr 1970

* Excluding the USA

Source: Music Information Database

Cliff Richard, Eden Kane and Engelbert Humperdinck, who were all born in India, would have qualified for the list but were UK citizens. The Seekers' Keith Potger was born in Ceylon, but is regarded as an Australian. Emile Ford's Checkmates were British, but Ford himself was from the West Indies.

Far left: Jo Stafford
Jo Stafford's 'You Belong to Me' was the UK's second No. 1 and the first by a female singer – a position it held for a single week.

Left: Doris Day
Doris Day's Oscar-winning 'Secret Love' from the film Calamity Jane (1953) held the UK No. 1 slot for 10 weeks.

Right: Prez Prado
The Cuban bandleader's 'Cherry Pink and Apple Blossom White' spent six weeks at UK No. 1.

THE 10 **FIRST RECORDS TO ENTER THE UK CHART AT NO. 1**

ARTIST	TITLE	DATE AT NO. 1
1 Elvis Presley	'Jailhouse Rock'	25 Jan 1958
2 Elvis Presley	'It's Now Or Never'	5 Nov 1960
3 Cliff Richard and the Shadows	'The Young Ones'	13 Jan 1962
4 Elvis Presley	'Can't Help Falling In Love'/ 'Rock-A-Hula-Baby'	3 Mar 1962
5 Beatles	'Get Back'	26 Apr 1969
6 Slade	'Cum On Feel the Noize'	3 Mar 1973
7 Slade	'Skweeze Me, Pleeze Me'	30 Jun 1973
8 Gary Glitter	'I Love You Love Me Love'	17 Nov 1973
9 Slade	'Merry Xmas Everybody'	15 Dec 1973
10 Jam	'Going Underground'/ 'The Dreams of Children'	22 Mar 1980

Source: Music Information Database

The instant chart topper was once a rarity, whereas more than 86 per cent of the chart toppers in the twenty-first century have entered at No. 1.

Male Singers

Justified *success*
Justin Timberlake's debut album Justified *was UK No. 1 for seven weeks, and the UK's bestselling in 2003, with certified sales of over 1.5 million copies.*

TOP 10 **LONGEST GAPS BETWEEN NO. 1 HIT SINGLES BY MALE SINGERS IN THE UK**

	SINGER	PERIOD	YRS	GAP MTHS	DAYS
1	George Harrison	2 Feb 1971–26 Jan 2002	30	11	24
2	Elvis Presley	1 Oct 1977–22 Jun 2002	24	8	21
3	Elton John	4 Sep 1976–16 Jun 1990	13	9	12
4	Frank Sinatra	1 Oct 1954–27 May 1966	11	7	26
5	Cliff Richard	17 Apr 1968–19 Aug 1979	11	4	2
6	Cliff Richard	22 Dec 1990–27 Nov 1999	8	11	5
7	Bryan Adams	2 Nov 1991–11 Mar 2000	8	4	9
8	Don McLean	1 Jul 1972–14 Jun 1980	7	11	13
9	Peter Andre	14 Dec 1996-6 Mar 2004	7	2	21
10	Elvis Presley	12 Sep 1970–27 Aug 1977	6	11	15

Source: Music Information Database

TOP 10 **YOUNGEST MALE SOLO SINGERS TO HAVE A NO. 1 SINGLE IN THE UK**

	ARTIST / TITLE	YEAR	YRS	AGE* MTHS	DAYS
1	Little Jimmy Osmond, 'Long Haired Lover from Liverpool'	1972	9	8	7
2	Donny Osmond, 'Puppy Love'	1972	14	6	30
3	Paul Anka, 'Diana'	1957	16	1	1
4	Sean Kingston, 'Beautiful Girls'	2007	17	7	5
5	Gareth Gates#, 'Unchained Melody'	2002	17	8	18
6	Glenn Medeiros, 'Nothing's Gonna Change My Love'	1988	18	0	15
7	Craig Douglas, 'Only Sixteen'	1959	18	0	27
8	Cliff Richard, 'Living Doll'	1959	18	9	18
9	Craig David, 'Fill Me In'	2000	18	11	0
10	Leon Jackson, 'When You Believe'	2007	18	11	29

* During first week of debut No. 1 UK single
\# Youngest British solo No. 1

Source: Music Information Database

Gareth Gates had two further No. 1s before he turned 19. If group members were eligible for the list, all three Hanson brothers would be in the Top 10. Isaac was 16 years and 6 months, Taylor 14 years and 2 months and Zachary 11 years and 7 months when 'Mmmbop' topped the charts in 1997.

TOP 10 **SINGLES BY MALE SOLO SINGERS IN THE UK**

	TITLE / ARTIST	YEAR
1	'Candle in the Wind (1997)'/'Something About the Way You Look Tonight', Elton John	1997
2	'Anything is Possible'/'Evergreen', Will Young	2002
3	'I Just Called to Say I Love You', Stevie Wonder	1984
4	'(Everything I Do) I Do it for You', Bryan Adams	1991
5	'Tears', Ken Dodd	1965
6	'Imagine', John Lennon	1975
7	'Careless Whisper', George Michael	1984
8	'Release Me', Engelbert Humperdinck	1967
9	'Unchained Melody', Gareth Gates	2002
10	'Diana', Paul Anka	1957

Source: The Official UK Charts Company

This list represents a timeshaft through the history of British popular music, with singles from each decade reflecting the sometimes unpredictable taste of the British public. The best Elvis Presley can do is No. 11 with 'It's Now or Never', which is just a few thousand behind Paul Anka's 'Diana'.

TOP 10 BESTSELLING ALBUMS BY A MALE ARTIST IN THE UK

TITLE / ARTIST	YEAR
1 Thriller, Michael Jackson	1982
2 Bad, Michael Jackson	1987
3 Back To Bedlam, James Blunt	2006
4 Bat Out of Hell, Meat Loaf	1978
5 White Ladder, David Gray	2000
6 But Seriously..., Phil Collins	1989
7 Tubular Bells, Mike Oldfield	1973
8 I've Been Expecting You, Robbie Williams	1998
9 Ladies and Gentlemen – The Best of, George Michael	1998
10 The Marshall Mathers EP, Eminem	2000

Source: The Official UK Charts Company

Stevie Wonder
'I Just Called to Say I Love You' stayed at UK No.1 for six weeks in 1984.

TOP 10 BESTSELLING ALBUMS BY MALE ARTISTS IN THE UK IN THE PAST 10 YEARS

2007	Life in Cartoon Motion, Mika
2006	Undiscovered, James Morrison
2005	Back to Bedlam, James Blunt
2004	Greatest Hits, Robbie Williams
2003	Justified, Justin Timberlake
2002	Escapology, Robbie Williams
2001	Swing When You're Winning, Robbie Williams
2000	Sing When You're Winning, Robbie Williams
1999	I've Been Expecting You, Robbie Williams
1998	Ladies and Gentlemen – The Best of, George Michael

Source: Music Information Database

TOP 10 MALE ARTISTS WITH THE MOST PLATINUM ALBUMS IN THE UK

ARTIST*	PLATINUM ALBUMS
1 Robbie Williams (9)	56
2 Michael Jackson (14)	43
3 Phil Collins (13)	35
4 Elton John (24)	28
5 George Michael (8)	27
6 Rod Stewart (30)	20
7 Meat Loaf (10)	18
8 Eminem (7)	17
9 = Chris Rea (10)	15
= Cliff Richard (25)	15

* Gold totals in brackets

Source: Music Information Database

Platinum albums in the UK are those that have achieved sales of 300,000 – roughly one per 202 inhabitants, compared with US platinum (sales of one million).

Female Singers

TOP 10 LONGEST GAPS BETWEEN NO. 1 SINGLES BY FEMALE SOLO ARTISTS IN THE UK

	ARTIST	PERIOD	GAP YRS	MTHS	DAYS
1	Diana Ross	18 Sep 1971–1 Mar 1986	14	5	11
2	Kylie Minogue	3 Feb 1990–24 June 2000	10	5	21
3	Madonna	12 May 1990–28 Feb 1998	7	9	16
4	Petula Clark	4 Mar 1961–11 Feb 1967	5	11	7
5	Madonna	2 Sep 2000–19 Nov 2005	5	2	18
6	Jennifer Lopez	20 Jan 2001–26 Feb 2005	4	1	7
7	Whitney Houston	29 Oct 1988–28 Nov 1992	4	0	30
8	Britney Spears	20 May 2000–13 Mar 2004	3	9	22
9	Cher	8 Jun 1991–18 Mar 1995	3	9	10
10	Cher	1 Apr 1995–24 Oct 1998	3	6	23

Source: Music Information Database

Mind the gap

Cher's spaced-out UK No. 1s span her only three singles to hit the top slot, 'The Shoop Shoop Song' (1991) to 'Love Can Build a Bridge' (1995) and 'Believe' (1998).

TOP 10 YOUNGEST FEMALE SOLO SINGERS TO HAVE A NO. 1 SINGLE IN THE UK

	ARTIST / TITLE	YEAR	AGE YRS	MTHS	DAYS
1	Helen Shapiro, 'You Don't Know'	1961	14	10	13
2	Billie, 'Because We Want To'	1998	15	9	20
3	Tiffany, 'I Think We're Alone Now'	1988	16	3	28
4	Nicole, 'A Little Peace'	1982	17	0	0
5	Britney Spears, '...Baby One More Time'	1999	17	2	25
6	Sandie Shaw, '(There's) Always Something There to Remind Me'	1964	17	7	26
7	LeAnn Rimes, 'Can't Fight the Moonlight'	2000	18	2	29
8	Mary Hopkin, 'Those Were the Days'	1968	18	4	22
9	Sonia, 'You'll Never Stop Me Loving You'	1989	18	5	9
10	Christina Aguilera, 'Genie in a Bottle'	1999	18	9	29

Source: Music Information Database

TOP 10 BESTSELLING ALBUMS BY FEMALE SOLO ARTISTS IN THE UK

TITLE / ARTIST	YEAR
1 The Immaculate Collection, Madonna	1990
2 Come on Over, Shania Twain	1998
3 No Angel, Dido	2000
4 Life For Rent, Dido	2003
5 Jagged Little Pill, Alanis Morissette	1995
6 Come Away With Me, Norah Jones	2002
7 Tracy Chapman, Tracy Chapman	1998
8 Whitney, Whitney Houston	1987
9 Simply the Best, Tina Turner	1991
10 Falling Into You, Celine Dion	1996

Source: The Official UK Charts Company

The top three albums listed here have all sold in excess of three million copies – in fact Dido's first two releases have a combined sale of almost 5.8 million.

More than one
Britney Spears' '...Baby One More Time', the UK's second bestselling by a female singer, hit No. 1 in every European country.

TOP 10 SINGLES BY FEMALE SOLO SINGERS IN THE UK

TITLE / ARTIST	YEAR
1 'Believe', Cher	1998
2 '...Baby One More Time', Britney Spears	1999
3 'I Will Always Love You', Whitney Houston	1992
4 'The Power of Love', Jennifer Rush	1985
5 'My Heart Will Go On', Celine Dion	1998
6 'Think Twice', Celine Dion	1994
7 'Saturday Night', Whigfield	1994
8 'Can't Get You Out of My Head', Kylie Minogue	2001
9 'Don't Cry For Me Argentina', Julie Covington	1976
10 'Torn', Natalie Imbruglia	1997

Source: The Official UK Charts Company

TOP 10 FEMALE ARTISTS WITH THE MOST PLATINUM ALBUMS IN THE UK

ARTIST*	PLATINUM ALBUMS
1 Madonna (21)	50
2 = Celine Dion (11)	22
= Tina Turner (9)	22
4 Kylie Minogue (8)	21
5 Whitney Houston (5)	19
6 Dido (2)	16
7 Shania Twain (3)	15
8 = Mariah Carey (12)	13
= Enya (6)	13
10 = Gloria Estefan (4)	12
= Katie Melua (4)	12

* Gold totals listed in brackets

Source: BPI

TOP 10 BESTSELLING ALBUMS BY FEMALE SOLO ARTISTS IN THE UK IN THE PAST 10 YEARS

YEAR	TITLE / ARTIST
2007	Back to Black, Amy Winehouse
2006	Corinne Bailey Rae, Corinne Bailey Rae
2005	Eye to the Telescope, KT Tunstall
2004	Call Off the Search, Katie Melua
2003	Life For Rent, Dido
2002	M!ssundaztood, P!nk
2001	No Angel, Dido
2000	The Greatest Hits, Whitney Houston
1999	Come on Over, Shania Twain
1998	Ray of Light, Madonna

Source: Music Information Database

Groups & Duos

TOP 10 **SINGLES BY GROUPS AND DUOS IN THE UK, 2007**

TITLE / GROUP/DUO

1 'Rule the World', Take That
2 'About You Now', Sugababes
3 '(I'm Gonna Be) 500 Miles', Proclaimers with Brian Potter and Andy Pipkin
4 'Ruby', Kaiser Chiefs
5 'How to Save a Life', The Fray
6 'Beautiful Liar', Beyonce and Shakira
7 'Hey There Delilah', Plain White T's
8 'Apologize', Timbaland presents OneRepublic
9 'Shine', Take That
10 'With Every Heartbeat', Robyn with Kleerup

Source: The Official UK Charts Company

Satisfaction guaranteed
In a career spanning 45 years, the Rolling Stones have had eight UK No. 1 chart hits and spent 18 weeks at No. 1.

TOP 10 **GROUPS AND DUOS WITH THE MOST NO. 1 SINGLES IN THE UK**

	GROUP/DUO	NO. 1 SINGLES
1	The Beatles	17
2	Westlife*	14
3	Take That	10
4	= Abba	9
	= Spice Girls	9
6	= Oasis	8
	= Rolling Stones	8
8	= U2	7
	= McFly	7
10	= Blondie	6
	= Boyzone	6
	= Queen#	6
	= Slade	6
	= Sugababes	6

* Including one with Mariah Carey
# Including No. 1s with David Bowie, George Michael and Five

Source: Music Information Database

TOP 10 **GROUPS AND DUOS WITH THE MOST WEEKS AT NO. 1 IN THE UK**

	GROUP/DUO	WEEKS AT NO. 1
1	The Beatles	69
2	Abba	31
3	Take That	26
4	Wet Wet Wet	23
5	The Spice Girls	22
6	Queen	21
7	= Slade	20
	= Westlife	20
9	Rolling Stones	18
10	= The Shadows	16*
	= T. Rex	16

* Excludes hits shared with Cliff Richard

Source: Music Information Database

TOP 10 **ALBUMS BY GROUPS AND DUOS IN THE UK, 2007**

TITLE / GROUP/DUO

1 Beautiful World, Take That
2 Back Home, Westlife
3 Long Road Out of Eden, Eagles
4 Yours Truly Angry Mob, Kaiser Chiefs
5 Favourite Worst Nightmare, Arctic Monkeys
6 Eyes Open, Snow Patrol
7 Echoes Silence Patience & Grace, Foo Fighters
8 Mothership – The Best of Led Zeppelin, Led Zeppelin
9 Sam's Town, Killers
10 Costello Music, Fratellis

Source: The Official UK Charts Company

TOP 10 **ALBUMS BY GROUPS AND DUOS IN THE UK**

TITLE / GROUP/DUO	YEAR
1 Greatest Hits (Volume One), Queen	1981
2 Sgt. Pepper's Lonely Hearts Club Band, The Beatles	1967
3 (What's the Story) Morning Glory, Oasis	1995
4 Gold – Greatest Hits, Abba	1992
5 Brothers in Arms, Dire Straits	1985
6 The Dark Side of the Moon, Pink Floyd	1973
7 Greatest Hits Volume II, Queen	1991
8 Stars, Simply Red	1991
9 Rumours, Fleetwood Mac	1977
10 Urban Hymns, Verve	1997

Source: The Official UK Charts Company

In the pink
While it failed to attain UK No. 1, Pink Floyd's iconic album The Dark Side of the Moon *has amassed domestic sales of over 3.8 million, with total worldwide sales estimated at more than 40 million.*

TOP 10 **GROUPS AND DUOS WITH THE LONGEST SINGLES CHART CAREERS IN THE UK**

GROUP/DUO / CHART SPAN	YEARS	MONTHS	DAYS
1 The Rolling Stones 27 Jul 1963–2 Sep 2006	43	1	6
2 The Kinks 15 Aug 1964–25 Sep 2004	40	1	10
3 Slade 19 Jun 1971–5 Jan 2008	37	6	17
4 Status Quo 24 Aug 1968–19 Nov 2005	37	2	26
5 Wizzard 8 Dec 1973–5 Jan 2008	35	0	28
6 Bee Gees 29 Apr 1967–5 May 2001	35	0	6
7 The Beatles 13 Oct 1962–27 Apr 1996	33	6	14
8 The Beach Boys 3 Aug 1963–23 Mar 1996	32	7	20
9 The Who 20 Feb 1965–3 Aug 1996	31	5	14
10 Abba 20 Apr 1974–12 Jun 2004	30	1	22

Source: Music Information Database

TOP 10 **SINGLES BY GROUPS AND DUOS IN THE UK**

TITLE / GROUP/DUO	YEAR
1 'Bohemian Rhapsody', Queen	1975
2 'Mull of Kintyre'/'Girls' School', Wings	1977
3 'Rivers of Babylon'/'Brown Girl in the Ring', Boney M	1978
4 'You're the That I Want', John Travolta and Olivia Newton-John	1978
5 'Relax', Frankie Goes to Hollywood	1984
6 'She Loves You, The Beatles	1963
7 'Unchained Melody'/'(There'll be Bluebirds Over the) White Cliffs of Dover', Robson Green and Jerome Flynn	1995
8 'Mary's Boy Child'/'Oh My Lord', Boney M	1978
9 'Love is All Around', Wet Wet Wet	1994
10 'I Want to Hold Your Hand', The Beatles	1963

Source: The Official UK Charts Company

Music Awards

THE 10 **ARTISTS WITH MOST MTV AWARDS**

	ARTIST	AWARDS
1	Madonna	20
2	Peter Gabriel	13
3	R.E.M.	12
4	Aerosmith	10
5	=Fatboy Slim	9
	=Janet Jackson	9
7	=Eminem	8
	=Green Day	8
	=Michael Jackson	8
10	=a-ha	7
	=En Vogue	7
	='NSync	7
	=Red Hot Chili Peppers	7
	=The Smashing Pumpkins	7

Source: MTV

THE 10 **ARTISTS WITH MOST GRAMMY AWARDS**

	ARTIST	AWARDS
1	Sir Georg Solti	31
2	Quincy Jones	27
3	Pierre Boulez	26
4	=Vladimir Horowitz	25
	=Stevie Wonder	25
6	U2	22
7	Alison Krauss	21
8	=Henry Mancini	20
	=John Williams	20
10	=Pat Metheny	18
	=Bruce Springsteen	18

Source: NARAS

The Grammy Awards ceremony has been held annually in the United States since its inauguration on 4 May 1959, and the awards are now considered to be the most prestigious in the music industry. The proliferation of classical artists in this Top 10 (not least, conductor Sir George Solti) is largely attributable to the large number of classical award categories at the Grammys, which have been latterly overshadowed by the rise of pop and rock.

THE 10 **LATEST RECIPIENTS OF THE NATIONWIDE MERCURY PRIZE***

	ARTIST / ALBUM	YEAR
1	Klaxons, Myths of the Near Future	2007
2	Arctic Monkeys, Whatever People Say I Am, That's What I'm Not	2006
3	Antony & the Johnsons, I Am a Bird Now	2005
4	Franz Ferdinand, Franz Ferdinand	2004
5	Dizzee Rascal, Boy in Da Corner	2003
6	Ms Dynamite, A Little Deeper	2002
7	PJ Harvey, Stories from the City, Stories from the Sea	2001
8	Badly Drawn Boy, The Hour of Bewilderbeast	2000
9	Talvin Singh, OK	1999
10	Gomez, Bring It On	1998

* Since 2004; originally Mercury Prize, later Mercury Music Prize

Source: Nationwide Mercury Prize

Coldplay and Radiohead have both been nominated three times, but never managed to win.

Madonna
Madonna, who performed at the inaugural MTV Video Music Awards in 1984, has amassed a record tally of 20 MTV awards, ranging from her 1986 Career Achievement Award to Best Video for 'Beautiful Stranger' (1999), plus Artist of the Decade special award in 1989.

Yesterday and today
Paul McCartney won two BRIT awards in 1983, but none for the next 25
years, until his Outstanding Contribution to British Music award in 2008.

THE 10 LATEST RECIPIENTS OF THE BRIT AWARD FOR OUTSTANDING CONTRIBUTION TO BRITISH MUSIC

	ARTIST	YEAR
1	Paul McCartney	2008
2	Oasis	2007
3	Paul Weller	2006
4	Bob Geldof	2005
5	Duran Duran	2004
6	Tom Jones	2003
7	Sting	2002
8	U2	2001
9	Spice Girls	2000
10	Eurythmics	1999

Source: BRIT Awards

Of the 10 listed artists, only Eurythmics and Fleetwood Mac have never also won a BRIT award.

THE 10 FIRST ARTISTS TO RECEIVE GRAMMY LIFETIME ACHIEVEMENT AWARDS

	ARTIST	YEAR
1	Bing Crosby	1962
2	Frank Sinatra	1965
3	Duke Ellington	1966
4	Ella Fitzgerald	1967
5	Irving Berlin	1968
6	Elvis Presley	1971
7 =	Louis Armstrong	1972
=	Mahalia Jackson	1972
9 =	Chuck Berry	1984
=	Charlie Parker	1984

Source: NARAS

The Grammy Lifetime Achievement Award is presented to 'performers who, during their lifetimes, have made creative contributions of outstanding artistic significance to the field of recording'

TOP 10 LONGEST-SPANNING GRAMMY WINNERS

	ARTIST	YEARS	SPAN
1 =	Tony Bennett	1962–2006	44
=	Ray Charles	1960–2004	44
3 =	The Beatles	1964–2007	43
=	Andre Previn	1961–2004	43
5	Al Schmitt	1962–2004	42
6	Phil Ramone	1964–2005	41
7 =	Johnny Cash	1967–2007	40
=	Aretha Franklin	1967–2007	40
9 =	Burt Bacharach	1967–2005	38
=	Quincy Jones	1963–2001	38
=	Joni Mitchell	1969–2007	38

Source: Music Information Database

Tony Bennett's 44-year span ranges from 1962 Record of the Year 'I Left My Heart in San Francisco' to his collaboration with Christina Aguilera, 'Steppin' Out With My Baby'

Movie Music

TOP 10 **FILM MUSICALS ADAPTED FROM STAGE VERSIONS**

	MUSICAL	THEATRE OPENING	FILM RELEASE
1	Grease	1972	1978
2	Chicago	1975	2002
3	Hairspray	2002	2007
4	The Sound of Music	1959	1965
5	The Phantom of the Opera	1986	2004
6	Evita	1978	1996
7	The Rocky Horror (Picture) Show	1973	1975
8	Dreamgirls	1981	2006
9	Fiddler on the Roof	1964	1971
10	Sweeney Todd: The Demon Barber of Fleet Street	1979	2007

The adapting of stage musicals as films has a long history, with these the most successful cinematic versions of what, in most instances, were previously long-running theatrical productions.

TOP 10 **MUSICIAN FILM BIOGRAPHIES**

	FILM	SUBJECT	YEAR
1	Walk the Line	Johnny Cash	2005
2	The Sound of Music	von Trapp family	1965
3	Ray	Ray Charles	2004
4	The Pianist	Wladyslaw Szpilman	2002
5	Shine	David Helfgott	1996
6	La Vie en Rose	Edith Piaf	2007
7	Coal Miner's Daughter	Loretta Lynn	1980
8	La Bamba	Ritchie Valens	1987
9	Amadeus	Wolfgang Amadeus Mozart	1984
10	What's Love Got to Do with It	Tina Turner	1993

Biopics on the lives of musicians have been a Hollywood staple for over 60 years, encompassing both classical and popular musicians, including Hank Williams (*Your Cheatin' Heart*, 1964), Peter Tchaikovsky (*The Music Lovers*, 1970), Buddy Holly (*The Buddy Holly Story*, 1978) and Jacqueline du Pré (*Hilary and Jackie*, 1998).

Above: Reverse role
Julie Andrews in Victor/Victoria, *which, in a reverse of the common route, became a musical.*

Left: Role reversal
Hairspray, *the film (2007) of the musical (2002) of the film (1988), starred John Travolta, uncharacteristically cast in a female role.*

TOP 10 **MGM MUSICALS**

MUSICAL	YEAR
1 Victor/Victoria	1982
2 That's Entertainment!	1974
3 The Wizard of Oz	1939
4 De-Lovely	2004
5 Gigi	1958
6 Seven Brides For Seven Brothers	1954
7 I'll Cry Tomorrow	1955
8 High Society	1956
9 The Unsinkable Molly Brown	1964
10 Meet Me in St Louis	1944

From the earliest years of talking pictures, MGM established itself as the pre-eminent studio for musicals, making some 200 and winning the first Best Picture Oscar for *The Broadway Melody* (1929) and subsequently for *The Great Ziegfeld* (1936), *An American in Paris* (1951) and *Gigi* (1958). MGM's *That's Entertainment*, like its two sequels (1976 and 1994), was a compilation of clips rather than a single narrative film, while *De-Lovely* is a musical biopic based on the life and songs of Cole Porter.

TOP 10 **BESTSELLING MUSICAL ALBUMS IN THE UK**

TITLE	YEAR OF RELEASE
1 The Sound of Music	1965
2 Grease	1978
3 South Pacific	1958
4 West Side Story	1962
5 Oklahoma	1955
6 The King and I	1956
7 Oliver	1968
8 Mary Poppins	1965
9 Evita	1996
10 My Fair Lady	1964

Source: Music Information Database

The Sound of Music stayed at No. 1 in the UK charts for a record 69 weeks and sold some 21 million copies worldwide.

TOP 10 **ORIGINAL SOUNDTRACK ALBUMS IN THE UK**

TITLE	YEAR OF RELEASE
1 The Sound of Music	1965
2 Dirty Dancing	1998
3 Grease	1978
4 Saturday Night Fever	1977
5 The Bodyguard	1992
6 South Pacific	1958
7 Titanic	1997
8 Bridget Jones's Diary	2001
9 Trainspotting	1996
10 The Commitments	1991

Source: Music Information Database

Classical Music & Opera

The Three Tenors
The Three Tenors' original 1990 concert recording became the world's bestselling classical album and led to a series of immensely popular performances.

THE 10 **LATEST CLASSICAL ALBUM GRAMMY WINNERS**

COMPOSER / TITLE	YEAR
1 Joan Tower, Made in America	2007
2 Gustav Mahler, Symphony No. 7	2006
3 William Bolcom, Songs of Innocence and of Experience	2005
4 John Adams, On the Transmigration of Souls	2004
5 Gustav Mahler, Symphony No. 3, Kindertotenlieder	2003
6 Ralph Vaughan Williams, A Sea Symphony (Symphony No. 1)	2002
7 Hector Berlioz, Les Troyens	2001
8 Dmitri Shostakovich, The String Quartets	2000
9 Igor Stravinsky, Firebird, The Rite of Spring, Persephone	1999
10 Samuel Barber, Prayers of Kierkegaard/ Ralph Vaughan Williams, Dona Nobis Pacem/ Bela Bartok, Cantata Profana	1998

Source: NARAS

TOP 10 **CLASSICAL ALBUMS IN THE UK**

TITLE	PERFORMER / ORCHESTRA	YEAR
1 The Three Tenors In Concert	José Carreras, Placido Domingo, Luciano Pavarotti	1990
2 The Essential Pavarotti	Luciano Pavarotti	1990
3 Vivaldi: The Four Seasons	Nigel Kennedy/English Chamber Orchestra	1989
4 The Three Tenors – In Concert 1994	José Carreras, Placido Domingo, Luciano Pavarotti, Zubin Mehta	1994
5 The Voice	Russell Watson	2000
6 Voice of an Angel	Charlotte Church	1998
7 Pure	Hayley Westenra	2003
8 Encore	Russell Watson	2002
9 The Essential Pavarotti, 2	Luciano Pavarotti	1991
10 The Pavarotti Collection	Luciano Pavarotti	1986

Source: Music Information Database

Fuelled by the new medium of CDs, sales of classical music boomed to unprecedented heights in the 1980s and early 1990s, with a select band of superstars led by Carreras, Domingo and Pavarotti (the latter even had a Top 3 single with 'Nessun Dorma') and violinist Nigel Kennedy soaring ahead of the field as a whole.

TOP 10 OPERAS MOST FREQUENTLY PERFORMED AT THE ROYAL OPERA HOUSE, COVENT GARDEN, 1833–2007

OPERA / COMPOSER	FIRST PERFORMANCE	TOTAL*
1 La Bohème Giacomo Puccini	2 Oct 1897	561
2 Carmen Georges Bizet	27 May 1882	511
3 Aïda Giuseppi Verdi	22 Jun 1876	481
4 Rigoletto Giuseppi Verdi	14 May 1853	471
5 Faust Charles Gounod	18 Jul 1863	448
6 Tosca Giacomo Puccini	12 Jul 1900	434
7 Don Giovanni Wolfgang Amadeus Mozart	17 Apr 1834	424
8 La Traviata Giuseppi Verdi	25 May 1858	408
9 Madama Butterfly Giacomo Puccini	10 Jul 1905	387
10 Norma Vincenzo Bellini	12 Jul 1833	355

* To 31 August 2007

TOP 10 OPERAS MOST FREQUENTLY PERFORMED AT THE METROPOLITAN OPERA HOUSE, NEW YORK

OPERA	COMPOSER	PERFORMANCES*
1 La Bohème	Giacomo Puccini	1,193
2 Aïda	Giuseppi Verdi	1,093
3 Carmen	Georges Bizet	936
4 La Traviata	Giuseppi Verdi	934
5 Tosca	Giacomo Puccini	891
6 Rigoletto	Giuseppi Verdi	815
7 Madama Butterfly	Giacomo Puccini	812
8 Faust	Charles Gounod	733
9 Pagliacci	Ruggero Leoncavallo	705
10 Cavalleria Rusticana	Pietro Mascagni	660

* As at end of the 2007 season

Source: Metropolitan Opera

The Metropolitan Opera House opened on 22 October 1883, with a performance of Charles Gounod's *Faust*.

Carmen
With over 500 performances at the Royal Opera House and more than 900 at the Metropolitan Opera House, New York, Bizet's Carmen, *which premiered in Paris on 3 March 1875, is one of the world's most-performed operas.*

ENTERTAINMENT

In the Long Run

The Bard in brief
Performed by the Reduced Shakespeare Company, the long-running comedy The Complete Works of William Shakespeare (Abridged) *holds the record for its 43-second version of* Hamlet.

TOP 10 LONGEST-RUNNING NON-MUSICALS ON BROADWAY

SHOW	PERFORMANCES
1 Oh! Calcutta! 24 Sep 1976–6 Aug 1989	5,959
2 Life with Father 8 Nov 1939–12 Jul 1947	3,224
3 Tobacco Road 4 Dec 1933–31 May 1941	3,182
4 Abie's Irish Rose 23 May 1922–1 Oct 1927	2,327
5 Gemini 21 May 1977–6 Sep 1981	1,819
6 Deathtrap 26 Feb 1978–13 Jun 1982	1,793
7 Harvey 1 Nov 1944–15 Jan 1949	1,775
8 Born Yesterday 4 Feb 1946–31 Dec 1949	1,642
9 Mary, Mary 6 Mar 1961–8 Mar 1964	1,572
10 The Voice of the Turtle 8 Dec 1943–3 Jan 1948	1,557

Off Broadway, *The Golden Horseshoe Revue* performed at Disneyland from 16 July 1955 to 12 October 1986, a record-breaking total of 47,250 performances.

TOP 10 LONGEST-RUNNING COMEDIES ON BROADWAY

COMEDY	PERFORMANCES
1 Life with Father 8 Nov 1939–12 Jul 1947	3,224
2 Abie's Irish Rose 23 May 1922–1 Oct 1927	2,327
3 Gemini 21 May 1977–6 Sep 1981	1,819
4 Harvey 1 Nov 1944–15 Jan 1949	1,775
5 Born Yesterday 4 Feb 1946–31 Dec 1949	1,642
6 Mary, Mary 8 Mar 1961–12 Dec 1964	1,572
7 The Voice of the Turtle 8 Dec 1943–3 Jan 1948	1,557
8 Barefoot in the Park 23 Oct 1963–25 Jun 1967	1,530
9 Same Time, Next Year 14 Mar 1975–3 Sep 1978	1,453
10 Brighton Beach Memoirs 27 Mar 1983–11 May 1986	1,299

Howard Lindsay and Russel Crouse's *Life with Father* owed its success in part to the show's nostalgic view of bygone America that appeared under threat as it opened on the eve of World War II.

TOP 10 LONGEST-RUNNING NON-MUSICALS IN THE UK

SHOW	PERFORMANCES
1 The Mousetrap (1952–)	23,026*
2 The Woman in Black (1989–)	7,635*
3 No Sex, Please – We're British (1971–81; 1982–86; 1986–87)	6,761
4 The Complete Works of William Shakespeare (Abridged) (1996–2005)	4,266
5 Oh! Calcutta! (1970–74; 1974–80)	3,918
6 Run for Your Wife (1983–91)	2,638
7 There's a Girl in My Soup (1966–69; 1969–72)	2,547
8 Pyjama Tops (1969–75)	2,498
9 Sleuth (1970; 1972; 1973–75)	2,359
10 Worm's Eye View (1945–51)	2,245

* Still running; total as at 1 March 2008

Oh! Calcutta! is included here as it is regarded as a revue with music, rather than a musical.

TOP 10 LONGEST-RUNNING COMEDIES IN THE UK

SHOW	PERFORMANCES
1 No Sex, Please – We're British (1971–81; 1982–86; 1986–87)	6,761
2 The Complete Works of William Shakespeare (Abridged) (1996–2005)	4,266
3 Run for Your Wife (1983–91)	2,638
4 There's a Girl in My Soup (1966–69; 1969–72)	2,547
5 Pyjama Tops (1969–75)	2,498
6 Worm's Eye View (1945–51)	2,245
7 Boeing Boeing (1962–65; 1965–67)	2,035
8 Blithe Spirit (1941–42; 1942; 1942–46)	1,997
9 Dirty Linen (1976–80)	1,667
10 Reluctant Heroes (1950–54)	1,610

The West End's longest-running comedy *No Sex Please – We're British* opened at the Strand Theatre on 3 June 1971. In contrast, its run at the Ritz Theatre, New York, closed after 14 performances.

Chorus of approval
In 2006 Les Misérables, *the musical based on Victor Hugo's 1862 novel, became the longest-running on the London stage. It has now played for 23 years.*

TOP 10 **LONGEST-RUNNING MUSICALS ON BROADWAY**

	SHOW	RUN	PERFORMANCES
1	The Phantom of the Opera	26 Jan 1988–	8,355*
2	Cats	23 Sep 1982–10 Sep 2000	7,485
3	Les Misérables	12 Mar 1987– 18 May 2003	6,680
4	A Chorus Line	25 Jul 1975–28 Apr 1990	6,137
5	Beauty and the Beast	9 Mar 1994–28 Jul 2007	5,461
6	Rent	29 Apr 1996–	4,908*
7	Chicago	14 Nov 1996–	4,685*
8	The Lion King	13 Nov 1997–	4,270*
9	Miss Saigon	11 Apr 1991–28 Jan 2001	4,092
10	42nd Street	18 Aug 1980–8 Jan 1989	3,486

* Still running, total as at 1 March 2008

All the longest-running musicals date from the past 40 years. Prior to these record-breakers, the longest runner of the 1940s was *Oklahoma!*, which debuted in 1943 and ran for 2,212 performances up to 1948, and from the 1950s *My Fair Lady*, which opened in 1956 and closed in 1962 after 2,717 performances.

TOP 10 **LONGEST-RUNNING MUSICALS IN THE UK**

	SHOW	PERFORMANCES*
1	Les Misérables (1985–)	9,934#
2	Cats (1981–2002)	8,949
3	The Phantom of the Opera (1986–)	8,900#
4	Blood Brothers (1988–)	8,142#
5	Starlight Express (1984–2002)	7,406
6	Miss Saigon (1989–99)	4,263
7	Mama Mia! (1999–)	3,500#
8	Jesus Christ, Superstar (1972–80)	3,357
9	Evita (1978–86)	2,900
10	Oliver! (1960–66)	2,618

* Continuous runs only
# Still running, total as at 1 March 2008

Movie Industry

TOP 10 **FILM-PRODUCING COUNTRIES**

	COUNTRY	FEATURE FILMS PRODUCED (2006)
1	India	1,091
2	USA	490
3	Japan	417
4	China	330
5	France	203
6	Russia	200
7	Spain	150
8	Brazil	142
9	UK	134
10	Germany	122

Source: *Screen Digest*

TOP 10 **COUNTRIES BY BOX-OFFICE REVENUE**

	COUNTRY	EST. TOTAL BOX-OFFICE GROSS 2006 ($)
1	USA	9,420,000,000
2	Japan	1,839,600,000
3	UK	1,397,000,000
4	France	1,387,600,000
5	Germany	1,018,300,000
6	Spain	788,300,000
7	Canada	685,900,000
8	Italy	680,200,000
9	Australia	661,000,000
10	Mexico	557,900,000

Source: *Screen Digest*

Lording the lists
The Lord of the Rings trilogy makes up three of the 14 highest-earning films of all time worldwide, and the top five in the UK.

TOP 10 **FILMS IN THE UK**

	FILM	YEAR	TOTAL UK BOX OFFICE GROSS (£)
1	Titanic	1998	69,025,646
2	Harry Potter and the Philosopher's Stone	2001	66,096,060
3	The Lord of the Rings: The Fellowship of the Ring	2001	63,051,172
4	The Lord of the Rings: The Return of the King*	2003	61,062,348
5	The Lord of the Rings: The Two Towers	2002	57,654,384
6	Casino Royale	2006	55,502,884
7	Harry Potter and the Chamber of Secrets	2002	54,780,731
8	The Full Monty	1997	52,232,058
9	Pirates of the Caribbean: Dead Man's Chest	2006	51,993,705
10	Star Wars: Episode I – The Phantom Menace	1999	51,063,811

* Won Best Picture Oscar

TOP 10 **BIGGEST FILM BUDGETS**

Up to 2007

	FILM	YEAR	BUDGET ($)
1	Pirates of the Caribbean: At World's End	2007	300,000,000
2	Superman Returns	2006	270,000,000
3	Spider-Man 3	2007	258,000,000
4	Pirates of the Caribbean: Dead Man's Chest	2006	225,000,000
5	X-Men: The Last Stand	2006	210,000,000
6	King Kong	2005	207,000,000
7	=Titanic	1997	200,000,000
	=Terminator 3: Rise of the Machines	2003	200,000,000
	=Spider-Man 2	2004	200,000,000
10	The Chronicles of Narnia: The Lion, the Witch and the Wardrobe	2005	180,000,000

Above: **World's End** *world's biggest*
Pirates of the Caribbean: At World's End *had the biggest budget ever, but earned almost $1 billion globally.*

Up to 1987

	FILM	YEAR	BUDGET ($)
1	War and Peace (Russia)	1967	100,000,000
2	=Superman	1978	55,000,000
	=Ishtar	1987	55,000,000
4	Superman II	1980	54,000,000
5	=Annie	1982	50,000,000
	=Santa Claus	1985	50,000,000
	=Zimnyaya Vishnya (Russia)	1985	50,000,000
8	The Cotton Club	1984	47,000,000
9	Inchon	1981	46,000,000
10	Dune	1984	45,000,000

The state-sponsored eight-hour Russian epic *War and Peace* took seven years to film. Allowing for inflation since 1967, it would cost over $630 million to make today. It was not until 1991 that a commercially produced film, *Terminator 2: Judgment Day*, commanded a budget of over $100 million. Its director, James Cameron, went on to make $200-million budget *Titanic*.

Opening Weekends

TOP 10 **OPENING WEEKENDS WORLDWIDE**

	FILM	YEAR	OPENING WEEKEND WORLD TOTAL ($ MILLION)
1	Spider-Man 3	2007	381.7
2	Pirates of the Caribbean: At World's End	2007	344.0
3	Harry Potter and the Order of the Phoenix	2007	332.7
4	Star Wars: Episode III – Revenge of the Sith	2005	303.9
5	The Lord of the Rings: The Return of the King	2003	250.0
6	The Da Vinci Code	2006	232.1
7	Harry Potter and the Prisoner of Azkaban	2004	207.2
8	War of the Worlds	2005	203.1
9	The Matrix Revolutions	2003	201.4
10	Transformers	2007	191.7

Above: Magic numbers
Potter stars Rupert Grint, Daniel Radcliffe and Emma Watson at the
Hollywood opening of Harry Potter and the Order of the Phoenix. *This
film and Harry Potter and the Prisoner of Azkaban are among the biggest-
opening films ever.*

Top right: Third time lucky
Spider-Man 3 broke all records with its opening weekend, setting a new
benchmark for worldwide daily and opening weekend earnings.

Right: Monster hit
The original Shrek earned only £4,686,210 during its opening weekend in
the UK, a total that was far exceeded by its two eagerly awaited sequels.

TOP 10 **ANIMATED OPENING WEEKENDS IN THE UK**

	FILM	YEAR	OPENING WEEKEND GROSS (£)
1	Shrek the Third	2007	16,671,727
2	Shrek 2	2004	16,220,752
3	The Simpsons Movie	2007	13,626,853
4	The Incredibles	2004	9,874,782
5	Ice Age: The Meltdown	2006	9,775,974
6	Wallis & Gromit: The Curse of the Were-Rabbit	2005	9,374,932
7	Monsters, Inc.	2002	9,200,257
8	Toy Story 2	2000	7,971,539
9	Finding Nemo	2003	7,590,845
10	Shark Tale	2004	7,545,074

TOP 10 **OPENING WEEKENDS IN THE UK**

	FILM	YEAR	OPENING WEEKEND GROSS (£)
1	Harry Potter and the Prisoner of Azkaban	2004	23,882,688
2	Harry Potter and the Chamber of Secrets	2002	18,871,829
3	Shrek the Third*	2007	16,671,727
4	Harry Potter and the Order of the Phoenix	2007	16,493,305
5	Harry Potter and the Philosopher's Stone	2001	16,335,627
6	Shrek 2*	2004	16,220,752
7	The Lord of the Rings: The Return of the King#	2003	15,021,761
8	Harry Potter and the Goblet of Fire	2005	14,933,901
9	Star Wars: Episode III – Revenge of the Sith	2005	14,361,469
10	X-Men: The Last Stand	2006	14,197,643

* Animated
# Won Best Picture Oscar

In the past decade, opening weekends have been increasingly viewed as a pointer to the ongoing success of a film, but are not a guarantee, since films may launch to great acclaim and die away rapidly, or start their run modestly before gathering momentum: *Titanic* (1998) made only £4,805,270 on its UK opening, before going on to become the highest-earning ever. The number of screens is also significant: most of those in the Top 10 were shown at more than 500 screens nationwide.

Film Genres

TOP 10 **WEDDING FILMS**

	FILM	YEAR
1	My Big Fat Greek Wedding	2002
2	Runaway Bride	1999
3	My Best Friend's Wedding	1997
4	Wedding Crashers	2005
5	Four Weddings and a Funeral	1994
6	American Wedding	2003
7	Sweet Home Alabama	2002
8	In & Out	1997
9	The Wedding Singer	1998
10	Father of the Bride Part II	1995

These are all films in which a wedding or weddings are central, rather than incidental, to the plot. All those in the Top 10 have earned upwards of $100 million worldwide.

TOP 10 **HORROR SPOOF FILMS**

	FILM	YEAR
1	Scary Movie	2000
2	Scary Movie 3	2003
3	Scary Movie 4	2006
4	Scream	1996
5	Scream 2	1997
6	Scream 3	2000
7	Scary Movie 2	2001
8	The Rocky Horror Picture Show	1975
9	Young Frankenstein	1974
10	Lake Placid	1999

While many films combine comedy and horror elements, those in this Top 10 represent the most successful of a species of parodies of classic horror films that began 60 years ago with such examples as *Abbott and Costello Meets Frankenstein* (1948).

TOP 10 **GHOST FILMS**

	FILM	YEAR
1	The Sixth Sense	1999
2	Ghost	1990
3	Ghostbusters	1984
4	What Lies Beneath	2000
5	Casper	1995
6	The Ring	2002
7	Scary Movie 3	2003
8	Ghostbusters II	1989
9	The Others	2001
10	Sleepy Hollow	1999

Wedding Crashers
The spectacle and social interaction offered by weddings has made them a popular and often successful staple of both Hollywood and – with films such as Monsoon Wedding (2001) – international cinema.

TOP 10 SUPERHERO FILMS

	FILM	YEAR
1	Spider-Man 3	2007
2	Spider-Man	2002
3	Spider-Man 2	2004
4	The Incredibles*	2004
5	X-Men: The Last Stand	2006
6	Batman	1989
7	X2: X-Men United	2003
8	Superman Returns	2006
9	Batman Begins	2005
10	The Mask	1994

* Animated

Marching on
The highest-earning natural-history film of all time, French-made March of the Penguins *has made in excess of $127 million worldwide.*

TOP DOCUMENTARY FILMS

	FILM	SUBJECT	YEAR
1	Fahrenheit 9/11	War on terrorism	2004
2	The Dream is Alive	Space Shuttle	1985
3	Everest	Mountaineering	1998
4	March of the Penguins	Emperor penguins	2005
5	To Fly	History of flying	1976
6	Grand Canyon: The Hidden Secrets	Exploration	1984
7	Mysteries of Egypt	Historical	1998
8	Space Station 3-D	International Space Station	2002
9	Jackass: Number Two	Comedy stunts	2006
10	Jackass: The Movie	Comedy stunts	2002

TOP 10 MAGIC, WITCHES AND WIZARDS FILMS

	FILM	YEAR
1	The Lord of the Rings: The Return of the King	2003
2	Harry Potter and the Philosopher's Stone	2001
3	Harry Potter and the Order of the Phoenix	2007
4	The Lord of the Rings: The Two Towers	2002
5	Shrek 2*	2004
6	Harry Potter and the Goblet of Fire	2005
7	Harry Potter and the Chamber of Secrets	2002
8	The Lord of the Rings: The Fellowship of the Ring	2001
9	Harry Potter and the Prisoner of Azkaban	2004
10	Shrek the Third*	2007

* Animated

Comedy Stars

TOP 10 **MIKE MYERS FILMS**

FILM	YEAR
1 Austin Powers: The Spy Who Shagged Me	1999
2 Austin Powers in Goldmember	2002
3 Wayne's World	1992
4 The Cat in the Hat	2003
5 Austin Powers: International Man of Mystery	1997
6 Wayne's World 2	1993
7 54	1998
8 View from the Top	2003
9 So I Married an Axe Murderer	1993
10 Mystery, Alaska	1999

The power of Austin
Mike Myers as Austin Powers, eponymous star of three of his highest-earning films.

TOP 10 **BILL MURRAY FILMS**

FILM	YEAR
1 Ghostbusters	1984
2 Charlie's Angels	2000
3 Ghostbusters II	1989
4 Tootsie	1982
5 Lost in Translation	2003
6 Groundhog Day	1993
7 Stripes	1981
8 The Royal Tenenbaums	2001
9 Wild Things	1998
10 Scrooged	1988

Bill Murray appeared, uncredited, as himself in *Space Jam* (1996) – if included in his personal Top 10, based on global box-office income, it would appear in third place. He also provided the voice of Garfield in the animated *Garfield: The Movie* (2004) and *Garfield: A Tail of Two Kitties* (2006).

TOP 10 **OWEN WILSON FILMS**

FILM	YEAR
1 Night at the Museum	2006
2 Armageddon	1998
3 Meet the Fockers	2004
4 Meet the Parents	2000
5 Wedding Crashers	2005
6 The Haunting	1999
7 Starsky and Hutch	2004
8 Anaconda	1997
9 You, Me and Dupree	2006
10 The Cable Guy	1996

Assuming his cameo role in *Meet the Fockers* is included (third in this Top 10), every one of Owen Wilson's films has earned more than $100 million – the first three more than $500 million – at the global box office. He also provided the voice of Lightning McQueen in the animated *Cars* (2006).

TOP 10 **JIM CARREY FILMS**

	FILM	YEAR
1	Bruce Almighty	2003
2	Dr Seuss's How the Grinch Stole Christmas	2000
3	The Mask	1994
4	Batman Forever	1995
5	Liar Liar	1997
6	The Truman Show	1998
7	Dumb & Dumber	1994
8	Ace Ventura: When Nature Calls	1995
9	Lemony Snicket's A Series of Unfortunate Events	2004
10	Fun with Dick and Jane	2005

One click
Adam Sandler's fantasy comedy Click *has earned more than 10 times its $25 million budget.*

TOP 10 **STEVE MARTIN FILMS**

	FILM	YEAR
1	Cheaper by the Dozen	2003
2	Bringing Down the House	2003
3	The Pink Panther	2006
4	Cheaper by the Dozen 2	2005
5	Parenthood	1989
6	Father of the Bride Part II	1995
7	Bowfinger	1999
8	HouseSitter	1992
9	Father of the Bride	1991
10	The Jerk	1979

TOP 10 **ADAM SANDLER FILMS**

	FILM	YEAR
1	Click	2006
2	Big Daddy	1999
3	50 First Dates	2004
4	Anger Management	2003
5	The Longest Yard	2005
6	The Waterboy	1998
7	I Now Pronounce You Chuck and Larry	2007
8	Mr Deeds	2002
9	The Wedding Singer	1998
10	Little Nicky	2000

TOP 10 **BEN STILLER FILMS**

	FILM	YEAR
1	Night at the Museum	2006
2	Meet the Fockers	2004
3	There's Something About Mary	1998
4	Meet the Parents	2000
5	Along Came Polly	2004
6	Starsky and Hutch	2004
7	DodgeBall: A True Underdog Story	2004
8	The Cable Guy	1996
9	The Heartbreak Kid	2007
10	The Royal Tenenbaums	2001

Oscar-winning Films

TOP 10 **FILMS TO WIN THE MOST OSCARS** *

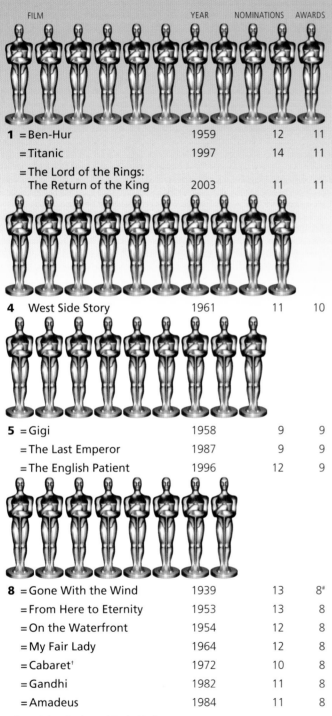

FILM	YEAR	NOMINATIONS	AWARDS
1 = Ben-Hur	1959	12	11
= Titanic	1997	14	11
= The Lord of the Rings: The Return of the King	2003	11	11
4 West Side Story	1961	11	10
5 = Gigi	1958	9	9
= The Last Emperor	1987	9	9
= The English Patient	1996	12	9
8 = Gone With the Wind	1939	13	8#
= From Here to Eternity	1953	13	8
= On the Waterfront	1954	12	8
= My Fair Lady	1964	12	8
= Cabaret†	1972	10	8
= Gandhi	1982	11	8
= Amadeus	1984	11	8

* Oscar® is a Registered Trade Mark
\# Plus two special awards
† Did not win Best Picture Oscar

Titanic matched the previous record of 14 nominations of *All About Eve* (1950), but outshone it by winning 11, compared with the latter's six. *Shakespeare in Love* (1998) and *Schindler's List* (1993) are the most recent of 10 films that have won seven Oscars each.

Titanic success
Kate Winslet was nominated as best actress for her role in Titanic. In addition to Oscars for Best Picture and Best Director, the film won nine others.

TOP 10 **FILMS NOMINATED FOR THE MOST OSCARS**

FILM	YEAR	AWARDS	NOMINATIONS
1 = All About Eve	1950	6	14
= Titanic	1997	11	14
3 = Gone With the Wind	1939	8*	13
= From Here to Eternity	1953	8	13
= Mary Poppins#	1964	5	13
= Who's Afraid of Virginia Woolf?#	1966	5	13
= Forrest Gump	1994	6	13
= Shakespeare in Love	1998	7	13
= The Lord of the Rings: The Fellowship of the Ring#	2001	4	13
= Chicago	2002	6	13

* Plus two special awards
\# Did not win Best Picture Oscar

Thirteen is not an unlucky number where Oscar nominations are concerned, no fewer than eight films having received that total. They and the two with 14 are those that received the greatest share of votes from Academy members (currently over 5,500, who include previous nominees and winners), using a system that creates a shortlist of five nominees in each of 24 categories.

'There are no clean getaways'
Josh Brolin as Llewelyn Moss in No Country for Old Men, *the Oscar-winning*
film based on Cormac McCarthy's novel.

TOP 10 **HIGHEST-EARNING BEST PICTURE OSCAR WINNERS**

	FILM	YEAR*	WORLD BOX OFFICE ($)
1	Titanic	1997	1,845,034,188
2	The Lord of the Rings: The Return of the King	2003	1,129,219,252
3	Forrest Gump	1994	677,386,686
4	Gladiator	2000	457,640,427
5	Dances With Wolves	1990	424,208,842
6	Rain Man	1988	416,011,462
7	Gone With the Wind	1939	400,176,459
8	American Beauty	1999	356,296,601
9	Schindler's List	1993	321,267,179
10	A Beautiful Mind	2001	313,542,341

* Of release; Academy Awards are made the following year

THE 10 **LATEST BEST PICTURE OSCAR WINNERS**

YEAR	FILM	DIRECTOR
2007	No Country for Old Men	Ethan Coen and Joel Coen
2006	The Departed	Martin Scorsese
2005	Crash	Paul Haggis*
2004	Million Dollar Baby	Clint Eastwood
2003	The Lord of the Rings: The Return of the King	Peter Jackson
2002	Chicago	Rob Marshall*
2001	A Beautiful Mind	Ron Howard
2000	Gladiator	Ridley Scott*
1999	American Beauty	Sam Mendes
1998	Shakespeare in Love	John Madden*

* Did not also win Best Director Oscar

Oscar-winning Stars

Hepburn's hat-trick
Katharine Hepburn is the only actress to win three Best Actress Oscars, with almost 50 years between her first and last.

TOP 10 **ACTORS AND ACTRESSES WITH THE MOST NOMINATIONS***

	ACTOR /	WINS: SUPPORTING/BEST / NOMINATIONS		
1	Meryl Streep	1	1	14
2	=Katharine Hepburn	0	4	12
	=Jack Nicholson	1	2	12
4	=Bette Davis	0	2	10
	=Laurence Olivier	0	1	10
6	=Paul Newman	0	1	9
	=Spencer Tracy	0	2	9
8	=Marlon Brando	0	2	8
	=Jack Lemmon	1	1	8
	=Peter O'Toole	0	0	8
	=Al Pacino	0	1	8
	=Geraldine Page	0	1	8

* In all acting categories

THE 10 **FIRST STARS TO WIN TWO BEST ACTOR/ACTRESS OSCARS**

	STAR	FIRST WIN / YEAR	SECOND WIN / YEAR
1	Luise Rainer	The Great Ziegfeld* 1936	The Good Earth 1937
2	=Bette Davis	Dangerous 1935	Jezebel 1938
	=Spencer Tracy	Captains Courageous 1937	Boys Town 1938
4	Fredric March	Dr Jekyll and Mr Hyde 1931/32	The Best Years of Our Lives* 1946
5	Olivia de Havilland	To Each His Own 1946	The Heiress 1949
6	Vivien Leigh	Gone With the Wind* 1939	A Streetcar Named Desire 1951
7	Gary Cooper	Sergeant York 1941	High Noon 1952
8	Ingrid Bergman	Gaslight 1944	Anastasia 1956
9	Elizabeth Taylor	Butterfield 8 1960	Who's Afraid of Virginia Woolf? 1966
10	Katharine Hepburn	Morning Glory 1932/33	Guess Who's Coming to Dinner? 1967

* Won Best Picture Oscar

Uniquely, Katharine Hepburn went on to win a third Best Actress Oscar with *The Lion in Winter* (1968) and a fourth for *On Golden Pond* (1981).

THE 10 **LATEST STARS TO WIN TWO BEST ACTOR/ACTRESS OSCARS**

	ACTRESS	FIRST WIN / YEAR	SECOND WIN / YEAR
1	Hilary Swank	Boys Don't Cry 1999	Million Dollar Baby* 2004
2	Jack Nicholson	One Flew Over the Cuckoo's Nest 1975	As Good as it Gets 1997
3	Tom Hanks	Philadelphia 1993	Forrest Gump* 1994
4	Jodie Foster	The Accused 1988	The Silence of the Lambs* 1991
5	Dustin Hoffman	Kramer vs. Kramer* 1979	Rain Man* 1988
6	Sally Field	Norma Rae 1979	Places in the Heart 1984
7	Jane Fonda	Klute 1971	Coming Home 1978
8	Glenda Jackson	Women in Love 1970	A Touch of Class 1973
9	Katharine Hepburn	The Lion in Winter 1968	On Golden Pond 1981
10	Marlon Brando	On the Waterfront* 1954	The Godfather* 1972

* Won Best Picture Oscar

THE 10 **LATEST BEST ACTOR OSCAR WINNERS**

YEAR	ACTOR	FILM
2007	Daniel Day-Lewis	There Will Be Blood
2006	Forest Whitaker	The Last King of Scotland
2005	Philip Seymour Hoffman	Capote
2004	Jamie Foxx	Ray
2003	Sean Penn	Mystic River
2002	Adrien Brody	The Pianist
2001	Denzel Washington	Training Day
2000	Russell Crowe	Gladiator*
1999	Kevin Spacey	American Beauty*
1998	Roberto Benigni	Life is Beautiful

* Won Best Picture Oscar

THE 10 **LATEST BEST ACTRESS OSCAR WINNERS**

YEAR	ACTRESS	FILM
2007	Marion Cotillard	La Vie en Rose
2006	Helen Mirren	The Queen
2005	Reese Witherspoon	Walk the Line
2004	Hilary Swank	Million Dollar Baby*
2003	Charlize Theron	Monster
2002	Nicole Kidman	The Hours
2001	Halle Berry	Monster's Ball
2000	Julia Roberts	Erin Brockovich
1999	Hilary Swank	Boys Don't Cry
1998	Gwyneth Paltrow	Shakespeare in Love*

* Won Best Picture Oscar

Blood and roses
Above: Daniel Day-Lewis (centre) won his second Best Actor Oscar for his role as oilman Daniel Plainview in There Will be Blood.
Below: French actress Marion Cotillard gained her Best Actress Oscar for her performance as Edith Piaf in La Vie en Rose.

Actors

TOP 10 **GEORGE CLOONEY FILMS**

	FILM	YEAR
1	Ocean's Eleven	2001
2	Ocean's Twelve	2004
3	The Perfect Storm	2000
4	Ocean's Thirteen	2007
5	Batman & Robin	1997
6	Spy Kids	2001
7	Intolerable Cruelty	2003
8	The Peacemaker	1997
9	Three Kings	1999
10	One Fine Day	1996

Already well-known as Dr Doug Ross in the TV series *ER* – as well as some best-forgotten early film parts, such as *Return of the Killer Tomatoes!* (1988) – George Clooney has appeared in a run of successful films during the past decade. His cameo role in *Spy Kids 3D: Game Over* (2003) has been discounted here. He also provided voices for the animated *South Park: Bigger, Longer & Uncut* (1999) and the title role in the forthcoming *The Fantastic Mr Fox* (2009).

TOP 10 **LEONARDO DICAPRIO FILMS**

	FILM	YEAR
1	Titanic*	1997
2	Catch Me If You Can	2002
3	The Departed	2006
4	The Aviator	2004
5	Gangs of New York	2002
6	The Man in the Iron Mask	1998
7	Blood Diamond	2006
8	Romeo + Juliet	1996
9	The Beach	2000
10	The Quick and the Dead	1995

* Won Best Picture Oscar

Leonardo DiCaprio is in the enviable position of having starred in *Titanic*, the highest-earning film of all time, in addition to eight further films that have generated more than $100 million at the global box office.

Ocean swell
George Clooney as crime caper hero Danny Ocean. The three Ocean's films have earned a total of over $1.1 billion at the world box office.

TOP 10 **JOHN TRAVOLTA FILMS**

	FILM	YEAR
1	Grease	1978
2	Look Who's Talking	1989
3	Saturday Night Fever	1977
4	Wild Hogs	2007
5	Face/Off	1997
6	Pulp Fiction	1994
7	Hairspray	2007
8	Phenomenon	1996
9	Broken Arrow	1996
10	The General's Daughter	1999

TOP 10 **NICOLAS CAGE FILMS**

	FILM	YEAR
1	National Treasure: Book of Secrets	2007
2	National Treasure	2004
3	The Rock	1996
4	Face/Off	1997
5	Gone in 60 Seconds	2000
6	Ghost Rider	2007
7	Con Air	1997
8	City of Angels	1998
9	World Trade Center	2006
10	The Family Man	2000

TOP 10 **BRAD PITT FILMS**

	FILM	YEAR
1	Troy	2004
2	Mr & Mrs Smith	2005
3	Ocean's Eleven	2001
4	Ocean's Twelve	2004
5	Se7en	1995
6	Ocean's Thirteen	2007
7	Interview with the Vampire: The Vampire Chronicles	1994
8	Twelve Monkeys	1995
9	Sleepers	1996
10	Legends of the Fall	1994

Bourne again
The Bourne Ultimatum, *the third outing for Matt Damon in the role of Jason Bourne, earned twice as much globally as the original film,* The Bourne Identity.

TOP 10 **MATT DAMON FILMS**

	FILM	YEAR
1	Saving Private Ryan	1998
2	Ocean's Eleven	2001
3	The Bourne Ultimatum	2007
4	Ocean's Twelve	2004
5	Ocean's Thirteen	2006
6	The Departed	2006
7	The Bourne Supremacy	2004
8	Good Will Hunting	1997
9	The Bourne Identity	2002
10	The Talented Mr Ripley	1999

TOP 10 **JOHNNY DEPP FILMS**

	FILM	YEAR
1	Pirates of the Caribbean: Dead Man's Chest	2006
2	Pirates of the Caribbean: At World's End	2007
3	Pirates of the Caribbean: The Curse of the Black Pearl	2003
4	Charlie and the Chocolate Factory	2004
5	Sleepy Hollow	1999
6	Platoon	1986
7	Chocolat	2000
8	Sweeney Todd: The Demon Barber of Fleet Street	2007
9	Donnie Brasco	1997
10	Finding Neverland	2004

TOP 10 **DANIEL CRAIG FILMS**

	FILM	YEAR
1	Casino Royale	2006
2	The Golden Compass	2004
3	Lara Croft: Tomb Raider	2001
4	Road to Perdition	2002
5	Munich	2005
6	Elizabeth	1998
7	The Invasion	2007
8	The Jacket	2005
9	I Dreamed of Africa	2000
10	A Kid in King Arthur's Court	1995

Actresses

TOP 10 **CATE BLANCHETT FILMS**

	FILM	YEAR
1	The Lord of the Rings: The Return of the King	2003
2	The Lord of the Rings: The Two Towers	2002
3	The Lord of the Rings: The Fellowship of the Ring	2001
4	The Aviator	2004
5	Babel	2006
6	The Talented Mr Ripley	1999
7	Elizabeth: The Golden Age	2007
8	Bandits	2001
9	Elizabeth	1998
10	Notes on a Scandal	2006

Cate Blanchett has been nominated for five Oscars, winning the 2004 Best Supporting Actress award for playing the part of a previous Oscar-winner, Katharine Hepburn, in *The Aviator*.

Screen queen
Cate Blanchett's Top 10 is dominated by the commercially successful Lord of the Rings trilogy.

TOP 10 **KEIRA KNIGHTLEY FILMS**

	FILM	YEAR
1	Pirates of the Caribbean: Dead Man's Chest	2006
2	Pirates of the Caribbean: At World's End	2007
3	Star Wars: Episode I – The Phantom Menace	1999
4	Pirates of the Caribbean: The Curse of the Black Pearl	2003
5	Love Actually	2003
6	King Arthur	2004
7	Atonement	2007
8	Pride and Prejudice	2005
9	Bend it Like Beckham	2003
10	Domino	2005

The Top 10 films in which Keira Knightley has starred have earned a total of $4.4 billion worldwide. All were made before she was 21, her Academy Award best actress nomination at 20 (for *Pride and Prejudice*) being the third youngest ever.

TOP 10 **DREW BARRYMORE FILMS**

	FILM	YEAR
1	E.T.: The Extra-Terrestrial	1982
2	Batman Forever	1995
3	Charlie's Angels	2000
4	Charlie's Angels: Full Throttle	2003
5	50 First Dates	2004
6	Scream	1996
7	Music and Lyrics	2007
8	The Wedding Singer	1998
9	Ever After: A Cinderella Story	1998
10	Never Been Kissed	1999

Granddaughter of Hollywood legend John Barrymore, Drew Barrymore's first film role was in *Altered States* (1980), when she was five; by the time of her part in *E.T.: The Extra-Terrestrial* she was aged seven. Her bankability has increased in recent years to enable her to command a reputed $15 million for her role in *Music and Lyrics* (2007).

TOP 10 **JUDI DENCH FILMS**

	FILM	YEAR
1	Casino Royale	2006
2	Die Another Day	2002
3	The World is Not Enough	1999
4	GoldenEye	1995
5	Tomorrow Never Dies	1997
6	Shakespeare in Love	1998
7	Chocolat	2000
8	Pride and Prejudice	2005
9	The Chronicles of Riddick	2004
10	Notes on a Scandal	2006

While her highest-earning films are her five Bond appearances as 'M', all but one in Dame Judi Dench's personal Top 10 earned in excess of $100 million worldwide. She won a Best Supporting Actress Oscar for an appearance in *Shakespeare in Love* that lasts barely six minutes. She also provided the voice of Mrs Calloway in the animated *Home on the Range*.

TOP 10 **CAMERON DIAZ FILMS**

	FILM	YEAR
1	There's Something About Mary	1998
2	The Mask	1994
3	My Best Friend's Wedding	1997
4	Charlie's Angels	2000
5	Charlie's Angels: Full Throttle	2003
6	The Holiday	2006
7	Vanilla Sky	2001
8	Gangs of New York	2002
9	Any Given Sunday	1999
10	In Her Shoes	2005

Cameron Diaz's Top 10 films include some of the highest-earning of recent years, the Top 10 cumulatively making $2.3 billion worldwide. She also provided the voice of Princess Fiona in all three *Shrek* films (2001–07), which have outearned those listed.

TOP 10 **RACHEL WEISZ FILMS**

	FILM	YEAR
1	The Mummy Returns	2001
2	The Mummy	1999
3	Constantine	2005
4	About a Boy	2002
5	Fred Claus	2007
6	Enemy at the Gates	2001
7	The Constant Gardener	2005
8	Runaway Jury	2003
9	Chain Reaction	1996
10	Confidence	2003

While the two *Mummy* films top Rachel Weisz's list based on earnings, it was her role in *The Constant Gardener* that earned her the Best Actress Oscar.

Dual role
Based on the comic Hellblazer, *horror film* Constantine *starred Rachel Weisz in two parts, as a detective and her deceased twin sister.*

TOP 10 **UMA THURMAN FILMS**

	FILM	YEAR
1	Batman & Robin	1997
2	Pulp Fiction	1994
3	Kill Bill: Vol. 1	2003
4	Kill Bill: Vol. 2	2004
5	Paycheck	2003
6	Be Cool	2005
7	Prime	2005
8	My Super Ex-Girlfriend	2006
9	The Truth About Cats & Dogs	1996
10	The Avengers	1998

Although in the Top 10 by virtue of its global-box office income, *The Avengers* did not earn back its substantial production budget, estimated at $60 million. Conversely, *Pulp Fiction* had a budget of some $8 million, but went on to make more than $200 million worldwide. Taken together, Uma Thurman's Top 10 films have earned a world total of more than $1.2 billion.

Directors

TOP 10 **FILMS DIRECTED BY RON HOWARD**

FILM	YEAR		FILM	YEAR
1 The Da Vinci Code	2006		**6** Backdraft	1991
2 Dr. Seuss's How the Grinch Stole Christmas	2000		**7** Far and Away	1992
3 Apollo 13	1995		**8** Parenthood	1989
4 A Beautiful Mind*	2001		**9** Cinderella Man	2005
5 Ransom	1996		**10** Cocoon	1985

* Won Best Director Oscar; film won Best Picture Oscar

Above: Ron Howard's The Da Vinci Code *Starring Tom Hanks, the film has earned over $750 million internationally.*

TOP 10 **FILMS DIRECTED BY RIDLEY SCOTT**

FILM	YEAR
1 Gladiator	2000
2 Hannibal	2001
3 American Gangster	2007
4 Kingdom of Heaven	2005
5 Black Hawk Down	2001
6 Black Rain	1989
7 Alien	1979
8 G.I. Jane	1997
9 Matchstick Men	2003
10 Thelma and Louise	1991

TOP 10 **FILMS DIRECTED OR PRODUCED BY GEORGE LUCAS**

FILM	YEAR
1 Star Wars: Episode I – The Phantom Menace*#	1999
2 Star Wars: Episode III – Revenge of the Sith*#	2005
3 Star Wars: Episode IV – A New Hope*#	1977
4 Star Wars: Episode II – Attack of the Clones*#	2002
5 Star Wars: Episode VI – Return of the Jedi#	1983
6 Star Wars: Episode V – The Empire Strikes Back#	1980
7 Indiana Jones and the Last Crusade#	1989
8 Raiders of the Lost Ark#	1981
9 Indiana Jones and the Temple of Doom#	
10 American Graffiti*	1973

* Directed
\# Produced

George Lucas made the move from directing to producing after the phenomenal success of the first of the *Star Wars* films, but he has a Midas touch in both fields, the first six on this list ranking among the 50 highest-earning films ever, and his Top 10 cumulatively earning more than $5.6 billion worldwide.

TOP 10 **FILMS DIRECTED BY CHRISTOPHER COLUMBUS**

FILM	YEAR
1 Harry Potter and the Philosopher's Stone	2001
2 Harry Potter and the Chamber of Secrets	2002
3 Home Alone	1990
4 Mrs Doubtfire	1993
5 Home Alone 2: Lost in New York	1992
6 Stepmom	1998
7 Nine Months	1995
8 Bicentennial Man	1999
9 Adventures in Babysitting	1987
10 Rent	2005

Burton directs
Tim Burton on the set of Batman Returns *(1992), with Michael Keaton as Batman and Michelle Pfeiffer as Catwoman. It had a budget of $80 million and earned over $283 million.*

TOP 10 **FILMS DIRECTED BY TIM BURTON**

	FILM	YEAR
1	Charlie and the Chocolate Factory	2005
2	Batman	1989
3	Batman Returns	1992
4	Planet of the Apes	2001
5	Sleepy Hollow	1999
6	Big Fish	2003
7	Sweeney Todd: The Demon Barber of Fleet Street	2007
8	Tim Burton's Corpse Bride	2005
9	Mars Attacks!	1996
10	Edward Scissorhands	1990

Director-producer-writer Tim Burton is one of a handful of successful Hollywood directors whose name features as part of the titles of films he has directed. The first two films in his list have each earned in excess of $400 million globally, and all but No. 10 in this list over $100 million. The recent success of *Sweeney Todd: The Demon Barber of Fleet Street* relegated cult film *Beetlejuice* from his Top 10.

TOP 10 **FILMS DIRECTED BY STEVEN SPIELBERG**

	FILM	YEAR
1	Jurassic Park	1993
2	E.T.: The Extra-Terrestrial	1982
3	The Lost World: Jurassic Park	1997
4	War of the Worlds	2005
5	Indiana Jones and the Last Crusade	1989
6	Saving Private Ryan	1998
7	Jaws	1975
8	Raiders of the Lost Ark	1981
9	Minority Report	2002
10	Catch Me If You Can	2002

If Spielberg's credits as producer were also included, further blockbusters such as *Transformers* (2007), *Shrek* (2001; uncredited) and *Men in Black* (1997) would rank highly. Spielberg has been nominated for Oscars on 12 occasions, winning Best Director and Best Picture for *Schindler's List* and Best Director for *Saving Private Ryan*. He has also received the Academy's Irving G. Thalberg Memorial Award.

TOP 10 **FILMS DIRECTED BY CLINT EASTWOOD**

	FILM	YEAR
1	Million Dollar Baby*	2004
2	The Bridges of Madison County	1995
3	Unforgiven*	1992
4	Mystic River	2003
5	A Perfect World	1993
6	Space Cowboys	2000
7	Absolute Power	1997
8	The Rookie	1990
9	Letters from Iwo Jima	2006
10	Sudden Impact	1983

* Won Best Director Oscar; film won Best Picture Oscar

Animation

Rat rates
Set in Paris, Best Animated Feature
Oscar-winning Ratatouille
established a new French record
for the highest-earning opening
weekend for an animated film.

TOP 10 **ANIMATED FILMS**

FILM	YEAR	WORLDWIDE TOTAL GROSS ($)
1 Shrek 2*	2004	920,665,658
2 Finding Nemo#	2003	864,625,978
3 Shrek the Third*	2007	797,750,521
4 The Lion King#	1994	783,841,776
5 Ice Age: The Meltdown†	2006	651,564,512
6 The Incredibles#	2004	631,442,092
7 Ratatouille#	2007	620,720,969
8 Madagascar*	2005	532,680,671
9 Monsters, Inc.#	2001	529,061,238
10 The Simpson's Movie†	1992	526,622,545

* DreamWorks
\# Disney
† 20th Century Fox Animation

TOP 10 **ANIMATED FILMS IN THE UK**

FILM	YEAR	UK TOTAL GROSS (£)
1 Shrek 2*	2004	48,243,628
2 Toy Story 2#	2000	44,306,070
3 The Simpsons Movie	2007	38,312,694
4 Shrek the Third*	2007	38,079,462
5 Monsters, Inc.#	2002	37,907,451
6 Finding Nemo#	2003	37,364,251
7 The Incredibles#	2004	32,277,041
8 Wallace & Gromit: The Curse of the Were-Rabbit*	2005	32,007,310
9 Chicken Run*	2000	29,514,237
10 Ice Age: The Meltdown†	2006	29,450,144

* DreamWorks
\# Disney
† 20th Century Fox Animation

THE 10 **LATEST WINNERS OF ANNIE AWARDS FOR BEST ANIMATED FEATURE**

YEAR* / FILM

YEAR	FILM
2007	Ratatouille
2006	Cars
2005	Wallace & Gromit in The Curse of the Were-Rabbit
2004	The Incredibles
2003	Finding Nemo
2002	Spirited Away
2001	Shrek
2000	Toy Story 2
1999	The Iron Giant
1998	Mulan

* Of film – awards are made the following year

The Annie Awards have been presented by the International Animated Film Society (ASIFA-Hollywood) since 1972. In addition to the individual and specialist category awards presented from then, it has been honouring Best Animated Feature (originally Outstanding Achievement in an Animated Theatrical Feature) since 1992, when it was won by *Beauty and the Beast*. The equivalent Academy Award (Oscar) for Best Animated Feature was first presented in 2001.

Worth the wait
It took 10 years from its original conception to release, but The Simpsons Movie *has earned a place in the Top 10 highest-earning animated films of all time.*

TOP 10 **ANIMATED FILM BUDGETS**

	FILM	YEAR	BUDGET ($)
1	The Polar Express	2004	170,000,000
2	Shrek the Third	2007	160,000,000
3	=Bee Movie	2007	150,000,000
	=Beowulf	2007	150,000,000
	=Ratatouille	2007	150,000,000
	=Shrek 2	2007	150,000,000
7	Flushed Away	2006	149,000,000
8	Tarzan	1999	145,000,000
9	Treasure Planet	2002	140,000,000
10	Final Fantasy: The Spirits Within	2001	137,000,000

Snow White and the Seven Dwarfs (1937) established a record animated film budget of $1.49 million. The $2.6 million budget for *Pinocchio* (1940) and $2.28 million for *Fantasia* (1940) were the two biggest of the 1940s, while *Sleeping Beauty* (1959) at $6 million was the highest of the 1950s. Since the 1990s budgets of $50 million or more have become commonplace: *The Lion King* (1994) cost $79.3 million, *Tarzan* becoming the first to break through $100 million.

TOP 10 **ANIMATED FILMS BASED ON TV SERIES**

	FILM	TV SERIES*	FILM YEAR
1	The Simpsons Movie	1987	2007
2	Pokemon: The First Movie	1997	1999
3	The Rugrats Movie	1991	1998
4	The SpongeBob SquarePants Movie	1999	2004
5	Pokemon: The Movie 2000	1997	2000
6	Rugrats in Paris: The Movie – Rugrats II	1991	2000
7	TMNT	1987	2007
8	South Park: Bigger, Longer & Uncut	1997	1999
9	Beavis and Butt-head Do America	1993	1996
10	Pokémon 3: The Movie	1997	2001

* Launched on TV in USA

Prior to these releases, popular animated TV series including *Flintstones*, *Jetsons* and *Transformers* made the transition to the big screen. Such is their long-established fan following that such films often attract huge audiences: the first six films in this list each earned in excess of $100 million.

Radio

THE 10 **LATEST WINNERS OF THE SONY RADIO COMEDY AWARD**

YEAR	PROGRAMME	PRODUCERS
2007	1966 And All That	BBC Radio Entertainment for Radio 4
2006	The Ape that Got Lucky	BBC Radio Entertainment for Radio 4
2005	The National Theatre of Brent's Complete and Utter History of the Mona Lisa	Above the Title Productions for BBC Radio 4
2004	I'm Sorry I Haven't a Christmas Carol	BBC Radio Entertainment for Radio 4
2003	Just a Minute	BBC Radio Entertainment for Radio 4
2002	I'm Sorry I Haven't a Clue	BBC Radio Entertainment for Radio 4
2001	Dead Ringers	BBC Radio Entertainment for Radio 4
2000	Blue Jam	TalkBack Productions for BBC Radio 1
1999	Old Harry's Game	BBC Radio 4
1998	Blue Jam	TalkBack Productions for BBC Radio 1

THE 10 **LATEST WINNERS OF THE SONY RADIO DRAMA AWARD**

YEAR	PROGRAMME	PRODUCERS
2007	Lorilei	BBC Radio Drama for BBC Radio 4
2006	No Background Music	BBC Radio Drama for BBC Radio 4
2005	Laughter in the Dark	Catherine Bailey Productions for BBC Radio 3
2004	The Loneliest Road	BBC Radio Drama for BBC Radio 3
2003	Runt	BBC Radio Drama for BBC World Service
2002	A Woman in Waiting	BBC Radio 4
2001	Alpha	BBC World Service Drama for BBC World Service
2000	Plum's War	The Fiction Factory for BBC Radio 4
1999	Bleak House	Goldhawk Universal Productions for BBC Radio 4
1998	The Trick is to Keep Breathing	BBC Scotland for BBC Radio 4

TOP 10 **RADIO STATIONS IN THE UK**

STATION / % 2006–07*

1	2	3	4	5
BBC Radio 2	BBC Radio 1	BBC Radio 4	BBC Radio 5 Live	Classic FM
26.5	21.4	18.7	12.0	11.8

6	7	8	9	10
Virgin (AM/FM)	talkSPORT	BBC Radio 3	BBC World Service	BBC 7
4.8	4.7	3.8	2.7	1.4

* Of people listening for at least 15 minutes per week

Source: *BBC Annual Report and Accounts 2006/2007*

THE 10 LATEST RECIPIENTS OF THE SONY RADIO GOLD AWARD

YEAR	RECIPIENT
2007	Paul Gambaccini
2006	Terry Wogan
2005	Steve Wright
2004	Johnnie Walker
2003	John Humphrys
2002	John Peel
2001	Chris Tarrant
2000	Ralph Bernard
1999	Zoë Ball
1998	Chris Evans

The Gold Award is presented for 'Outstanding Contribution to Radio Over the Years'. The first award, in 1983, was presented to Frank Muir and Denis Norden.

TOP 10 LONGEST-RUNNING PROGRAMMES ON BBC RADIO

PROGRAMME	FIRST BROADCAST
1 The Week's Good Cause	24 Jan 1926
2 The Shipping Forecast	26 Jan 1926
3 Choral Evensong	7 Oct 1926
4 Daily Service	2 Jan 1928*
5 The Week in Westminster	6 Nov 1929
6 Sunday Half Hour	14 Jul 1940
7 Desert Island Discs	29 Jan 1942
8 Saturday Night Theatre	3 Apr 1943
9 Composer of the Week#	2 Aug 1943
10 From Our Own Correspondent	4 Oct 1946

* Experimental broadcast; national transmission began December 1929
# Formerly *This Week's Composer*

In addition to these 10 long-running programmes, a further six that started in the 1940s are still on the air, with *Woman's Hour*, first broadcast on 7 October 1946, and *Down Your Way* (29 December 1946) the oldest.

Sound waves
Telecommunication towers for radio and TV broadcasts, as well as mobile phone masts, are now a notable feature of the world's skylines.

TV

THE 10 **LATEST WINNERS OF THE BAFTA TV BEST ACTRESS AWARD**

YEAR	ACTRESS / PROGRAMME
2008	Eileen Atkins, Cranford
2007	Victoria Wood, Housewife, 49
2006	Anna Maxwell Martin, Bleak House
2005	Anamaria Marinca, Sex Traffic
2004	Julie Walters, The Canterbury Tales: The Wife of Bath's Tale
2003	Julie Walters, Murder
2002	Julie Walters, My Beautiful Son (ITV1)
2001	Judi Dench, Last of the Blonde Bombshells
2000	Thora Hird, Lost for Words
1999	Thora Hird, Talking Heads: Waiting for the Telegram

In 1959 the Society of Film and Television Arts was formed by the amalgamation of the British Film Academy (founded 1948) and the Guild of Television producers and Directors (1954), changing its name to BAFTA (the British Academy of Film and Television Arts) in 1975.

THE 10 **LATEST WINNERS OF THE BAFTA TV BEST COMEDY PROGRAMME OR SERIES AWARD**

2008	Fonejacker
2007	That Mitchell and Webb Look
2006	Help
2005	Little Britain
2004	Little Britain
2003	Alistair McGowan's Big Impression
2002	The Sketch Show
2001	Da Ali G Show
2000	The League of Gentlemen
1999	Father Ted

THE 10 **LATEST WINNERS OF THE BAFTA TV BEST ACTOR AWARD**

YEAR	ACTOR / PROGRAMME
2008	Andrew Garfield, Boy A
2007	Jim Broadbent, Longford
2006	Mark Rylance, The Government Inspector
2005	Rhys Ifans, Not Only But Always
2004	Bill Nighy, State of Play
2003	Albert Finney, The Gathering Storm
2002	Michael Gambon, Perfect Strangers
2001	Michael Gambon, Longitude
2000	Michel Gambon, Wives & Daughters
1999	Tom Courtenay, A Rather English Marriage

TOP 10 **SATELLITE TV COUNTRIES**

	COUNTRY / SATELLITE TV HOUSEHOLDS*
1	USA 43,574,750
2	Japan 23,777,360
3	Germany 16,533,870
4	Egypt 10,587,910
5	India 9,925,410
6	UK 9,913,460
7	Italy 7,144,960
8	France 7,132,170
9	Turkey 6,397,580
10	Algeria 5,328,320

Top 10 total 140,315,790
World total 205,503,210

* Households with satellite TV, 2009 forecast

Source: Euromonitor International, Global Market Information Database

TOP 10 **CABLE TV COUNTRIES**

COUNTRY / CABLE TV HOUSEHOLDS*

1 China 191,998,950
2 USA 85,017,870
3 India 76,216,660
4 Japan 31,684,190
5 Germany 22,367,950
6 Russia 20,551,350
7 South Korea 16,608,320
8 Canada 8,237,540
9 Philippines 6,886,740
10 Netherlands 6,418,690

*Top 10 total 465,988,260
UK 3,735,860
World total 556,067,040*

* Households with cable TV, 2009 forecast

Source: Euromonitor International, Global Market Information Database

TOP 10 **TELEVISION AUDIENCES IN THE UK**

	PROGRAMME	BROADCAST	AUDIENCE
1	1966 World Cup Final: England v. West Germany	30 Jul 1966	32,300,000
2	Funeral of Diana, Princess of Wales	6 Sep 1997	32,100,000
3	The Royal Family documentary	21 Jun 1969	30,690,000
4	EastEnders Christmas episode (Den divorces Angie)	25 Dec 1986	30,150,000
5	Apollo 13 splashdown	17 Apr 1970	28,600,000
6	Cup Final Replay: Chelsea v Leeds United	28 Apr 1970	28,490,000
7	Wedding of Prince Charles and Lady Diana Spencer	29 Jul 1981	28,400,000
8	Wedding of Princess Anne and Capt Mark Phillips	14 Nov 1973	27,600,000
9	Coronation Street (Alan Bradley killed by a tram)	19 Mar 1989	26,930,000
10	Only Fools and Horses (Batman and Robin episode)	29 Dec 1996	24,350,000

Source: British Film Institute

THE 10 **LATEST WINNERS OF THE BAFTA TV DRAMA SERIES/SERIAL AWARD**

YEAR	SERIES	SERIAL
2008	Life on Mars	Britz
2007	The Street	See No Evil: The Moors Murders
2006	Doctor Who	Bleak House
2005	Shameless	Sex Traffic
2004	Buried	Charles II: The Power and The Passion
2003	Spooks	Shackleton
2002	Cold Feet	The Way We Live Now
2001	Clocking Off	Longitude
2000	The Cops	Warriors
1999	The Cops	Our Mutual Friend

In its early years, the BAFTA drama award went to such classic series as *Upstairs Downstairs* (1971 and 1973) and *Brideshead Revisited* (1981). Prior to 1992, no distinction was made between series and serials.

DVD & Video

Gold disc
After earning almost $300 million worldwide from its cinema release and winning four Oscars, The
Departed, *starring Jack Nicholson and Matt Damon, went on to become the year's most-rented DVD.*

TOP 10 **MOST-RENTED DVDS IN THE UK, 2007**

TITLE

1 The Departed
2 Click
3 Casino Royale
4 The Devil Wears Prada
5 Borat: Cultural Learnings of America for Make Benefit Glorious Nation of Kazakhstan
6 Night at the Museum
7 Children of Men
8 The Holiday
9 Little Miss Sunshine
10 You, Me & Dupree

TOP 10 **BESTSELLING DVDS IN THE UK, 2007**

TITLE

1 Casino Royale
2 The Queen
3 Happy Feet
4 Hot Fuzz
5 Night at the Museum
6 Borat: Cultural Learnings of America for Make Benefit Glorious Nation of Kazakhstan
7 The Devil Wears Prada
8 Flushed Away
9 The Departed
10 Click

TOP 10 **MOST-RENTED VIDEOS IN THE UK***

TITLE

1 Four Weddings and a Funeral
2 Dirty Dancing
3 Basic Instinct
4 Crocodile Dundee
5 Gladiator
6 Sister Act
7 Forrest Gump
8 The Sixth Sense
9 Home Alone
10 Ghost

* To 1 January 2006; includes VHS and DVD formats

Source: British Video Association/MRIB

TOP 10 **BESTSELLING DVDS OF ALL TIME IN THE UK**

TITLE

1 Pirates of the Caribbean: The Curse of the Black Pearl

2 The Lord of the Rings: The Fellowship of the Ring

3 The Lord of The Rings: The Two Towers

4 Pirates of the Caribbean: Dead Man's Chest

5 The Lord of the Rings: The Return of the King

6 Shrek 2

7 The Shawshank Redemption

8 Gladiator

9 Casino Royale

10 Harry Potter and the Goblet of Fire

Source: British Video Association/The Official UK Charts Company

It is estimated that while some 25 per cent of UK homes owned a DVD player in 2002, this figure grew to 45 per cent in 2003, 62 per cent in 2004, 75 per cent in 2005 and close to 80 per cent in 2007, with the UK market for DVDs the largest in Europe.

Big fish
Finding Nemo *(2003)* was the bestselling DVD of an animated film until overtaken by Shrek 2 *(2004)*.

TOP 10 **VIDEO COUNTRIES**

	COUNTRY	% OF TOTAL SPENT ON DVD	TOTAL VIDEO SPENDING ($)*
1	USA	93.8	24,915,000,000
2	Japan	84.1	6,408,000,000
3	UK	96.8	4,973,000,000
4	Canada	93.3	2,483,000,000
5	France	98.6	2,465,000,000
6	Germany	97.1	2,099,000,000
7	Australia	96.4	1,347,000,000
8	Spain	97.2	917,000,000
9	Italy	92.7	880,000,000
10	Netherlands	98.8	623,000,000

* 2005, DVD and VHS

Source: *Screen Digest*

TOP 10 **BESTSELLING VIDEOS IN THE UK***

TITLE

1 The Lord of the Rings: The Fellowship of the Ring

2 Titanic

3 Shrek

4 The Lord of the Rings: The Two Towers

5 The Jungle Book

6 Dirty Dancing

7 Pirates of the Caribbean: The Curse of the Black Pearl

8 Gladiator

9 The Matrix

10 The Lion King

* To 1 January 2006; includes VHS and DVD formats

Source: British Video Association/The Official UK Charts Company

Already 55 years old when it appeared on video in 1992, animated Disney classic *Snow White and the Seven Dwarfs* once topped the all-time list. It was soon eclipsed by the 1993 release of the 1967 film *The Jungle Book*, but was only recently knocked out of the Top 10 altogether.

TOP 10 **MOST-RENTED DVDS AT LOVEFILM**

TITLE

1 The Shawshank Redemption

2 Pulp Fiction

3 The Lord of The Rings: The Return of the King

4 Leon

5 The Usual Suspects

6 Schindler's List

7 The Godfather

8 Star Wars Trilogy

9 The Lord of The Rings: The Two Towers

10 The Matrix

THE COMMERCIAL WORLD

Workers of the World

A million workers
Created in 1988, the China National Petroleum Corporation is one of the world's biggest employers.

TOP 10 **COMPANIES WITH THE MOST EMPLOYEES**

	COMPANY / COUNTRY	INDUSTRY	EMPLOYEES
1	Wal-Mart Stores, USA	Retail	1,900,000
2	State Grid, China	Electric power	1,504,000
3	China National Petroleum, China	Oil and gas	1,086,966
4	US Postal Service, USA	Mail	796,199
5	Sinopec, China	Oil and gas	681,900
6	Siemens, Germany	Electronics	475,000
7	McDonald's, USA	Fast-food restaurants	465,000
8	Deutsche Post, Germany	Post and courier	463,350
9	Carrefour, France	Hypermarkets	456,295
10	Agricultural Bank of China, China	Banking	452,464

Source: *Fortune Global 500 2007*

TOP 10 **OCCUPATIONS IN THE UK**

	JOB SECTOR	EMPLOYEES
1	Real-estate renting and business activities	4,507,000
2	Health and social work	3,365,000
3	Manufacturing	2,999,000
4	Retail (except motor and repair of personal/ household goods)	2,899,000
5	Education	2,414,000
6	Hotels and restaurants	1,839,000
7	Transport, storage and communication	1,601,000
8	Public administration and defence	1,519,000
9	Construction	1,288,000
10	Wholesale and commission trade (excluding motor)	1,141,000
	Total (including sectors outside Top 10)	*27,035,000*

Source: National Statistics

TOP 10 **COUNTRIES WORKING THE LONGEST HOURS**

	COUNTRY	AVERAGE ANNUAL HOURS PER PERSON*
1	South Korea	2,354
2	Greece	2,053
3	Czech Republic	2,002
4 =	Hungary	1,994
=	Poland	1,994
6	Mexico	1,909
7	New Zealand	1,809
8	USA	1,804
9	Italy	1,801
10	Iceland	1,794
	UK	*1,672*

* In employment, 2005 – total (employed and self-employed) or employed only, depending on source; OECD countries only

Source: OECD

Among OECD member countries, Norway works the fewest hours per annum – an average of 1,360. Historical assessments of hours worked show that in the mid-nineteenth century, the average US employee worked up to 3,650 hours a year, equivalent to 10 hours a day, seven day a week, or more than double the contemporary figure.

TOP 10 **COUNTRIES WITH THE MOST WORKERS**

	COUNTRY	WORKERS*
1	China	803,300,000
2	India	516,400,000
3	USA	153,100,000
4	Indonesia	108,000,000
5	Brazil	99,470,000
6	Russia	75,100,000
7	Bangladesh	69,400,000
8	Japan	66,070,000
9	Nigeria	50,130,000
10	Pakistan	49,180,000
	UK	*30,710,000*
	World total	*3,001,000,000*

* 2007 or latest year available; based on people aged 15–64 who are currently employed; excluding unpaid groups

Source: CIA, *The World Factbook 2008*/International Labour Organization

As defined by the ILO, the 'labour force' includes people aged 15 to 64 currently employed and those who are unemployed, but excludes unpaid groups such as students, housewives and retired people.

Call centre
Although a fraction of its huge labour force, over one million Indians are employed in call centres, such as this one in Bangalore.

TOP 10 **COUNTRIES WITH THE HIGHEST PROPORTION OF WORKERS**

	COUNTRY	WORKERS PER 1,000 OF POPULATION
1	Monaco	1,347
2	San Marino	691
3	United Arab Emirates	668
4	Azerbaijan	639
5	China	604
6	Myanmar	601
7	Papua New Guinea	600
8	Andorra	591
9	Trinidad and Tobago	585
10	The Bahamas	577
	UK	*512*

Source: CIA, *The World Factbook 2008*

Wealth – Countries

TOP 10 AREAS OF UK GOVERNMENT EXPENDITURE

DEPARTMENT	DEPARTMENTAL EXPENDITURE LIMITS 2008–09 (£)
1 Health	94,000,000,000
2 Children, Schools and Families	46,900,000,000
3 Defence	33,600,000,000
4 Local Government	24,700,000,000
5 Scotland	24,500,000,000
6 Innovation, Universities and Skills	16,900,000,000
7 Wales	13,000,000,000
8 Justice	9,300,000,000
9 Home Office	9,000,000,000
10 Northern Ireland Executive	7,900,000,000
Top 10 total	*279,800,000,000*
Total estimated expenditure (including those not in Top 10)	*324,300,000,000*

Source: HM Treasury

TOP 10 SOURCES OF UK GOVERNMENT INCOME

SOURCE	EST. INCOME 2008–09 (£)
1 Income tax	161,800,000,000
2 National Insurance	101,000,000,000
3 VAT	85,800,000,000
4 Corporation tax	51,500,000,000
5 Fuel duty	26,200,000,000
6 Stamp duty	15,800,000,000
7 Alcohol duty	8,500,000,000
8 Tobacco duty	7,800,000,000
9 Capital gains tax	5,400,000,000
10 Inheritance tax	3,300,000,000
Top 10 total	*467,100,000,000*
Total estimated expenditure (including those not in Top 10)	*473,700,000,000*

Source: HM Treasury

TOP 10 COINS AND NOTES IN CIRCULATION IN THE UK BY VALUE

UNIT	VALUE IN CIRCULATION 2006 (£)
1 £20 note	22,690,000,000
2 £50 note	6,510,000,000
3 £10 note	5,591,000,000
4 £1 coin	1,452,000,000
5 £5 note	1,051,000,000
6 £2 coin	536,000,000
7 20p coin	438,000,000
8 50p coin	384,500,000
9 5p coin	182,295,000
10 10p coin	158,700,000

THE 10 COUNTRIES WITH THE HIGHEST INFLATION

COUNTRY	ANNUAL INFLATION RATE (%, 2007)
1 Zimbabwe	16,170
2 Myanmar	36.9
3 Guinea	23.4
4 Eritrea	22.7
5 Iran	19.0
6 Venezuela	18.0
7 Ethiopia	17.8
8 Dem. Rep. of Congo	17.5
9 Sri Lanka	17.0
10 = Azerbaijan	16.6
= São Tomé and Príncipe	16.6
UK	*2.4*

Source: International Monetary Fund

These figures indicate the rise in consumer prices over the previous year. An inflation rate of 100 per cent would mean that consumer prices had doubled since the previous year. High though they are, and immensely painful to consumers and governments alike, these levels seem almost insignificant when compared with the multimillion per cent hyperinflation experienced by Germany in 1923, or Hungary in 1946. Britain's highest annual rate of inflation was in 1974–75, when it reached almost 27 per cent.

TOP 10 **RICHEST COUNTRIES**

	COUNTRY	GROSS DOMESTIC PRODUCT PER CAPITA 2008 ($)
1	Luxembourg	110,032
2	Norway	83,702
3	Qatar	80,211
4	Iceland	63,875
5	Ireland	62,482
6	Denmark	59,728
7	Switzerland	58,412
8	Sweden	49,091
9	Netherlands	48,169
10	UK	48,072

Source: International Monetary Fund, World Economic Outlook Database

Sky high
Qatar has a population of fewer than one million, but its oil wealth results in a substantial GDP, reflected in its high-rise and exotic architecture, such as the coffee-pot monument – a symbol of welcome – in Doha, the capital city.

African tragedy
Despite its considerable natural resources, warfare and other problems have so damaged the economy of the Democratic Republic of Congo that, while it has a population similar to that of the UK, its GDP is just 1/276th.

THE 10 **POOREST COUNTRIES**

	COUNTRY	GROSS DOMESTIC PRODUCT PER CAPITA, 2008 ($)
1	Burundi	140
2	Dem. Rep. of Congo	174
3	Liberia	206
4	Guinea-Bissau	211
5	Ethiopia	225
6	Myanmar	230
7	The Gambia	259
8	Malawi	269
9	Sierra Leone	287
10	Niger	331

Source: International Monetary Fund, World Economic Outlook Database

Richest of the Rich

TOP 10 COUNTRIES WITH THE MOST DOLLAR BILLIONAIRES

COUNTRY* / $ BILLIONAIRES

1 USA
435

2 Russia
82

3 China (including Hong Kong)
78

4 India
50

5 = Germany 49
= UK 49

7 Turkey
35

8 Switzerland
27

9 Japan
25

10 Canada
23

World total 946

* Of residence, irrespective of citizenship

Source: *Forbes* magazine, *The World's Billionaires*, 2008

TOP 10 RICHEST MEN*

	NAME / COUNTRY (CITIZEN/ RESIDENCE, IF DIFFERENT)	SOURCE	NET WORTH ($)
1	Warren Edward Buffett, USA	Berkshire Hathaway (investments)	62,000,000,000
2	Carlos Slim Helu, Mexico	Communications	60,000,000,000
3	William H. Gates III, USA	Microsoft (software)	58,000,000,000
4	Lakshmi Mittal, India/UK	Mittal Steel	45,000,000,000
5	Mukesh Ambani, India	Reliance Industries (petrochemicals)	43,000,000,000
6	Anil Ambani, India	Reliance Communications (petrochemicals)	42,000,000,000
7	Ingvar Kamprad, Sweden/Switzerland	Ikea (home furnishings)	31,000,000,000
8	K. P. Singh, India	DLF (property)	30,000,000,000
9	Oleg Deripaska, Russia	UC Russal (aluminium)	28,000,000,000
10	Karl Albrecht, Germany	Aldi (supermarkets)	27,000,000,000

* Excluding rulers and family fortunes

Source: *Forbes* magazine, *The World's Billionaires*, 2008

TOP 10 **HIGHEST-EARNING CELEBRITIES**

	CELEBRITY*	PROFESSION	EARNINGS* ($)
1	Oprah Winfrey	Talk-show host/producer	260,000,000
2	Jerry Bruckheimer	Film and TV producer	120,000,000
3	Steven Spielberg	Film producer/director	110,000,000
4	Tiger Woods	Golfer	100,000,000
5	Johnny Depp	Film actor	92,000,000
6	Jay-Z	Rap artist	83,000,000
7	Tom Hanks	Film actor	74,000,000
8	Madonna	Singer	72,000,000
9	Howard Stern	Radio shock jock	70,000,000
10	Bon Jovi	Singer	67,000,000

* Individuals, excluding groups; all US
\# 2006–07

Source: *Forbes* magazine, *The Celebrity 100*, 2007

Earning élite
Oprah and Elvis, respectively the world's highest-earning living and deceased celebrities. Elvis is one of a select group of individuals who, through ongoing royalty and other earnings, are worth more dead than alive.

TOP 10 **HIGHEST-EARNING SPORTSMEN**

	SPORTSMAN / COUNTRY*	SPORT	ESTIMATED EARNINGS, 2006–07
1	Tiger Woods	Golf	100,000,000
2	Oscar de la Hoya	Boxing	43,000,000
3	Phil Mickelson	Golf	42,200,000
4	Kimi Räikkönen, Finland	Motor racing	40,000,000
5	Michael Schumacher, Germany	Motor racing	36,000,000
6	David Beckham, UK	Football	33,000,000
7	Kobe Bryant	Basketball	32,900,000
8	Shaquille O'Neal	Basketball	31,900,000
9 =	Michael Jordan	Basketball	31,000,000
=	Ronaldinho, Brazil	Football	31,000,000

* All from the USA unless otherwise stated

Source: *Forbes* magazine

TOP 10 **HIGHEST-EARNING DEAD CELEBRITIES**

	CELEBRITY / PROFESSION	DEATH	EARNINGS 2006–07 ($)
1	Elvis Presley Rock star	16 Aug 1977	49,000,000
2	John Lennon Rock star	8 Dec 1980	44,000,000
3	Charles Schultz 'Peanuts' cartoonist	12 Feb 2000	35,000,000
4	George Harrison Rock star	29 Nov 2001	22,000,000
5	Albert Einstein Scientist	18 Apr 1955	18,000,000
6	Andy Warhol Artist	22 Feb 1987	15,000,000
7	Theodor 'Dr Seuss' Geisel Author	24 Sep 1991	13,000,000
8	Tupac Shakur Musician	13 Sep 1996	9,000,000
9	Marilyn Monroe Actress	5 Aug 1962	7,000,000
10	Steve McQueen Actor	30 Nov 1980	6,000,000

Source: *Forbes* magazine, *Top-Earning Dead Celebrities*, 2007

Natural Resources

TOP 10 **ALUMINIUM PRODUCERS**

COUNTRY / PRODUCTION 2006 (TONNES)

1 China   8,700,00

2 Russia 3,720,000

3 Canada 3,000,000

4 USA 2,300,000

5 Australia 1,900,000

9 South Africa 890,000

6 Brazil 1,600,000

7 Norway 1,360,000

8 India 1,000,000

10 Bahrain 830,000

World 33,100,000

Source: US Geological Survey, *Minerals Yearbook*

TOP 10 **SALT PRODUCERS**

COUNTRY / PRODUCTION* 2006 (TONNES)

1 China 48,000,000

2 USA 46,000,000

3 Germany 18,600,000

4 India 16,000,000

5 Canada 15,000,000

6 Australia 12,400,000

7 Mexico 8,500,000

8 Brazil 7,300,000

9 France 7,000,000

10 UK 5,800,000

World 240,000,000

* Includes salt in brine

Source: US Geological Survey, *Minerals Yearbook*

TOP 10 **CEMENT PRODUCERS**

COUNTRY / PRODUCTION 2006 (TONNES)

1 China 1,100,000,000

2 India 155,000,000

3 USA* 101,000,000

4 Japan 68,000,000

5 Russia 54,000,000

6 South Korea 52,000,000

7 Spain 50,000,000

8 Italy 46,000,000

9 Turkey 45,000,000

10 = Indonesia 40,000,000 = Thailand 40,000,000

* Including Puerto Rico   Source: US Geological Survey, *Minerals Yearbook*

World 2,500,000,000

TOP 10 **STEEL PRODUCERS**

COUNTRY / PRODUCTION (TONNES 2007)

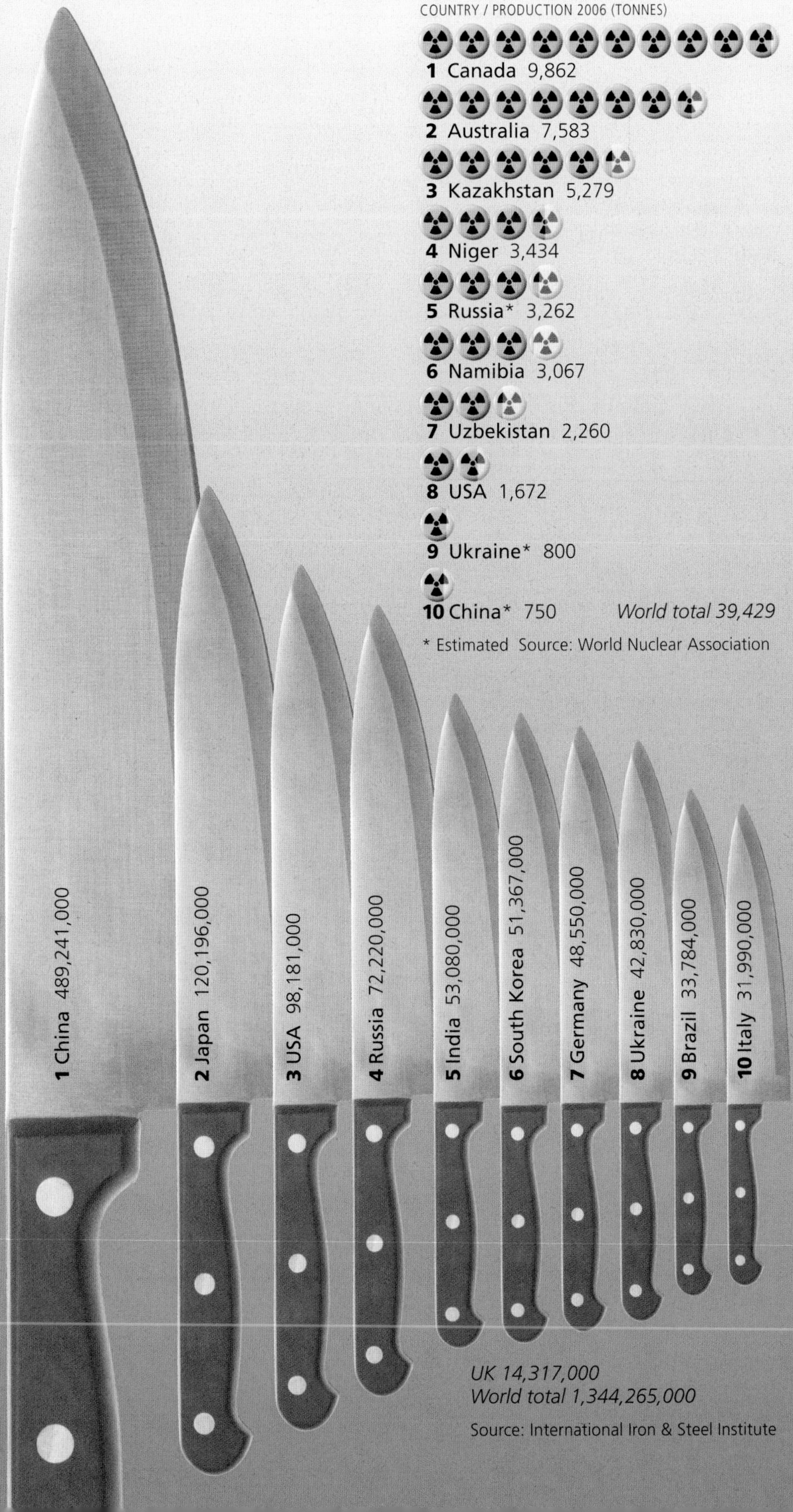

1 China 489,241,000
2 Japan 120,196,000
3 USA 98,181,000
4 Russia 72,220,000
5 India 53,080,000
6 South Korea 51,367,000
7 Germany 48,550,000
8 Ukraine 42,830,000
9 Brazil 33,784,000
10 Italy 31,990,000

UK 14,317,000
World total 1,344,265,000

Source: International Iron & Steel Institute

TOP 10 **URANIUM-PRODUCING COUNTRIES**

COUNTRY / PRODUCTION 2006 (TONNES)

1 Canada 9,862
2 Australia 7,583
3 Kazakhstan 5,279
4 Niger 3,434
5 Russia* 3,262
6 Namibia 3,067
7 Uzbekistan 2,260
8 USA 1,672
9 Ukraine* 800
10 China* 750   *World total 39,429*

* Estimated Source: World Nuclear Association

TOP 10 **LEAD PRODUCERS**

COUNTRY / PRODUCTION 2006 (TONNES)

1 China 1,050,000
2 Australia 780,000
3 USA 430,000
4 Peru 320,000
5 Mexico 140,000
6 Canada 79,000
7 Ireland 65,000
8 Sweden 61,000
9 = India 60,000
   = Poland 60,000

Precious Things

TOP 10 **LARGEST UNCUT DIAMONDS**

DIAMOND / DATE / LOCATION OF DISCOVERY / DETAILS   CARATS

1 Cullinan, 1905, Premier Mine, South Africa   3,106.75
Measuring approximately 100 x 65 x 50 mm (4 x 2.5 x 2 in) and weighing
621 g (1 lb 6 oz) it was bought by the Transvaal government for £150,000
and presented to King Edward VII, who had it cut. The most important of
the separate gems are now among the British Crown Jewels.

2 Excelsior, 30 Jun 1893, Jagersfontein Mine, South Africa   971.75
Cut by the celebrated Amsterdam firm of I. J. Asscher in 1903, the Excelsior
produced 21 superb stones, which were sold mainly through Tiffany's of
New York.

3 Star of Sierra Leone, 14 Feb 1972, Sierra Leone   968.90
The uncut diamond weighed 225 g (8 oz) and measured 63.5 x 38.1 mm
(2.5 x 1.5 in).

4 Incomparable, *c.* 1980, Mbuji-Mayi ('Goat Water') village,
Dem. Rep. of Congo (then Zaïre)   890.00
The four-year cutting process yielded a stone of 407.48 carats and 14 'satellite'
gems. In 2002 it was offered for sale on eBay with a reserve of $15 million.
It did not reach its reserve and was unsold.

5 Great Mogul, 1650, Kollur Diggings, India   787.50
Upon its discovery, this diamond was presented to Shah Jahan, the builder
of the Taj Mahal.

6 De Beers Millennium Star, 1990, near Mbuji-Mayi,
Dem. Rep. of Congo (then Zaïre)   777.00
The dimensions of the rough diamond from which the Millennium Star was
cut are shrouded in secrecy. The polished stone, which was featured in the
celebrations at the Millennium Dome, London, on 31 December 1999
(and later figured in an averted attempt by an armed gang to steal it), is
203.04 carats and measures 50.06 x 36.56 x 18.5 mm (2 x 1.5 x 0.75 in).

7 Woyie River, 1945, Woyie River, Sierra Leone   770.00
Cut into 30 stones, the largest of which, known as Victory and weighing
31.35 carats, was auctioned at Christie's, New York, in 1984 for $880,000.

8 Golden Jubilee, *c.* 1985–86, Premier Mine, South Africa   755.50
Found in 1986 in the Premier Mine (the home of the Cullinan), the polished
diamond cut from it is, at 545.67 carats, the largest in the world.

9 Presidente Vargas, 1938, San Antonio River, Brazil   726.60
Named after the then president, Getúlio Dornelles Vargas.

10 Jonker, 17 Jan 1934, Elandsfontein, South Africa   726.00
This massive diamond was found on a claim owned by Johannes Jacobus
Jonker, after it had been exposed by a heavy storm. Acquired by Harry Winston,
it was exhibited in the American Museum of Natural History and attracted
enormous crowds.

Source: De Beers

The weight of diamonds is measured in carats (the word derives from the carob bean,
which was once used as a measure). There are approximately 142 carats to the ounce.
Fewer than 1,000 rough diamonds weighing more than 100 carats have ever been
recorded. In 2007, an 8,000-carat diamond was alleged to have been discovered in an
unnamed mine in South Africa. As the world's press speculated on what could have been
a stone more than twice the size of the record-holding Cullinan, it was exposed as a fake.

TOP 10 **DIAMOND PRODUCERS**

COUNTRY	VOLUME 2006 (CARATS)
1 Russia	38,400,000
2 Botswana	32,000,000
3 Australia	29,220,000
4 Dem. Rep. of Congo	28,000,000
5 South Africa	15,370,000
6 Canada	12,350,000
7 Angola	7,800,000
8 Namibia	2,200,000
9 China	1,065,000
10 Ghana	970,000
World total	*171,200,000*

Source: The Diamond Registry

TOP 10 **SILVER PRODUCERS**

COUNTRY	% OF WORLD TOTAL	PRODUCTION 2006 (TONNES)
1 Peru	17.2	3,471
2 Mexico	14.9	2,998
3 China	11.5	2,317
4 Australia	8.6	1,729
5 Chile	8.0	1,602
6 Poland	6.3	1,257
7 Russia	6.1	1,232
8 USA	5.7	1,141
9 Canada	4.8	970
10 Kazakhstan	4.0	812
World total	*100.0*	*20,096*

Source: The Silver Institute/GFMS, *World Silver Survey 2007*

Good as gold
The manufacture of gold jewellery in India has a long tradition. Although some gold is recycled, the country's total demand is equivalent to more than one-fifth of all the gold mined in a year worldwide.

TOP 10 **GOLD JEWELLERY MANUFACTURING COUNTRIES**

	COUNTRY	GOLD CONSUMPTION 2006* (TONNES)
1	India	521.5
2	USA	308.7
3	China	244.7
4	Turkey	165.3
5	Saudi Arabia	104.3
6	United Arab Emirates	88.2
7	Russia	69.5
8	Italy	63.9
9	Indonesia	57.7
10	Pakistan	54.7
	UK and Ireland	*54.2*

* Including scrap

Source: Gold Fields Mineral Services Ltd, Gold Survey 2007

TOP 10 **COUNTRIES WITH THE MOST GOLD**

COUNTRY / GOLD RESERVES* (TONNES)

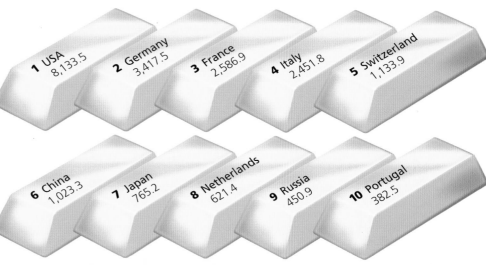

1 USA 8,133.5
2 Germany 3,417.5
3 France 2,586.9
4 Italy 2,451.8
5 Switzerland 1,133.9
6 China 1,023.3
7 Japan 765.2
8 Netherlands 621.4
9 Russia 450.9
10 Portugal 382.5

UK 310.3
World total 29,873

* As at March 2008

Source: World Gold Council

Gold reserves are the government holdings of gold in each country – which are often far greater than the gold owned by private individuals. Although less important today, in the days of the 'Gold Standard', this provided a way of measuring a country's wealth, guaranteeing the convertibility of its currency, and determined such factors as exchange rates.

Shopping Lists

TOP 10 **GLOBAL RETAILERS**

COMPANY / BASE / RETAIL SALES 2006* ($)

* Financial year

Source: *Stores* magazine,
2008 Global Powers of Retailing

2 Carrefour, France
97,861,000,000

3 Home Depot, Inc., USA
90,837,000,000

4 Tesco plc, UK
79,976,000,000

5 METRO AG,
Germany
74,857,000,000

6 Kroger Co., USA
66,111,000,000

7 Target Corp., USA
59,490,000,000

8 Costco Wholesale
Corp., USA
58,963,000,000

9 Sears Holdings,
USA
53,012,000,000

10 Schwarz Unternehmen
Treuhand KG, Germany
52,422,000,000

1 Wal-Mart Stores, Inc., USA
344,992,000,000

TOP 10 **CATEGORIES OF CONSUMER SPENDING IN THE UK**

CATEGORY	AS % OF TOTAL	WEEKLY EXPENDITURE PER HOUSEHOLD (£)
1 Housing	18	80.90
2 Food	15	67.90
3 Motoring	14	63.80
4 Leisure services	14	63.00
5 Household goods	9	33.50
6 Household services	6	27.10
7 Clothing and footwear	5	22.40
8 Leisure goods	4	19.40
9 Personal goods and services	4	16.90
10 Alcoholic drink	3	14.80

Average weekly household expenditure on commodities and services in the UK in 2005–06 was £441.40. Households with the lowest incomes spend a higher proportion of the total on essentials such as food, fuel, light and power than households with higher incomes.

TOP 10 **CATGEORIES OF CONSUMER COMPLAINTS IN THE UK**

CATEGORY	% OF TOTAL*	COMPLAINTS
1 Second-hand cars purchased from independent dealers	5.1	41,880
2 Mobile phones (service agreements)	4.2	34,679
3 TVs	2.4	19,744
4 Mobile phones (hardware)	2.2	17,760
5 Personal goods and services (various)	2.1	16,976
6 General building work	1.9	15,598
7 Car repairs and servicing from independent garages	1.9	15,253
8 Upholstered furniture	1.7	14,024
9 Internet service providers	1.7	13,536
10 Second-hand cars purchased from franchise dealers	1.6	13,322

* Of 819,815 recorded by Consumer Direct, the government's telephone and online advice service, in 2007

Great Mall of China
Until recently the world's largest shopping complex, the Jin Yuan shopping Mall, Beijing, with more than 1,000 stores, caters for the Chinese capital's emerging middle class.

TOP 10 **LARGEST SHOPPING MALLS IN THE WORLD**

	MALL / LOCATION	OPENED	GLA* SQ M
1	South China Mall, Dongguan, China	2005	660,000
2	Jin Yuan, Beijing, China	2004	560,000
3	Mall of Asia, Pasay City, Philippines	2006	386,000
4	West Edmonton Mall, Edmonton, Alberta, Canada	1981	350,000
5	Cevahir Istanbul, Istanbul, Turkey	2005	348,000
6	= City North Edsa, Quezon City, Philippines	1985	332,000
	= Megamall, Mandaluyong City, Philippines	1991	332,000
8	= Beijing Mall, Beijing, China	2005	320,000
	= Berjaya Times Square, Kuala Lumpur, Malaysia	2003	320,000
10	Zhengjia Plaza, Guangzhou, China	2005	280,000

* Gross Leasable Area

Source: Emil Pocock, Eastern Connecticut State University

TOP 10 **RETAILERS IN THE UK**

	STORE GROUP	ANNUAL SALES (£)*
1	Tesco	39,454,000,000
2	J. Sainsbury	16,061,000,000
3	W. M. Morrison	12,461,500,000
4	Kingfisher (B&Q, etc.)	8,675,900,000
5	Marks & Spencer	7,797,700,000
6	DSG (Dixons)	7,403,400,000
7	John Lewis Partnership	6,400,000,000
8	Home Retail (Argos, Homebase)	5,851,000,000
9	Boots	5,027,400,000
10	Inchcape (automotive)	4,842,100,000

* To year ending 31 December 2006 or closest accounting period

Advertising & Brands

TOP 10 COUNTRIES SPENDING THE MOST ON ADVERTISING

COUNTRY	TOTAL AD SPEND FORECAST (2009)
1 USA	210,955,280,000
2 Japan	41,755,480,000
3 UK	26,620,310,000
4 Germany	23,311,560,000
5 China	22,702,710,000
6 France	16,014,470,000
7 Russia	13,931,960,000
8 Italy	13,340,400,000
9 Brazil	11,659,150,000
10 Spain	11,337,030,000
Top 10 total	*391,628,350,000*
World total	*549,627,610,000*

Source: Euromonitor International, Global Market Information Database

TOP 10 GROCERY BRANDS IN THE UK

BRAND	SALES 2006 (£)
1 Coca-Cola	959,900,000
2 Warburton's bakery	609,500,000
3 Walker's crisps	424,500,000
4 Hovis bakery	386,600,000
5 Cadbury's Dairy Milk	371,800,000
6 Nescafé instant coffee	346,900,000
7 Lucozade	337,700,000
8 Andrex toilet tissue	336,100,000
9 Kingsmill bakery	302,100,000
10 Robinsons soft drinks	283,800,000

Source: ACNielsen/Checkout, *Top 100 Grocery Brands 2007*

The Top 10 brands remained unchanged between 2006 and 2007, almost all experiencing growth.

TOP 10 COUNTRIES SPENDING THE MOST ON ONLINE ADVERTISING

COUNTRY	ONLINE AD SPEND FORECAST (2009)
1 USA	21,937,370,000
2 UK	5,721,140,000
3 Japan	5,712,250,000
4 Canada	1,427,310,000
5 Australia	1,158,430,000
6 South Korea	1,143,150,000
7 Germany	1,027,510,000
8 Norway	926,120,000
9 France	790,990,000
10 Italy	788,730,000
Top 10 total	*40,633,000,000*
World total	*45,470,600,000*

Source: Euromonitor International, Global Market Information Database

TOP 10 ONLINE ADVERTISERS IN THE UK

ADVERTISER	TOTAL AD SPEND (£)	TOTAL ONLINE SPEND (£)	ADVERTISER	TOTAL AD SPEND (£)	TOTAL ONLINE SPEND (£)
1 BskyB	93,403,263	19,547,407	**6** O2	52,145,446	11,085,679
2 Virgin Money	28,494,227	18,665,274	**7** Orange	84,720,854	10,571,489
3 Personal Loan Express	16,539,777	16,539,777	**8** BT	71,528,804	6,658,645
4 Experian	16,302,983	16,297,337	**9** e-loanshop.com	6,509,173	6,509,173
5 Microsoft	38,212,675	14,997,867	**10** RAC	23,591,176	4,941,038

Signs of the times
While the USA dominates world advertising expenditure by a considerable margin, Japan is solidly in second place.

Russian bear brand
Once regarded a symbol of the decadent West, Coca-Cola, the world's
most valuable brand, is now widely available throughout Russia, as this,
one of 18 such advertisements in Irkutsk, Siberia, testifies.

TOP 10 **GLOBAL MARKETERS**

COMPANY / COUNTRY	WORLD ADVERTISING* SPENDING, 2006 ($)
1 Procter & Gamble Company, USA	8,522,000,000
2 Unilever, UK/Netherlands	4,537,000,000
3 General Motors Corporation, USA	3,353,000,000
4 L'Oréal, France	3,119,000,000
5 Toyota Motor Corporation, Japan	3,098,000,000
6 Ford Motor Company, USA	2,869,000,000
7 Time Warner, USA	2,136,000,000
8 Nestlé, Switzerland	2,114,000,000
9 Johnson & Johnson, USA	2,025,000,000
10 DaimlerChrysler, Germany/USA	2,003,000,000

* Includes newspapers, magazines, billboards, television, radio, Internet and
Yellow Pages

Source: *Advertising Age*, 'Global Marketers', 2007

TOP 10 **MOST VALUABLE GLOBAL BRANDS**

BRAND NAME*	INDUSTRY	BRAND VALUE 2007 ($)
1 Coca-Cola	Beverages	65,324,000,000
2 Microsoft	Technology	58,709,000,000
3 IBM	Technology	57,091,000,000
4 General Electric	Diversified	51,569,000,000
5 Nokia (Finland)	Technology	33,696,000,000
6 Toyota (Japan)	Automotive	32,070,000,000
7 Intel	Technology	30,594,000,000
8 McDonald's	Food retail	29,398,000,000
9 Disney	Leisure	29,210,000,000
10 Mercedes-Benz (Germany)	Automotive	23,568,000,000

* All US-owned unless otherwise stated

Source: Interbrand/*BusinessWeek*

Brand consultants Interbrand use a method of estimating value
that takes account of the profitability of individual brands within
a business (rather than the companies that own them), as well as
such factors as their potential for growth.

Food

TOP 10 ICE-CREAM CONSUMERS

	COUNTRY	CONSUMPTION PER CAPITA (2007) LITRES	PINTS
1	USA	13.95	24.55
2	Australia	13.55	23.84
3	Finland	11.99	21.10
4	Norway	10.48	18.44
5	Sweden	10.11	17.79
6	Canada	9.94	17.49
7	Italy	8.59	15.12
8	New Zealand	8.53	15.01
9	Chile	7.09	12.48
10	UK	7.08	12.46

Source: Euromonitor International, Global Market Information Database

TOP 10 BEAN* CONSUMERS

	COUNTRY	EST. CONSUMPTION PER CAPITA (2007) KG	LB	OZ
1	UK	5.78	12	12
2	Ireland	4.18	9	3
3	Portugal	3.13	6	14
4	Australia	2.25	4	15
5	Spain	2.10	4	10
6	Canada	2.09	4	10
7	USA	1.79	3	15
8	New Zealand	1.68	3	11
9	Saudi Arabia	1.66	3	11
10	France	1.49	3	5
	World average	*0.29*	*0*	*10*

* Including baked beans, flageolet beans, kidney beans, chick peas, lentils, broad beans, white beans, black beans, etc.; excludes beans canned with sausages, which are categorized as 'canned ready meals'

Source: Euromonitor International, Global Market Information Database

The world eats 1,890,610 tonnes of beans a year, of which the UK consumes 350,810 tonnes, including 1.2 million cans of Heinz baked beans per day.

TOP 10 CHOCOLATE CONSUMERS

	COUNTRY	EST. CONSUMPTION PER CAPITA (2007) KG	LB	OZ
1	UK	10.37	22	14
2	Ireland	10.11	22	5
3	Switzerland	9.65	21	4
4	Germany	8.09	17	13
5	Norway	6.64	14	10
6	Austria	6.15	13	9
7	USA	5.72	12	10
8	Belgium	5.67	12	8
9	Denmark	5.44	12	0
10	Sweden	5.05	11	2
	World average	*1.04*	*2*	*5*

Source: Euromonitor International, Global Market Information Database

The estimated world total consumption of chocolate in 2007 was 6,872,780 tonnes.

TOP 10 BREAD CONSUMERS

COUNTRY / RETAIL VOLUME PER CAPITA (2007) KG/LB OZ

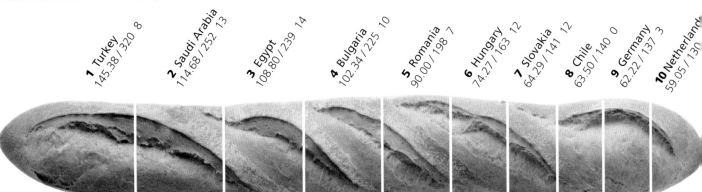

1 Turkey 145.38 / 320 8
2 Saudi Arabia 114.68 / 252 13
3 Egypt 108.80 / 239 14
4 Bulgaria 102.34 / 225 10
5 Romania 90.00 / 198 7
6 Hungary 74.27 / 163 12
7 Slovakia 64.29 / 141 12
8 Chile 63.50 / 140 0
9 Germany 62.22 / 137 3
10 Netherlands 59.05 / 130

UK 26.47 / 58 6

Source: Euromonitor International, Global Market Information Database

Breadwinner
Making bread by traditional methods in Egypt, one of the world's foremost consumers: some of the earliest archeological evidence of breadmaking comes from the region.

TOP 10 **FOOD, DRINK AND RESTAURANT BRANDS**

BRAND*	BRAND VALUE, 2007 ($)
1 Coca-Cola	65,324,000,000
2 McDonald's	29,398,000,000
3 Nescafé, Switzerland	12,950,000,000
4 Pepsi	12,888,000,000
5 Budweiser	11,652,000,000
6 Kellogg's	9,341,000,000
7 Heinz	6,544,000,000
8 Wrigley's	5,777,000,000
9 KFC	5,682,000,000
10 Nestlé, Switzerland	5,314,000,000

* US unless otherwise stated

Source: Interbrand, *Best Global Brands 2007*

TOP 10 **MEAT* CONSUMERS**

		AVERAGE CONSUMPTION PER CAPITA (2007)		
	COUNTRY	KG	LB	OZ
1	Spain	113.85	251	0
2	Argentina	113.02	249	3
3	Australia	106.07	233	14
4	New Zealand	103.18	227	8
5	Austria	102.55	226	1
6	Portugal	102.32	225	9
7	Greece	101.66	224	2
8	USA	93.51	206	2
9	Ireland	83.80	184	12
10	France	83.67	184	7
	UK	*50.87*	*112*	*2*
	World average	*36.74*	*81*	*0*

* Includes beef, veal, lamb, mutton, goat, pork, poultry and other meat

Source: Euromonitor International, Global Market Information Database

The world devours a total of 240,702,850 tonnes of meat a year.

TOP 10 **FOODS CONSUMED IN THE UK**

		AVERAGE WEEKLY CONSUMPTION PER HEAD*	
	ITEM	G	OZ
1	Milk and cream	2,022	71.32
2	Soft drinks	1,807	63.74
3	Fresh fruit	1,313	46.31
4	Vegetables (excl. potatoes)	1,142	40.28
5	Meat and meat products	1,042	36.76
6	Cereals#	914	32.24
7	Fresh and processed potatoes	810	28.57
8	Alcoholic drinks	760	26.81
9	Bread	692	24.41
10	Fats	184	6.49

* Household purchases (excluding eating out) 2005–06
# Excluding bread

Source: Department of Environment, Food and Rural Affairs (DEFRA), *Family Food 2006*, 2008

Drink

TOP 10 **SPIRIT DRINKERS**

COUNTRY / CONSUMPTION PER CAPITA (2007) LITRES/PINTS

1 South Korea
13.90 / 24.46

2 Russia
13.09 / 23.04

3 Ukraine
8.89 / 15.64

4 Thailand
8.10 / 14.25

5 Poland
6.56 / 11.54

6 Japan
6.34 / 11.16

7 Finland
5.87 / 10.33

8 Czech Republic
5.32 / 9.36

9 Bulgaria
4.86 / 8.55

10 France
4.64 / 8.17

UK 3.41 / 6.00   World average 2.02 / 3.55

Source: Euromonitor International, Global Market Information Database

TOP 10 **WINE DRINKERS**

| | COUNTRY | CONSUMPTION PER CAPITA (2005) | |
		LITRES	PINTS
1	Vatican	62.02	35.24
2	Andorra	60.13	34.17
3	France	55.85	31.74
4	Luxembourg	52.70	29.95
5	Italy	48.16	27.37
6	Portugal	46.67	26.52
7	Slovenia	43.77	24.87
8	Croatia	42.27	24.02
9	Switzerland	39.87	22.66
10	Spain	34.66	19.70
	UK	*18.97*	*10.78*

Source: Wine Institute

TOP 10 **BEER DRINKERS (PER CAPITA)**

COUNTRY / CONSUMPTION PER CAPITA (2004) LITRES/PINTS

Ireland
131.1 / 230.7

Germany
115.8 / 203.8

Czech Republic
156.9 / 276.1

Australia
109.9 / 193.4

Source: Kirin

Tea break
Tea-drinking is part in of the culture of Morocco and other Islamic countries where alcohol is prohibited.

TOP 10 **TEA DRINKERS**

	COUNTRY	CONSUMPTION PER CAPITA (2007) KG	LB	OZ	CUPS*
1	Ireland	2.48	5	8	1,091
2	UK	1.92	4	4	849
3	Turkey	1.52	3	6	669
4	Poland	1.27	2	13	559
5	Russia	1.15	2	9	506
6	Morocco	1.02	2	4	449
7	Egypt	1.01	2	4	444
8	Japan	0.75	1	10	330
9	New Zealand	0.69	1	8	304
10	Australia	0.67	1	8	295
	World average	*0.27*	*0*	*10*	*119*

* Based on 440 cups per kg/2 lb 3 oz

Source: Euromonitor International, Global Market Information Database

TOP 10 **COFFEE DRINKERS**

	COUNTRY	CONSUMPTION PER CAPITA (2007) KG	LB	OZ	CUPS*
1	Finland	8.46	18	10	1,269
2	Norway	6.66	14	11	999
3	Sweden	6.20	13	11	930
4	Denmark	4.91	10	13	737
5	Netherlands	4.85	10	11	728
6	Switzerland	4.64	10	4	696
7	Austria	4.58	10	2	687
8	Germany	4.20	9	4	630
9	Belgium	4.16	9	3	624
10	Brazil	3.57	7	14	536
	World average	*0.62*	*1*	*6*	*93*
	UK	*0.87*	*1*	*15*	*131*

* Based on 150 cups per kg (2 lb 3 oz)

Source: Euromonitor International, Global Market Information Database

TOP 10 **CARBONATED SOFT DRINK CONSUMERS**

	COUNTRY	ANNUAL CONSUMPTION PER CAPITA (2007) LITRES	PINTS
1	USA	137.61	303.38
2	Mexico	117.01	257.96
3	Norway	113.36	249.92
4	Argentina	112.72	248.50
5	Chile	103.39	227.94
6	New Zealand	83.87	184.90
7	Belgium	83.83	184.81
8	Canada	83.62	184.35
9	Australia	81.57	179.83
10	Saudi Arabia	70.24	154.85
	UK	*68.88*	*151.85*
	World average	*23.06*	*50.84*

Source: Euromonitor International, Global Market Information Database

Austria
108.3 / 190.6

UK
99.0 / 174.2

Belgium
93.0 / 163.7

Denmark
89.9 / 158.2

Finland
85 / 149.6

Luxembourg
84.4 / 148.5

Communications

TOP 10 COUNTRIES WITH THE MOST TELEPHONES

COUNTRY / TELEPHONE LINES PER 100 / TOTAL 2006

1 China 27.79
367,786,000

2 USA 28.31
172,031,900

3 Japan 43.02
55,165,000

4 Germany 65.94
54,550,000

5 India 3.64
40,770,000

6 Russia 27.94
40,100,000

7 Brazil 20.54
38,799,200

8 France 55.82
33,897,000

9 UK 56.15
33,602,500

* Top 10 —
861,750,600

10 Italy 43.12
25,049,000

World 19.34
1,267,252,000

Source: International Telecommunications Union

2007 NOW & THEN 1988

TOP 10 MOBILE PHONE COUNTRIES

2007		1988	
COUNTRY	MOBILE SUBSCRIBERS	COUNTRY	MOBILE SUBSCRIBERS
1 China	500,000,000	**1** USA	1,230,000
2 USA	233,000,000	**2** UK	290,000
3 India	166,000,000	**3** Sweden	160,000
4 Russia	150,000,000	**4** Japan	150,773
5 Japan	100,000,000	**5** Norway	120,029
6 Brazil	99,919,000	**6** Canada	120,000
7 Germany	84,300,000	**7** Denmark	77,432
8 Italy	71,500,000	**8** Finland	71,598
9 UK	69,675,000	**9** West Germany	48,747
10 Indonesia	63,803,000	**10** France	39,234
World total	*3,300,000,000*		

Source: Siemens, International Telecom Statistics

The first mobile phone network was established in Japan in 1979. Within a decade, most industrialized countries had established national systems, but increasingly, in many developing countries, mobile phones have replaced often defunct, inefficient or non-existent fixed lines, enabling their telephone systems rapidly to adopt twenty-first-century technology.

Phone line
Like-minded commuters in Japan, where the ownership of mobile phones has grown by a factor of 663 in the past 20 years.

U.S. Mail
Despite the growth of e-mail, texting and other forms of communication, the number of domestic mail items in the USA has increased in recent years.

TOP 10 COUNTRIES SENDING AND RECEIVING THE MOST LETTERS (DOMESTIC)

1 ENVELOPE REPRESENTS APPROX 5,000,000,000 ITEMS

COUNTRY	ITEMS OF MAIL HANDLED (2006)
1 USA	201,001,000,000
2 Japan	22,284,166,000
3 Germany	20,887,000,000
4 UK	20,323,000,000
5 France	17,165,000,000
6 Brazil	8,095,400,000
7 China	7,090,414,021
8 Italy	6,779,772,929
9 India	5,923,300,000
10 Spain	5,446,600,000
Top 10 total	*314,995,652,950*
World total	*429,769,752,361*

Source: Universal Postal Union

TOP 10 OLDEST PILLARBOXES IN DAILY USE IN THE UK

LOCATION	DATE
1 Union Street, St Peter Port, Guernsey	1853
2 Barnes Cross, Bishops Caundle, Dorset	1853
3 Mount Pleasant/College Road, Framlingham, Suffolk	1856
4 Double Street, Framlingham, Suffolk	1856
5 Market Place, Banbury, Oxfordshire	1856
6 Mudeford Green, Christchurch, Dorset	1856
7 Cornwallis/Victoria Road, Milford-on-Sea, Hampshire	1856
8 Eastgate, Warwick	1856
9 Westgate, Warwick	1856
10 High Street, Eton, Berkshire	1856

The Penny Post was introduced in 1840, and soon afterwards the public pressed for roadside posting boxes, which already existed in Belgium and France. In 1851, Anthony Trollope (best known as the author of *Barchester Towers* and other novels, but at this time a Post Office Surveyor's clerk) first suggested their use in St Helier, Jersey. They were set up in four locations there on 23 November 1852, but no trace of them survives.

THE 10 FIRST CITIES AND COUNTRIES TO ISSUE POSTAGE STAMPS

CITY/COUNTRY	STAMPS ISSUED
1 Great Britain	1 May 1840
2 New York City, USA	1 Feb 1842
3 Zurich, Switzerland	1 Mar 1843
4 Brazil	1 Aug 1843
5 Geneva, Switzerland	30 Sep 1843
6 Basle, Switzerland	1 Jul 1845
7 USA	1 Jul 1847
8 Mauritius	21 Sep 1847
9 Bermuda	unknown date 1848
10 France	1 Jan 1849

The first adhesive postage stamps issued in the UK were the Penny Blacks that went on sale on 1 May 1840. The first issued in the USA were designed for local delivery (as authorized by an 1836 Act of Congress) and produced by the City Despatch Post, New York City, inaugurated on 1 February 1842, and later that year incorporated into the US Post Office Department. The rest of the United States followed suit in 1847 when the Post Office Department issued its first national stamps.

Tourism

TOP 10 **TOURIST DESTINATIONS**

	COUNTRY	INTERNATIONAL VISITORS (2006)
1	France	79,100,000
2	Spain	58,500,000
3	USA	51,100,000
4	China	49,600,000
5	Italy	41,100,000
6	UK	30,700,000
7	Germany	23,600,000
8	Mexico	21,400,000
9	Austria	20,300,000
10	Russia	20,200,000
	World total	*846,000,000*

Source: World Tourism Organization

French leave
Tourists on the Seine, Paris. France has long been the world's most-visited country for international travellers.

TOP 10 **TOURISM SPENDING COUNTRIES**

	COUNTRY	INTERNATIONAL TOURISM EXPENDITURE, 2006 ($)
1	Germany	74,800,000,000
2	USA	72,000,000,000
3	UK	63,100,000,000
4	France	32,200,000,000
5	Japan	26,900,000,000
6	China	24,300,000,000
7	Italy	23,100,000,000
8	Canada	20,500,000,000
9	Russia	18,800,000,000
10	South Korea	16,200,000,000
	World total	*733,000,000,000*

Source: World Tourism Organization

TOP 10 **TOURIST EARNING COUNTRIES**

	COUNTRY	INTERNATIONAL TOURISM RECEIPTS, 2006 ($)
1	USA	85,694,000,000
2	Spain	51,115,000,000
3	France	42,910,000,000
4	Italy	38,129,000,000
5	China	33,949,000,000
6	UK	33,695,000,000
7	Germany	32,760,000,000
8	Australia	17,840,000,000
9	Turkey	16,853,000,000
10	Austria	16,658,000,000
	World total	*733,000,000,000*

Source: World Tourism Organization

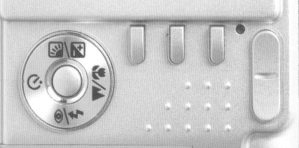

TOP 10 **COUNTRIES WITH THE BIGGEST INCREASE IN TOURISM**

COUNTRY	VISITORS INCREASE, 2005–06 (%)
1 Zimbabwe	46.7
2 Sudan	33.4
3 Syria	31.3
4 Cape Verde	22.3
5 Panama	20.1
6 Thailand	20.0
7 Cambodia	19.6
8 Lesotho	17.6
9 El Salvador	17.4
10 Bahrain	15.5

On the beach
Thailand's bustling resorts and unspoilt beaches have made the country an increasingly popular long-haul tourist destination.

TOP 10 **TOURIST DESTINATIONS OF UK RESIDENTS**

COUNTRY	VISITORS (2006)
1 Spain	14,428,000
2 France	10,854,000
3 Ireland	4,682,000
4 USA	3,986,000
5 Italy	3,380,000
6 Germany	2,698,000
7 Greece	2,436,000
8 Netherlands	2,410,000
9 Portugal	1,937,000
10 Belgium	1,815,000

Source: National Statistics, *Travel Trends 2006*

TOP 10 **TOURIST ATTRACTIONS IN THE UK**

ATTRACTION / LOCATION	VISITORS (2007)
1 Blackpool Pleasure Beach, Blackpool	5,500,000
2 British Museum, London	5,418,265
3 Tate Modern, London	4,915,000
4 The National Gallery, London	4,159,485
5 Natural History Museum, London	3,600,119
6 London Eye, London	3,500,000
7 Science Museum, London	2,714,021
8 Victoria & Albert Museum, London	2,435,300
9 Alton Towers, Staffordshire	2,400,000
10 Tower of London, London	2,064,126

Source: Association of Leading Visitor Attractions (ALVA)/London Eye

World Wide Web

TOP 10 **FASTEST SUPERCOMPUTERS**

COMPUTER / LOCATION	SPEED*
1 IBM eServer Blue Gene Solution BlueGene/L Department of Energy National Nuclear Security Administration, Lawrence Livermore National Laboratory, Livermore, California, USA	478.2
2 IBM Blue Gene/P Solution JUGENE Jülich Research Centre, Jülich, Germany	167.3
3 SGI Altix ICE 8200 New Mexico Computing Applications Center, Rio Rancho, New Mexico, USA	126.9
4 Hewlett-Packard Cluster Platform 3000 EKA Computational Research Laboratories, Tata Sons, Ltd, Pune, India	117.9
5 Hewlett-Packard Cluster Platform 3000 Swedish National Defence Radio Establishment, Lovön, Sweden	102.8
6 Cray XT3 Red Storm Sandia National Laboratories, Albuquerque, New Mexico, USA	
7 Cray XT4/XT3 Jaguar Oak Ridge National Laboratory, Tennessee, USA	101.7
8 IBM – eServer Blue Gene Solution BGW Thomas J. Watson Research Center, Yorktown Heights, New York, USA	91.29
9 Cray XT4 Franklin National Energy Rsearch Scientific Computing Center, Oakland, California, USA	85.37
10 eServer Blue Gene Solution New York Blue Brookhaven National Laboratory, Stony Brook, New York, USA	82.16

* Teraflops (trillions of calculations per second)

Source: TOP500® Supercomputer Sites, TOP500.org

TOP 10 **MOST-VISITED WEBSITES***

WEBSITE

1 Yahoo – yahoo.com
2 YouTube – youtube.com
3 Windows Live – live.com
4 Google – google.com
5 Myspace – myspace.com
6 Facebook – facebook.com
7 Microsoft Network – msn.com
8 Hi5 – hi5.com
9 Wikipedia – wikipedia.org
10 Orkut – orkut.com

* Based on Alexa traffic rankings

Founded in 1996, California-based Internet information company Alexa was acquired by Amazon.com in 1999. Its traffic rankings are widely regarded as providing the most accurate snapshot of the world's most-visited websites and indicate the variations from country to country: in the UK, for example, Google UK heads the list, with Facebook at No. 2.

Search engine
Established in 1998, Google has become a major corporation with almost 17,000 employees and annual revenue of $16.6 billion.

Brazilian surfer
The Internet has been avidly adopted as valuable educational tool in countries such as Brazil, which now ranks with many industrialized nations for its computer usage.

TOP 10 **INTERNET** COUNTRIES

	COUNTRY	% OF WORLD TOTAL	INTERNET USERS (2007)
1	USA	18.0	210,575,287
2	China	13.8	162,000,000
3	Japan	7.4	86,300,000
4	Germany	4.3	50,426,117
5	India	3.6	42,000,000
6	Brazil	3.3	39,140,000
7	UK	3.2	37,600,000
8	South Korea	2.9	34,120,000
9	France	2.8	32,925,953
10	Italy	2.7	31,481,928
	Top 10 total	*62.0*	*726,569,285*
	World total	*100.0*	*1,173,109,925*

Source: Internet World Stats

TOP 10 **BROADBAND** COUNTRIES

	COUNTRY	BROADBAND SUBSCRIBERS*
1	USA	72,914,000
2	China	66,464,000
3	Japan	28,426,000
4	Germany	19,965,000
5	UK	15,679,000
6	France	15,551,000
7	South Korea	14,710,000
8	Italy	10,861,000
9	Canada	8,659,000
10	Spain	8,035,000
	World total	*349,966,000*

* As at 1 January 2008

Source: OECD/Point Topic, *World Broadband Statistics*

TOP 10 **COMPUTER** COUNTRIES

	COUNTRY	% OF WORLD TOTAL	COMPUTERS (2006)
1	USA	25.15	240,500,000
2	Japan	7.83	77,950,000
3	China	7.44	74,110,000
4	Germany	5.47	54,480,000
5	UK	4.17	41,530,000
6	France	3.61	35,990,000
7	South Korea	3.07	30,620,000
8	Italy	2.94	29,310,000
9	Russia	2.71	26,970,000
10	Brazil	2.61	25,990,000
	Top 10 total	*65.00*	*637,450,000*
	World total	*100.00*	*996,100,000*

Source: Computer Industry Almanac Inc.

Energy

Below: City lights
The world's major cities at night graphically portray the extent of the planet's energy consumption.

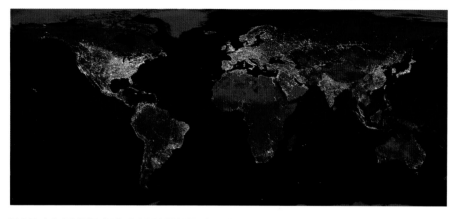

TOP 10 **ENERGY-CONSUMING COUNTRIES**

	COUNTRY	OIL	GAS	ENERGY CONSUMPTION (2006)* COAL	NUCLEAR	HEP#	TOTAL
1	USA	938.8	566.9	567.3	187.5	65.9	2,326.4
2	China†	363.0	52.2	1,198.8	12.3	94.3	1,720.6
3	Russia	128.5	388.9	112.5	35.4	39.6	704.9
4	Japan	235.0	76.1	119.1	68.6	21.5	520.3
5	India	120.3	35.8	237.7	4.0	25.4	423.2
6	Germany	123.5	78.5	82.4	37.9	6.3	328.5
7	Canada	98.8	87.0	25.0	22.3	79.3	322.3
8	France	92.8	40.6	13.1	102.1	13.9	262.6
9	UK	82.2	81.7	43.8	17.0	1.9	226.6
10	South Korea	105.3	30.8	54.8	33.7	1.2	225.8
	World total	*3,889.8*	*2,574.9*	*3,090.1*	*635.5*	*688.1*	*10,878.5*

* Millions of tonnes of oil equivalent # Hydroelectric power † Including Hong Kong

Source: *BP Statistical Review of World Energy 2007*

TOP 10 **WIND-POWER COUNTRIES**

	COUNTRY	% OF TOTAL	CAPACITY (MEGAWATTS)
1	Germany	27.8	20,622
2	Spain	15.6	11,615
3	USA	15.6	11,603
4	India	8.4	6,270
5	Denmark	4.2	3,136
6	China	3.5	2,604
7	Italy	2.9	2,123
8	UK	2.6	1,963
9	Portugal	2.3	1,716
10	France	2.1	1,567
	World total		*74,223*

Source: Global Wind 2006 Report

TOP 10 **COUNTRIES MOST RELIANT ON NUCLEAR POWER**

	COUNTRY	NUCLEAR ELECTRICITY AS % OF TOTAL (2005)
1	France	78.1
2	Lithuania	69.6
3	Slovakia	56.1
4	Belgium	55.6
5	Ukraine	48.5
6	Sweden	44.9
7	South Korea	44.7
8	Bulgaria	44.1
9	Armenia	42.7
10	Slovenia	42.4
	UK	*19.9*

Source: International Atomic Energy Agency

TOP 10 **RENEWABLE POWER-CONSUMING COUNTRIES***

	COUNTRY	CONSUMPTION KW/HR (2004)
1	USA	97,090,000,000
2	Germany	39,410,000,000
3	Spain	21,170,000,000
4	Brazil	17,200,000,000
5	Japan	15,010,000,000
6	Italy	12,800,000,000
7	Finland	10,230,000,000
8	Canada	10,020,000,000
9	Philippines	9,770,000,000
10	Denmark	9,720,000,000
	UK	*8,100,000,000*
	World total	*334,270,000,000*

* Includes geothermal, solar, wind, wood and waste electric power

Source: Energy Information Administration

TOP 10 **OIL-CONSUMING COUNTRIES**

	COUNTRY	2006	1986
		CONSUMPTION (TONNES)	
1	USA	938,800,000	749,300,000
2	China*	363,000,000	100,000,000
3	Japan	235,000,000	208,500,000
4	Russia	128,500,000	247,600,000
5	Germany	123,500,000	133,300,000
6	India	120,300,000	45,500,000
7	South Korea	105,300,000	27,400,0000
8	Canada	98,800,000	71,000,000
9	France	92,800,000	86,000,000
10	Saudi Arabia	92,600,000	46,300,000
	World total	*3,889,800,000*	*2,892,500,000*
	UK	*82,200,000*	*77,400,000*

* Including Hong Kong

Source: *BP Statistical Review of World Energy 2007*

In the past 20 years, such factors as population expansion, economic growth, increased industrial production and especially transport – the number of vehicles on the world's roads almost doubled in this period – have resulted in a 34 per cent increase in global oil consumption. This has been most marked in China and South Korea, which contrast sharply with a decline in Russia as its once-mighty industrial base has shrunk. It has been forecast that the inexorable rise in vehicle use in China and India will see these countries' demand for oil for transport alone increase by 75 per cent by 2025. It is predicted that worldwide demand for oil will increase from 86 million barrels a day to 118 million by 2030.

TOP 10 **NATURAL GAS-PRODUCING COUNTRIES**

	COUNTRY	PRODUCTION 2006 (TONNES OF OIL EQUIVALENT)
1	Russia	550,900,000
2	USA	479,300,000
3	Canada	168,300,000
4	Iran	94,500,000
5	Norway	78,900,000
6	Algeria	76,000,000
7	UK	72,000,000
8	Indonesia	66,600,000
9	Saudi Arabia	66,300,000
10	Turkmenistan	56,000,000
	World total	*2,586,400,000*

Source: *BP Statistical Review of World Energy 2007*

Above: Water power
Still under construction, the Three Gorges Dam on the Yangtze River, China, controls flooding and generates 22,500 megawatts of electricity, making it the world's greatest hydroelectric plant.

Below: Wind of change
Globally, the number of wind turbines has increased fourfold since the beginning of the twenty-first century, but still accounts for only one per cent of all electricity.

Environment

TOP 10 CARBON DIOXIDE-EMITTING COUNTRIES

	COUNTRY	CO$_2$ EMISSIONS (2004) (TONNES OF CO$_2$)
1	USA	1,650,020,000
2	China	1,366,554,000
3	Russia	415,951,000
4	India	366,301,000
5	Japan	343,117,000
6	Germany	220,596,000
7	Canada	174,401,000
8	UK	160,179,000
9	South Korea	127,007,000
10	Italy	122,726,000
	Top 10 total	*4,946,852,000*
	World total	*7,497,252,000*

Carbon emissions

CO$_2$ and other contaminants from steel production in Benxi, China, make it one of the country's most polluted cities. Such problems were highlighted in 2008 as Olympic athletes considered the health hazards posed.

TOP 10 COMPONENTS OF HOUSEHOLD WASTE IN THE UK*

	MATERIAL	% BY WEIGHT
1	Food waste	16.8
2	Garden waste	13.8
3	Misc. non-combustible waste	15.3
4	Non-packaging paper	10.7
5	Glass packaging	8.8
6	Misc. combustible waste	6.4
7	Cardboard and paper packaging	6.1
8	Dense plastic packaging	4.1
9	Textiles	3.8
10	Ferrous packaging (cans, etc.)	3.2

Source: *The Open University Household Waste Study*, 2006

According to this survey, each household in the UK generated an average of 22.4 kg (49.4 lb) of waste per week, of which only 0.6 kg (1.3 lb), or 2.7 per cent, was reused or recycled.

TOP 10 RUBBISH PRODUCERS

COUNTRY* / DOMESTIC WASTE PER CAPITA 2003# KG/LB

Ireland
760 / 1,676

USA
740 / 1,631

Iceland
730 / 1,609

Norway
700 / 1,543

Australia
690 / 1,521

Denmark
670 / 1,477

Switzerland
660 / 1,455

Luxembourg
650 / 1,433

Spain
650 / 1,433

Germany
640 / 1,411

UK 610 / 1,345

* OECD countries only
\# Or latest year for which data available

Source: Organization for Economic Co-operation and Development

Urban slum
Along with certain other African countries, Angola scores poorly on the EPI. Extensive slum areas known locally as musseques, with high levels of pollution, blight its capital, Luanda.

TOP 10 **PAPER-RECYCLING COUNTRIES**

COUNTRY	PRODUCTION 2006 (TONNES)
1 USA	45,231,926
2 Japan	22,315,408
3 China	16,894,000
4 Germany	14,413,000
5 UK	7,758,000
6 South Korea	7,086,000
7 France	5,953,000
8 Italy	5,488,224
9 Spain	4,323,000
10 Brazil	3,497,000
Top 10 total	*132,959,558*
World total	*164,329,031*

Source: Food and Agrigulture Organization of the United Nations

TOP 10 **ENVIRONMENTAL PERFORMANCE INDEX COUNTRIES**

	COUNTRY	EPI SCORE*
1	Switzerland	95.5
2	= Norway	93.1
	= Sweden	93.1
4	Finland	91.4
5	Costa Rica	90.5
6	Austria	89.4
7	New Zealand	88.9
8	Latvia	88.8
9	Colombia	88.3
10	France	87.8
	UK	*86.3*

* Environmental Performance Index score out of 100

Source: Environmental Performance Index 2008

THE 10 **WORST ENVIRONMENTAL PERFORMANCE INDEX COUNTRIES**

	COUNTRY	EPI SCORE*
1	Niger	39.1
2	Angola	39.5
3	Sierra Leone	40.0
4	Mauritania	44.2
5	= Burkina Faso	44.3
	= Mali	44.3
7	Chad	45.9
8	Dem. Rep. of Congo	47.3
9	= Guinea-Bissau	49.7
	= Yemen	49.7

* Environmental Performance Index score out of 100

Source: Environmental Performance Index

The Environmental Performance Index is a measure of environmental health and ecosystem vitality based on an assessment of 16 indicators in each country. These include air quality, water resources, biodiversity and habitat, productive natural resources and sustainable energy.

Hazards

Danger zone
Factory explosion in Gresik, Indonesia. The country is among the world's worst for the number and rate of work fatalities.

THE 10 **ITEMS MOST FREQUENTLY INVOLVED IN ACCIDENTS IN THE UK**

ARTICLE	ESTIMATED ANNUAL ACCIDENTS
1 Outdoor surface (grass, road, ice, etc.)	1,291,295
2 Clothing/footwear	894,251
3 Person (excl. injured person)	657,374
4 Sports equipment	575,845
5 Construction of a building feature	437,163
6 Transport	345,671
7 Animal/insect	137,678
8 Natural feature of landscape/garden	113,160
9 Food/drink	106,600
10 Built feature in garden/street	102,808

* National estimates based on actual Leisure Accident Surveillance System figures for sample population

These general categories provide fewer surprises than the often improbable sub-categories: among clothing and personal items, for example, 283 people managed to injure themselves with their spectacles, 201 with their trousers, 22 with a hat and 15 with false teeth, while the animals involved in injuries necessitating hospital visits included fish (12), pigs (11) and rabbits and hamsters (9).

The Great Molasses Flood
One of the strangest industrial accidents was that in Boston, USA, on 15 January 1919, when a gigantic tank containing some 8.7 million litres (2.3 million US gallons) of molasses burst and a 12-m (40-ft) wave surged through the streets killing 21 and injuring 150, while horses were drowned, a train derailed and buildings destroyed.

THE 10 **COUNTRIES WITH THE MOST WORK FATALITIES**

COUNTRY	RATE (FATALITIES PER 100,000)	TOTAL FATALITIES
1 China	10.5	73,615
2 India	11.5	48,176
3 Indonesia	20.9	18,220
4 Bangladesh	26.4	14,403
5 Brazil	16.6	11,304
6 Vietnam	27.0	9,988
7 Nigeria	20.1	9,631
8 Thailand	23.3	7,490
9 Russia	11.0	6,974
10 USA	5.2	6,821
Top 10 total		*206,622*
UK	*0.8*	*225*
World total		*345,719*

Source: International Labour Organization, *Global Estimates of Occupational Accidents*, 2005

THE 10 **MOST COMMON ACCIDENTS IN UK HOMES**

ACCIDENT	ESTIMATED ANNUAL ACCIDENTS
1 Tripping over	417,893
2 Falls on or from stairs or steps	306,168
3 Contact with static object	270,600
4 Cut or tear from sharp object	234,643
5 Struck by moving object	160,351
6 Foreign body	128,023
7 Acute overexertion	90,118
8 Thermal effect	84,460
9 Pinched or crushed by blunt object	79,171
10 Bite/sting	72,673

* National estimates based on actual Home Accident Surveillance System figures for sample population

Guadalajara gas blast
The catastrophic 1992 explosion resulted in an official death toll of 206,
but was believed to be as high as 230, with almost 500 injured.

THE 10 **WORST EXPLOSIONS***

LOCATION / DATE / INCIDENT	ESTIMATED NO. KILLED
1 Rhodes, Greece, 3 Apr 1856 Lightning strike of gunpowder store	4,000
2 Breschia, Italy, 18 Aug 1769 Church of San Nazaire caught fire after being struck by lightning, gunpowder store exploded	>3,000
3 Salang Tunnel, Afghanistan, 3 Nov 1982 Petrol tanker collision	>2,000
4 Lanchow, China, 26 Oct 1935 Arsenal	2,000
5 Halifax, Nova Scotia, 6 Dec 1917 Ammunition ship *Mont Blanc*	1,963
6 Hamont Station, Belgium, 3 Aug 1918 Ammunition trains	1,750
7 Memphis, USA, 27 Apr 1865 *Sultana* paddlesteamer boiler explosion	1,547
8 =Archangel, Russia, 20 Feb 1917 Munitions ship	1,500
=Smederovo, Yugoslavia, 9 Jun 1941 Ammunition dump	1,500
10 Bombay, India, 14 Apr 1944 Ammunition ship *Fort Stikine*	1,376

* Excluding mining disasters, terrorist and military bombs and natural
explosions, such as volcanoes

THE 10 **WORST INDUSTRIAL DISASTERS***

LOCATION / DATE / INCIDENT	NO. KILLED
1 Bhopal, India, 3 Dec 1984 Methylisocyante gas escape at Union Carbide plant	3,849
2 Jesse, Nigeria, 17 Oct 1998 Oil pipeline explosion	>700
3 Oppau, Germany, 21 Sep 1921 Bradishe Aniline chemical plant explosion	561
4 San Juanico, Mexico, 19 Nov 1984 Explosion at a PEMEX liquefied petroleum gas plant	540
5 Cubatão, Brazil, 25 Feb 1984 Oil pipeline explosion	508
6 Durunkah, Egypt, 2 Nov 1994 Fuel storage depot fire	>500
7 Mexico City, Mexico, 19 Nov 1984 Butane storage explosion	>400
8 Adeje, Nigeria, 10 Jul 2000 Oil pipeline explosion	>250
9 Guadalajara, Mexico, 22 Apr 1992 Explosions caused by a gas leak into sewers	230
10 Oakdale, Pennsylvania, 18 May 1918 TNT explosion at Aetna Chemical Company	210

* Including industrial sites, factories, fuel depots and pipelines; excluding
military, munitions, bombs, mining, marine and other transport disasters,
dam failures and mass poisonings

ON THE MOVE

The Need for Speed

THE 10 **LATEST HOLDERS OF THE WATER-SPEED RECORD**

DRIVER* / BOAT / LOCATION / DATE	SPEED KM/H	MPH
1 Dave Villwock, Miss Budweiser, Lake Oroville, California, USA 13 Mar 2004	354.849	220.493
2 Russ Wicks, Miss Freei, Lake Washington, Washington, USA 15 Jun 2000	330.711	205.494
3 Roy Duby, Miss US1, Lake Guntersville, Alabama, USA 17 Apr 1962	322.543	200.419
4 Bill Muncey, Miss Thriftaway, Lake Washington, 16 Feb 1960	308.996	192.001
5 Jack Regas, Hawaii Kai III, Lake Washington, 30 Nov 1957	301.956	187.627
6 Art Asbury (Canada), Miss Supertest II, Lake Ontario, Canada, 1 Nov 1957	296.988	184.540
7 Stanley Sayres, Slo-Mo-Shun IV, Lake Washington, 7 Jul 1952	287.263	178.497
8 Stanley Sayres, Slo-Mo-Shun IV, Lake Washington, 26 Jun 1950	258.015	160.323
9 Malcolm Campbell (UK), Bluebird K4, Coniston Water, UK, 19 Aug 1939	228.108	141.740
10 Malcolm Campbell, Bluebird K3, Hallwiler See, Switzerland, 17 Aug 1938	210.679	130.910

* USA unless otherwise stated

THE 10 **LATEST HOLDERS OF THE LAND-SPEED RECORD**

DRIVER (COUNTRY) / CAR	DATE	SPEED KM/H	MPH
1 Andy Green (UK), ThrustSSC*	15 Oct 1997	1,227.99	763.04
2 Richard Noble (UK), Thrust2*	4 Oct 1983	1,013.47	633.47
3 Gary Gabelich (USA), The Blue Flame	23 Oct 1970	995.85	622.41
4 Craig Breedlove (USA), Spirit of America – Sonic 1	15 Nov 1965	960.96	600.60
5 Art Arfons (USA), Green Monster	7 Nov 1965	922.48	576.55
6 Craig Breedlove (USA), Spirit of America – Sonic 1	2 Nov 1965	888.76	555.48
7 Art Arfons (USA), Green Monster	27 Oct 1964	858.73	536.71
8 Craig Breedlove (USA), Spirit of America	15 Oct 1964	842.04	526.28
9 Craig Breedlove (USA), Spirit of America	13 Oct 1964	749.95	468.72
10 Art Arfons (USA), Green Monster	5 Oct 1964	694.43	434.02

* Location Black Rock Desert, Nevada, USA; all other speeds were achieved at Bonneville Salt Flats, Utah, USA

Land-Speed Pioneers

The first official Land Speed Record of 62.78 km/h (39.24 mph) was set on 18 December 1898 by Comte Gaston de Chasseloup-Laubat in an electric car. In 1902 a steam-driven car, driven by Leon Serpollet, broke the record. In the same year William Vanderbilt became the first to take the record in a petrol-engined vehicle.

Fastest man on wheels
British jet pilot Wing Commander Andy Green was the first to break the sound barrier on land, setting the latest Land-Speed Record.

Higher and faster
The SR-71 Blackbird was both the fastest and highest-flying aircraft ever, reaching over 25.9 km (16 miles).

THE 10 **LATEST AIR-SPEED RECORDS HELD BY JETS***

	PILOT	COUNTRY	LOCATION	AIRCRAFT	SPEED KM/H	MPH	DATE
1	Eldon W. Joersz/ George T. Morgan Jr	USA	Beale AFB, California, USA	Lockheed SR-71A	3,529.560	2,193.167	28 Jul 1976
2	Adolphus Bledsoe/ John T. Fuller	USA	Beale AFB, USA	Lockheed SR-71A	3,367.221	2,092.294	27 Jul 1976
3	Robert L. Stephens/ Daniel Andre	USA	Edwards AFB, California, USA	Lockheed YF-12A	3,331.507	2,070.102	1 May 1965
4	Georgi Mossolov	USSR USSR	Podmoskownoe, Mikoyan E-166		2,681.000	1,665.896	7 Jul 1962
5	Robert B. Robinson	USA	Edwards AFB, USA	McDonnell F4H-1F Phantom II	2,585.425	1,606.509	22 Nov 1961
6	Joseph W. Rogers	USA	Edwards AFB, USA	Convair F-106A Delta Dart	2,455.736	1,525.924	15 Dec 1959
7	Georgi Mossolov	USSR	Jukowski-Petrowskol, USSR	Mikoyan E-66	2,388.000	1,483.834	31 Oct 1959
8	Walter W. Irwin	USA	Edwards AFB, USA	Lockheed YF-104A Starfighter	2,259.538	1,404.012	16 May 1958
9	Adrian E. Drew	USA	Edwards AFB, USA	McDonnell F-101A Voodoo	1,943.500	1,207.635	12 Dec 1957
10	Peter Twiss	UK	Chichester, UK	Fairey Delta Two	1,822.000	1,132.138	10 Mar 1956

* Ground-launched only, hence excluding X-15 records

On the Road

TOP 10 **CAR-PRODUCING COUNTRIES**

COUNTRY	CAR PRODUCTION (2007)
1 Japan	9,944,637
2 China	6,381,116
3 Germany	5,709,139
4 USA	3,924,268
5 South Korea	3,723,482
6 France	2,554,000
7 Brazil	2,388,402
8 Spain	2,195,780
9 India	1,707,839
10 UK	1,534,567

Source: OICA Statistics Committee

1 steering wheel = approx. 1,000,000

Driving force

The Volkswagen group, which also owns marques from Bentley to Skoda, is a major component of the internationally important German car industry.

TOP 10 **MOTOR VEHICLE-OWNING COUNTRIES**

COUNTRY	CARS	COMMERCIAL VEHICLES	TOTAL (2005)
1 USA	132,908,828	104,788,269	237,697,097
2 Japan	57,090,789	16,733,871	73,824,660
3 Germany	46,090,303	3,133,197	49,223,500
4 Italy	34,667,485	4,422,269	39,089,754
5 France	29,990,000	6,139,000	36,039,000
6 UK	30,651,700	3,942,700	34,594,400
7 Russia	25,285,000	5,705,000	30,990,000
8 China	8,900,000	21,750,000	30,650,000
9 Spain	20,250,377	4,907,867	25,158,244
10 Brazil	18,370,000	4,653,000	23,023,000
World total	*617,020,169*	*245,108,745*	*862,128,914*

Source: *Ward's Motor Vehicle Facts & Figures 2007*

1 car key = approx. 10,000,000

TOP 10 **CAR MANUFACTURERS**

COMPANY / COUNTRY	PASSENGER CAR PRODUCTION (2006)
1 Toyota (Japan)	6,800,228
2 General Motors (USA)	5,708,038
3 Volkswagen group (Germany)	5,429,896
4 Ford (USA)	3,800,633
5 Honda (Japan)	3,549,787
6 PSA Peugeot Citroën (France)	2,961,437
7 Nissan (Japan)	2,512,519
8 Hyundai (South Korea)	2,231,313
9 Renault-Dacia-Samsung (France)	2,085,837
10 Suzuki (Japan)	2,004,310
World total (including manufacturers outside Top 10)	51,953,234

Source: OICA Statistics Committee

THE 10 **COUNTRIES WITH MOST PEOPLE PER CAR**

COUNTRY	CARS	PEOPLE PER CAR (2005)
1 Myanmar	7,750	6,012.4
2 Bangladesh	35,950	4,014.5
3 Central African Republic	2,000	2,119.0
4 Tanzania	21,450	1,714.0
5 Mali	8,250	1,379.3
6 Malawi	11,650	1,113.7
7 Sudan	37,800	1,063.1
8 Afghanistan	28,600	1,046.5
9 Ethiopia	73,500	993.9
10 Côte d'Ivoire	21,000	823.7
UK	*30,651,700*	*2.0*
World average	*617,020,169*	*10.0*

Source: *Ward's Motor Vehicle Facts & Figures 2007*

As the total number of vehicles on the world's roads has grown out of proportion to population increases, the average ratio of people to cars has fallen from 23 in 1960 to 10 per car. Despite a recent surge in ownership in China, there are still 146.8 people for every car.

TOP 10 **COUNTRIES WITH THE LONGEST ROAD NETWORKS**

COUNTRY / TOTAL ROAD NETWORK KM/MILES

1 USA 6,430,366 / 3,995,644

2 India 3,383,344 / 2,102,312

3 China 1,870,661 / 1,162,375

4 Brazil 1,751,868 / 1,088,560

5 Japan 1,183,000 / 735,082

6 Canada 1,042,300 / 647,655

7 France 956,303 / 594,219

8 Russia 871,000 / 541,214

9 Australia 810,641 / 503,709

10 Spain 666,292 / 414,015

Top 10 18,965,775 / 11,784,785
UK 388,008 / 241,097
World 32,345,165 / 20,098,351

Source: CIA,
The World Factbook 2008

The CIA's assessment of road lengths includes both paved (mostly tarmac-surfaced) and unpaved highways (gravel and earth-surfaced). In many developing countries the proportion of unpaved is greater than paved. The world total is equivalent to over 800 times the circumference of the Earth at the Equator. It has been estimated that Great Britain's roads occupy 1.4 per cent of the country's total land area.

On Track

THE 10 FIRST UNDERGROUND RAILWAY SYSTEMS

CITY / FIRST LINE ESTABLISHED

1 London, UK
10 Jan 1863

2 Budapest, Hungary
2 May 1896

3 Glasgow, UK
14 Dec 1896

4 Boston, USA
1 Sep 1897

5 Paris, France
19 Jul 1900

6 Berlin, Germany
15 Feb 1902

7 New York, USA
27 Oct 1904

8 Philadelphia, USA
4 Mar 1907

9 Hamburg, Germany
15 Feb 1912

10 Buenos Aires, Argentina
1 Dec 1913

TOP 10 BUSIEST UNDERGROUND RAILWAY NETWORKS

CITY / PASSENGERS PER ANNUM (2006)

1 Tokyo, Japan
2,646,000,000

2 Moscow, Russia
2,475,000,000

3 New York, USA
1,850,000,000

4 Seoul, South Korea
1,654,000,000

5 Mexico City, Mexico
1,417,000,000

6 Paris, France
1,409,000,000

7 London, UK
1,094,000,000

8 Osaka, Japan
912,000,000

9 Hong Kong, China
867,000,000

10 São Paulo, Brazil
774,000,000

TOP 10 LONGEST UNDERGROUND RAILWAY NETWORKS

CITY / OPENED / STATIONS / TOTAL TRACK LENGTH KM/MILES

1 London, UK
(1863) 268
408 / 254

2 New York, USA
(1904) 468
368 / 229

3 Moscow, Russia
(1935) 176
293 / 182

4 Tokyo, Japan
(1927) 282
292 / 182

5 Seoul, South Korea
(1974) 266
287 / 179

6 Madrid, Spain
(1919) 316
282 / 175

7 Paris, France
(1900) 298
213 / 132

8 Mexico City, Mexico
(1969) 175
177 / 110

9 Hong Kong, China
(1979) 82
175 / 109

10 Chicago, USA
(1943) 144
173 / 107

Mumbai station

The Indian railway system is one of the world's most extensive and busiest, transporting over 15 million passengers a day.

TOP 10 **BUSIEST RAIL NETWORKS**

	LOCATION	PASSENGER/ KM PER ANNUM*
1	China	606,200,000,000
2	India	575,700,000,000
3	Japan	245,960,000,000
4	Russia	170,900,000,000
5	France	79,400,000,000
6	Germany	74,300,000,000
7	Ukraine	52,660,000,000
8	UK	46,760,000,000
9	Italy	46,440,000,000
10	Egypt	40,840,000,000

* Number of passengers multiplied by distance carried in 2006 or latest year for which figures available; totals include national and local services where applicable

Source: UIC Railisa Database

THE 10 **FIRST COUNTRIES WITH RAILWAYS**

	COUNTRY	FIRST RAILWAY ESTABLISHED
1	UK	27 Sep 1825
2	France	7 Nov 1829
3	USA	24 May 1830
4	Ireland	17 Dec 1834
5	Belgium	5 May 1835
6	Germany	7 Dec 1835
7	Canada	21 Jul 1836
8	Russia	30 Oct 1837
9	Austria	6 Jan 1838
10	Netherlands	24 Sep 1839

Although there were earlier horse-drawn railways, the Stockton & Darlington Railway inaugurated the world's first steam service. In their early years, some of those in the 10 first offered only limited services, often over short distances, but their opening dates mark the generally accepted beginning of each country's steam railway system.

TOP 10 **LONGEST RAIL NETWORKS**

	LOCATION	TOTAL RAIL LENGTH KM	MILES
1	USA	226,656	141,367
2	Russia	87,157	54,156
3	China	75,438	47,051
4	India	63,221	39,431
5	Germany	48,215	30,072
6	Canada	48,068	29,980
7	Australia	38,550	24,044
8	Argentina	31,902	19,897
9	France	29,370	18,318
10	Brazil	29,295	18,271
	UK	*16,567*	*10,333*
	World	*1,370,782*	*854,971*

Source: CIA, *The World Factbook 2008*

The total length of the world rail networks is equivalent to 34 times round the Earth at the Equator. Several countries have networks of under 100 km (62 miles), among them Nicaragua – 6 km (3.7 miles), and Paraguay – 36 km (22.4 miles).

Water

TOP 10 **LARGEST OIL TANKERS**

	TANKER	YEAR BUILT	OPERATOR'S COUNTRY	DEADWEIGHT TONNAGE*
1	=TI# Africa	2002	Belgium	441,893
	=TI Asia	2002	USA	441,893
	=TI Europe	2002	Belgium	441,893
4	TI Oceania	2003	USA	441,585
5	Marine Pacific	1979	USA	404,536
6	Enterprise	1981	Hong Kong	360,700
7	Nisa	1983	Saudi Arabia	322,912
8	Settebello	1983	Brazil	322,446
9	Aries Voyager	2006	Greece	320,870
10	Andromeda Voyager	2005	Greece	320,472

* Total weight of vessel, including cargo, crew, passengers and supplies
\# Tankers International

TOP 10 **LARGEST WOODEN SHIPS***

	SHIP / COUNTRY	LAUNCHED	LENGTH M	LENGTH FT
1	Eureka, USA	1890	91.3	299.5
2	Al Hashemi II, Kuwait	2000	83.8	274.8
3	Zheng He, China	2008	71.1	233.3
4	Jylland, Denmark	1860	71.0	233.0
5	Vasa, Sweden	1627#	69.0	226.3
6	SV Tenacious, UK	2000	65.0	213.3
7	Cutty Sark, UK	1869	64.8	212.5
8	Neptune, Italy	1985	61.9	203.0
9	Zinat Al Bihaar, Oman	1988	61.0	200.0
10	HMS Victory, UK	1765	56.7	186.0

* Surviving vessels only
\# Sunk, recovered 1959

TOP 10 **LARGEST MOTOR YACHTS**

	YACHT	OWNER	BUILT/ REFITTED	LENGTH M	LENGTH FT	LENGTH IN
1	Dubai	Sheikh Mohammed, Dubai	2006	160.0	524	10
2	Sunflower	–	2007	155.0	508	6
3	Eclipse	Roman Abramovich, Russia/UK	2008	147.1	482	6
4	Prince Abdulaziz	King Fahd, Saudi Arabia	1984	147.0	482	3
5	Al Salamah	Prince Sultan bin Abdul Aziz, Saudi Arabia	1999	139.8	456	10
6	Rising Sun	Larry Ellison, USA	2004	138.4	452	8
7	Octopus	Paul Allen, USA	2003	126.1	414	0
8	Savarona	Kahraman Sadikoglu, Turkey (charter)	1931/1992	124.3	408	0
9	Alexander	Latsis family, Greece	1976/1986	122.0	400	
10	Turama	Latsis family, Greece	1990/2004	116.9	381	9

Sheikh's Star

Formerly the *Golden Star*, Sheikh Mohammed bin Rashid Al Maktoum of Dubai's German-built motor yacht *Dubai* features a helicopter pad, submarine, garage, gym, squash court, cinema, theatre and pool. It is 18 m (58 ft) longer than a British Royal Navy Type 42 destroyer and has had an island with a berth for it specially built in Dubai.

Berth in Venice
Longer than a football pitch, Microsoft billionaire Paul Allen's motor yacht Octopus *is one of the world's largest private vessels.*

TOP 10 **LARGEST PASSENGER SHIPS**

2008

	SHIP	ENTERED SERVICE	COUNTRY BUILT	PASSENGER CAPACITY	GROSS TONNAGE
1	Independence of the Seas	2008	Finland	4,370	160,000
2	= Liberty of the Seas	2007	Finland	4,370	154,407
	= Freedom of the Seas	2006	Finland	4,370	154,407
4	Queen Mary 2	2004	France	3,090	148,528
5	= Mariner of the Seas	2004	Finland	3,840	138,279
	= Navigator of the Seas	2003	Finland	3,840	138,279
7	Explorer of the Seas	2000	Finland	3,840	137,308
8	= Adventure of the Seas	2001	Finland	3,838	137,276
	= Voyager of the Seas	1999	Finland	3,838	137,276
10	Crown Princess	2006	Italy	3,800	117,477

1988

	SHIP*	ENTERED SERVICE	COUNTRY BUILT	PASSENGER CAPACITY	GROSS TONNAGE#
1	Sovereign of the Seas	1988	France	2,852	73,192
2	Norway†	1961	France	1,944	70,202
3	Queen Elizabeth II	1969	Scotland	1,892	66,450
4	= Celebration	1987	Sweden	1,486	47,262
	= Jubilee	1986	Sweden	1,950	47,262
6	Holiday	1985	Denmark	_	46,052
7	Canberra	1961	N. Ireland	1,737	44,807
8	Royal Princess	1984	Finland	1,200	44,348
9	Seaward	1988	Finland	1,480	42,276
10	Westerdam	1986	W. Germany	1,494	42,092

* Name in 1988 – some later changed
\# In 1988 – some were smaller at launch but increased during refitting
† Formerly France

Ocean giant
Cruise line Royal Caribbean's Freedom of the Seas *accommodates 4,370 passengers and 1,360 crew on its 15 decks.*

Top Flight

THE 10 **FIRST COUNTRIES TO HAVE BALLOON FLIGHTS***

1 France   21 Nov 1783
The Montgolfier brothers, Joseph and Etienne, tested their
first unmanned hot-air balloon in the French town of Annonay
on 5 June 1783. On 21 November 1783, the first manned flight
of a Montgolfier balloon covered a distance of about 9 km
(5.5 miles) in 23 minutes, landing safely near Gentilly.

2 Italy   25 Feb 1784
The Chevalier Paolo Andreani and the brothers Augustino
and Carlo Giuseppe Gerli (the builders of the balloon) made
the first flight outside France, at Moncucco near Milan, Italy.

3 Austria   6 Jul 1784
Johann Georg Stuwer made the first Austrian flight from
the Prater, Vienna.

4 Scotland   27 Aug 1784
James Tytler (known as 'Balloon Tytler'), a doctor and
newspaper editor, took off from Comely Gardens, Edinburgh,
in a hot-air balloon, achieving an altitude of 107 m (350 ft)
in a 0.8-km (0.5-mile) hop in a home-made balloon.

5 England   15 Sep 1784
Watched by a crowd of 200,000, Italian balloonist
Vincenzo Lunardi ascended from the Artillery
Company Ground, Moorfields, London, flying
to Standon near Ware in Hertfordshire.
On 4 October 1784 James Sadler flew a
Montgolfier balloon at Oxford, thereby
becoming the first English-born pilot.

6 Ireland   19 Jan 1785
Although there are earlier claims, it is likely that Richard
Crosbie's hydrogen balloon flight from Ranelagh Gardens,
Dublin, was the first in Ireland.

7 Holland   11 Jul 1785
French balloon pioneer Jean-Pierre Blanchard, took off from
The Hague in a hydrogen balloon.

8 Germany   3 Oct 1785
Blanchard made the first flight in Germany from Frankfurt.

9 Belgium   20 Oct 1785
Blanchard flew his hydrogen balloon from Ghent.

10 Switzerland   5 May 1788
Blanchard flew from Basel. As well as flights from other
European cities, Blanchard made the first in the USA,
from Philadelphia, on 9 January 1793, watched by George
Washington – as well as future presidents John Adams,
Thomas Jefferson and James Monroe.

* Several of the balloonists listed also made subsequent flights, but in each
instance only their first flights are included

Up and Away
On 21 November 1783 François Laurent,
Marquis d'Arlandes and Jean-François Pilâtre
de Rozier took off from the Bois de Boulogne,
Paris, in a Montgolfier hot-air balloon, covering
a distance of about 9 km (5.5 miles).

TOP 10 **BUSIEST AIRPORTS**

2007

	AIRPORT	LOCATION	PASSENGERS
1	Atlanta Hartsfield International	Atlanta, USA	84,846,639
2	Chicago O'Hare	Chicago, USA	77,028,134
3	London Heathrow	London, UK	67,530,197
4	Tokyo International	Tokyo, Japan	65,810,672
5	Los Angeles, International	Los Angeles, USA	61,041,066
6	DFW International	Dallas/Fort Worth, USA	60,226,138
7	Charles De Gaulle	Paris, France	56,849,567
8	Frankfurt	Frankfurt, Germany	52,810,683
9	Beijing	Beijing, China	48,654,770
10	Denver International	Denver, USA	47,325,016

1987

	AIRPORT	LOCATION	PASSENGERS
1	Chicago O'Hare	Chicago, USA	53,338,056
2	Atlanta Hartsfield International	Atlanta, USA	45,191,480
3	Los Angeles, International	Los Angeles, USA	41,417,867
4	DFW International	Dallas/Fort Worth, USA	39,945,326
5	London Heathrow	London, UK	34,700,000
6	Denver International	Denver, USA	34,685,944
7	Newark	New Jersey, USA	29,433,046
8	San Francisco	San Francisco, USA	28,607,363
9	JFK	New York, USA	27,223,733
10	Tokyo International	Tokyo, Japan	27,217,761

Source: Airports Council International

TOP 10 **AIRLINES WITH THE MOST PASSENGERS**

AIRLINE / COUNTRY	PASSENGERS CARRIED (2006)*
1 American Airlines, USA	99,835,000
2 Southwest Airlines, USA	96,277,000
3 Delta Air Lines, USA	73,584,000
4 United Airlines, USA	69,265,000
5 Northwest Airlines, USA	55,925,000
6 Lufthansa, Germany	51,213,000
7 Air France, France	49,411,000
8 All Nippon Airways, Japan	49,226,000
9 Japan Airlines International, Japan	48,911,000
10 China Southern Airlines, China	48,512,000

* Total of international and domestic

Source: International Air Transport Association

Aircrash!

THE 10 WORST AIR COLLISIONS IN THE WORLD

1 Charkhi Dadrio, India, 12 Nov 1996   349
Soon after taking off from New Delhi's India Gandhi International Airport, a Saudi Arabian Airlines Boeing 747 collided with a Kazakh Airlines Ilyushin IL76 cargo aircraft on its descent and exploded, killing all 312 on the Boeing and all 37 on the Ilyushin in the world's worst mid-air crash.

2 Near Dneprodzerzhinsk, Ukraine, USSR, 11 Aug 1979   178
Two Soviet Tupolev-134 Aeroflot airliners collided in mid-air.

3 Vrbovec, Croatia, 10 Sep 1976   177
A British Airways Trident and a Yugoslav DC-9 collided, killing all 176 on board and a woman on the ground.

4 Morioko, Japan, 30 Jul 1971   162
An air collision occurred between an All Nippon Boeing 727 and Japanese Air Force F-86F. The student pilot and instructor in the fighter survived, but both were found guilty of negligence and imprisoned.

5 Near Souq as-Sabt, Libya, 22 Dec 1992   157
A Libyan Boeing 747 and a Libyan air force MiG-23 fighter collided. The fighter crew reportedly ejected to safety, but all passengers and crew on the airliner were killed.

6 San Diego, California, USA, 25 Sep 1978   144
A Pacific Southwest Boeing 727 collided in the air with a Cessna 172 light aircraft with a student pilot, killing 135 in the airliner, two in the Cessna and seven on the ground.

7 New York, USA, 16 Dec 1960   135
A United Airlines DC-8 with 77 passengers and a crew of seven, and a TWA Super Constellation with 39 passengers and five crew, collided in a snowstorm. The DC-8 crashed in Brooklyn, killing six on the ground; the Super Constellation crashed in Staten Island harbour, killing all passengers and crew on board.

8 Tehran, Iran, 8 Feb 1993   132
As it took off, a passenger aircraft carrying pilgrims was struck by a military aircraft, causing it to crash, killing all on board.

9 Grand Canyon, Arizona, USA, 30 Jun 1956   128
A United Airlines DC-7 and a TWA Super Constellation collided in the air, killing all on board both airliners in the worst civil aviation disaster to that date, and the first ever commercial aviation accident with more than 100 fatalities.

10 Ankara, Turkey, 1 Feb 1963   104
A Middle East Airlines Viscount 754 and a Turkish Air Force C-47 collided and plunged on to the city. All 14 on the airliner, three in the fighter and 87 on the ground were killed by the crash and fire that followed.

The first air collision resulting in more than 50 deaths occurred on 1 November 1949, when a Bolivian Air Force P-38 fighter and an Eastern Airlines DC-4 collided at Washington, DC, USA, killing 56.

THE 10 WORST AIR DISASTERS IN THE UK

1 Lockerbie, Scotland, 21 Dec 1988   270
Pan Am Flight 103 from London Heathrow to New York exploded in mid-air as a result of a terrorist bomb, killing 243 passengers, 16 crew and 11 on the ground in the UK's worst-ever air disaster.

2 Staines, Middlesex, 18 Jun 1972   118
A British European Airways Trident crashed after takeoff.

3 Siginstone, Glamorgan, 12 Mar 1950   81
An Avro Tudor V carrying Welsh rugby fans from Belfast inexplicably crashed while attempting to land at Llandow; three survived, one dying later in the worst air crash in the world up to this date.

4 Stockport, Cheshire, 4 Jun 1967   72
A British Midland Argonaut airliner carrying holidaymakers returning from Majorca crashed en route to Manchester Airport, killing all but 12 on board.

5 Freckelton, Lancashire, 23 Aug 1944   61
A US Air Force B-24 crashed on to a school after being struck by lightning, killing 10 USAAF personnel on board, 38 children, two teachers and other civilians on the ground.

6 Manchester Airport, 22 Aug 1985   55
A British Airtours Boeing 737 caught fire on the ground.

7 Near Gatwick Airport, West Sussex, 5 Jan 1969   50
An Ariana Afghan Airlines Boeing 727 crash-landed; the deaths included two on the ground.

8 M1 motorway, Kegworth, Leicestershire, 8 Jan 1989   47
A British Midland Boeing 737-400 attempting to land without engine power crashed on the motorway embankment.

9 = Isle of Wight, 15 Nov 1957   45
Following an engine fire, an Aquila Airlines Solent flying boat G-AKNU crashed in Chessel Down quarry.

= Off Sumburgh, Shetland Islands, 6 Nov 1986   45
A Boeing 234 Chinook helicopter ferrying oil-rig workers ditched in the sea, making this the worst-ever civilian helicopter accident. Two passengers were rescued by coastguards.

* Including ground casualties

In addition to disasters within the UK, a number of major air crashes involving British aircraft have occurred overseas. One of the earliest was that of British airship *R101* on 5 October 1930, near Beauvais, France, when 50 were killed after it crashed into a hillside. The crash of a Dan-Air Boeing 727 at Santa Cruz de Tenerife, Canary Islands, on 25 April 1980 left 146 dead. The collision of a British Airways Trident and an Inex Adria DC-9 over Zagreb on 10 September 1976 killed 176: 54 passengers and nine crew in the British aircraft and 108 passengers and five crew in the Yugoslavian aircraft.

THE 10 WORST AIRSHIP DISASTERS

LOCATION / DATE / INCIDENT   NO. KILLED

1 Coast off New Jersey, USA, 4 Apr 1933   73
US Navy airship *Akron* crashed into the sea in a storm, leaving only three survivors.

2 Over the Mediterranean, 21 Dec 1923   52
French airship *Dixmude* is assumed to have been struck by lightning, broke up and crashed into the sea.

3 Near Beauvais, France, 5 Oct 1930   50
British airship *R101* crashed into a hillside leaving 48 dead, with two dying later, and six survivors.

4 Coast off Hull, UK, 24 Aug 1921   44
Airship *R38* broke in two on a training and test flight.

5 Lakehurst, New Jersey, USA, 6 May 1937   36
German zeppelin *Hindenburg* caught fire when mooring. Remarkably, 62 people survived the blaze.

6 Hampton Roads, Virginia, USA, 21 Feb 1922   34
Roma, an Italian airship bought by the US Army, hit power lines and crashed, killing all but 11 men on board.

7 Berlin, Germany, 17 Oct 1913   28
The first air disaster with more than 20 fatalities, German airship *LZ18* crashed after engine failure and an explosion during a test flight at Berlin-Johannisthal.

8 Baltic Sea, 30 Mar 1917   23
German airship *SL9* was struck by lightning on a flight from Seerappen to Seddin and crashed into the sea.

9 Mouth of the River Elbe, Germany, 3 Sep 1915   19
German airship *L10* was struck by lightning and plunged into the sea.

10 Coast off Barnegat City, New Jersey, USA, 6 Jul 1960   18
Largest-ever non-rigid airship US Navy *Goodyear ZPG-3W* crashed into the sea. There were three survivors.

'Oh, the humanity…'
Radio commentator Herbert Morrison's memorable remark summarized the horror of eyewitnesses to the conflagration that engulfed German airship Hindenburg *as it prepared to moor, leaving 36 dead.*

SPORT & LEISURE

Summer Olympics

TOP 10 COUNTRIES WINNING THE MOST GOLD MEDALS AT ONE OLYMPICS*

	COUNTRY	YEAR	GOLD MEDALS
1	USA#	1984	83
2	Soviet Union#	1980	80
3	USA#	1904	79
4	Great Britain#	1908	56
5	Soviet Union	1988	55
6	Soviet Union	1972	50
7	Soviet Union	1976	49
8	East Germany	1980	47
9	= USA	1924	45
	= USA	1968	45
	= Unified Team	1992	45

* All Summer Olympic Games 1896–2004
# Host nation

East Germany (1980) is the only country on the list not to have topped the gold medal-winning table.

TOP 10 LEADING MEDAL-WINNING COUNTRIES, 2004

	COUNTRY	GOLD	SILVER	BRONZE	TOTAL
1	USA*	36	39	27	102
2	Russia	27	27	38	92
3	China	32	17	14	63
4	= Australia	17	16	16	49
	= Germany	13	16	20	49
6	Japan	16	9	12	37
7	France	11	9	13	33
8	Italy	10	11	11	32
9	= South Korea	9	12	9	30
	= UK	9	9	12	30

* Host nation

The 1984 Olympics were boycotted by Soviet countries as a protest against the boycotting of the 1980 Moscow Olympics by the United States and other nations. The only two countries to appear on the list in 2004 and not in 1984 are Russia and South Korea, while Romania, which finished third in 1984, and Canada (fourth) failed to make the Top 10 in 2004.

TOP 10 MEDAL-WINNING COUNTRIES AT THE SUMMER PARALYMPICS

	COUNTRY	GOLD	SILVER	BRONZE	TOTAL
1	USA	665	579	607	1,851
2	UK	470	468	454	1,392
3	Germany/West Germany	437	431	413	1,281
4	Canada	445	275	294	1,014
5	France	326	300	283	909
6	Australia	292	306	272	870
7	Holland	238	200	169	607
8	Poland	204	209	167	580
9	Sweden	206	203	145	554
10	Spain	176	166	182	524

The first international games for the disabled took place at Stoke Mandeville, UK, in 1952, when 130 athletes from just two countries – the UK and Netherlands – competed. The first Paralympics to take place at the same venue as the Olympic Games was in Rome in 1960, since when they have been held every four years, and since Seoul in 1988, at the same venue as the Summer Olympics. Some 400 athletes from 23 countries took part in 1960, while at Athens in 2004 a total of 3,806 athletes from 136 nations competed. The most medals won at one Games is 388 by the USA in the 'dual' Paralympics of 1984. Their total of 131 gold medals is also a record for one Games.

TOP 10 MOST GOLD MEDALS BY A MALE ATHLETE AT ONE OLYMPIC GAMES*

	ATHLETE / NATIONALITY	SPORT	YEAR	GOLDS
1	Mark Spitz, USA	Swimming	1972	7
2	= Vitaly Scherbo, Unified Team	Gymnastics	1992	6
	= Michael Phelps, USA	Swimming	2004	6
4	= Anton Heida, USA	Gymnastics	1904	5
	= Willis Lee, USA	Shooting	1920	5
	= Paavo Nurmi, Finland	Athletics	1924	5
	= Matt Biondi, USA	Swimming	1988	5
8	= Hubert Van Innis, Belgium	Archery	1920	4
	= Carl Osburn, USA	Shooting	1920	4
	= Lloyd Spooner, USA	Shooting	1920	4
	= Ville Ritola, Finland	Athletics	1924	4
	= Viktor Chukarin, USSR	Gymnastics	1956	4
	= Boris Shakhlin, USSR	Gymnastics	1960	4
	= Don Schollander, USA	Swimming	1964	4
	= Akinori Nakayama, Japan	Gymnastics	1968	4
	= Nikolay Andrianov, USSR	Gymnastics	1976	4
	= Carl Lewis, USA	Track & Field	1984	4

* All Summer Olympics 1896–2004

TOP 10 **SUMMER OLYMPIC GOLD MEDAL-WINNERS (MEN)**

	ATHLETE / COUNTRY	SPORT	YEARS	GOLDS
1	= Paavo Nurmi, Finland	Athletics	1920–28	9
	= Mark Spitz, USA	Swimming	1968–72	9
	= Carl Lewis, USA	Athletics	1984–96	9
4	= Sawao Kato, Japan	Gymnastics	1968–76	8
	= Matt Biondi, USA	Swimming	1984–92	8
	= Ray Ewry, USA	Athletics	1900–08	8
7	= Nikolay Andrianov, USSR	Gymnastics	1972–80	7
	= Boris Shakhlin, USSR	Gymnastics	1956–64	7
	= Viktor Chukarin, USSR	Gymnastics	1952–56	7
	= Aladàr Gerevich, Hungary	Fencing	1932–60	7

TOP 10 **SUMMER OLYMPIC GOLD MEDAL-WINNERS (WOMEN)**

	ATHLETE / COUNTRY	SPORT	YEARS	GOLDS
1	Larissa Latynina, USSR	Gymnastics	1956–64	9
2	= Birgit Fischer (*née* Schmidt) East Germany/Germany	Canoeing	1980–2004	8
	= Jenny Thompson, USA	Swimming	1992–2000	8
4	Vera Casalavska, Czechoslovakia	Gymnastics	1964–68	7
5	= Kristin Otto, Germany	Swimming	1988	6
	= Amy van Dyken, USA	Swimming	1996–2000	6
7	= Agnes Keleti, Hungary	Gymnastics	1952–56	5
	= Polina Astakhova, USSR	Gymnastics	1965–64	5
	= Nadia Comaneci, Romania	Gymnastics	1976–80	5
	= Nelli Kim, USSR	Gymnastics	1976–80	5
	= Elisabeta Oleniuc-Lipa, Romania	Rowing	1984–2004	5
	= Krisztina Egerszegi, Hungary	Swimming	1988–96	5

Above: Paddle power
German kayak star Birgit Fischer won eight gold and four silver medals in six consecutive Olympic Games.

Below: Seventh heaven
Carl Lewis's 1992 4 x 100 m relay victory added the seventh gold to his ultimate tally of nine.

Athletics

	COUNTRY	GOLD	SILVER	BRONZE	TOTAL
1	USA	14	4	8	26
2	Russia	4	9	3	16
3	Kenya	5	3	5	13
4	Jamaica	1	6	3	10
5	Germany	2	2	3	7
6	UK	1	1	3	5
7	Ethiopia	3	1	0	4
8	= Bahamas	1	2	0	3
	= Belarus	1	1	1	3
	= China	1	1	1	3
	= Cuba	1	1	1	3
	= Czech Republic	2	1	0	3

Brad Walker
American pole vaulter Brad Walker, winner of the 2007 World Championship gold medal with a vault of 5.86 m. It was just 28 cm short of Sergey Bubka's world record.

TOP 10 **MOST IMPROVED WOMEN'S IAAF WORLD RECORDS, 1988–2008***

	EVENT	1988	2008	% IMPROVEMENT
1	Pole vault	3.59m	5.01m	39.55
2	Hammer throw	58.94m	78.61m	33.37
3	20 km walk	1h 36m 19s	1h 25m 41s	11.04
4	Triple jump	14.04m	15.50m	10.40
5	Javelin throw#	67.09m	71.70m	6.87
6	Marathon	2h 21m 06s	2h 15m 25s	4.03
7	Discus throw	74.56m	76.80m	3.00
8	100 m	10.76s	10.49s	2.51
9	5,000 m	14m 37.33s	14m 16.63	2.36
10	10,000 m	30m 13.74s	29m 31.78s	2.31

* In events as contested at the Olympic Games and outdoor World Championships, based on the IAAF world records as at 1 January 1988 and 1 January 2008
\# Based on the present-day weight of the javelin, in force since 18 November 1991

Source: International Association of Athletics Federations (IAAF)

The 800 m, high jump and shot put are the only three women's world records that were not broken in the period 1988–2008. The women's world record for the discus throw is the only event that is better than the men's world record, as at 1 January 2008.

TOP 10 **MOST IMPROVED MEN'S IAAF WORLD RECORDS, 1988–2008***

	EVENT	1988	2008	% IMPROVEMENT
1	Javelin throw#	91.46m	98.48m	7.68
2	10,000 m	27m 13.81s	26m 17.53s	3.44
3	5,000 m	12m 58.39s	12m 37.35s	2.70
4	20 km walk	1h 19m 12s	1h 17m 16s	2.44
5	3,000 m steeplechase	8m 05.4s	7m 53.63s	2.42
6	Marathon	2h 07m 12s	2h 04m 26s	2.18
7	200 m	19.72s	19.32s	2.03
8	Decathlon	8,847 pts	9,026 pts	2.02
9	100 m	9.93s	9.74s	1.91
10	Pole vault	6.03m	6.14m	1.82

* In events as contested at the Olympic Games and outdoor World Championships, based on the IAAF world records as at 1 January 1988 and 1 January 2008
\# Based on the present-day weight of the javelin, in force since 18 November 1991

Source: International Association of Athletics Federations (IAAF)

The discus throw and hammer throw are the only two men's world records that have not been broken in the period 1988–2008. The current discus world record has stood since 6 June 1986.

Haile Gebrselassie
Ethiopia's Haile Gebrselassie, winner of two Olympic golds and four World Championship golds
at the 10,000 m. He has also won four indoor World Championship gold medals.

TOP 10 **MOST IAAF WORLD CHAMPIONSHIP MEDALS (MEN)***

	ATHLETE / COUNTRY	YEARS	GOLD	SILVER	BRONZE	TOTAL
1	Carl Lewis, USA	1983–93	8	1	1	10
2	Michael Johnson, USA	1991–99	9	0	0	9
3	Haile Gebrselassie, Ethiopia	1993–2003	4	2	1	7
4 =	Sergey Bubka, USSR/Ukraine	1983–97	6	0	0	6
=	Butch Reynolds, USA	1987–95	3	2	1	6
=	Lars Riedel, Germany	1991–2001	5	0	1	6
7 =	Colin Jackson, UK	1987–99	2	2	1	5
=	Jan Zelezny, Czechoslovakia/ Czech Republic	1987–2001	3	0	2	5
=	Dennis Mitchell, USA	1991–2001	3	0	2	5
=	Antonio Pettigrew, USA	1991–2001	4	1	0	5
=	Jonathan Edwards, UK	1993–2001	2	1	2	5
=	Bruny Surin, Canada	1995–99	2	2	1	5
=	Allen Johnson, USA	1995–2003	4	0	1	5
=	Maurice Greene, USA	1997–2001	5	0	0	5
=	Hicham El Guerrouj, Morocco	1997–2003	4	1	0	5

* Up to and including the 2007 Championships in Osaka, Japan

TOP 10 **MOST IAAF WORLD CHAMPIONSHIP MEDALS (WOMEN)***

	ATHLETE / COUNTRY	YEARS	GOLD	SILVER	BRONZE	TOTAL
1	Merlene Ottey, Jamaica	1983–95	3	4	7	14
2	Jearl Miles-Clark, USA	1991–2003	4	3	2	9
3 =	Gail Devers, USA	1993–2001	5	3	0	8
=	Gwen Torrence, USA	1991–95	3	4	1	8
5 =	Heike Daute (née Dreschler), GDR/Germany	1983–93	2	2	2	6
=	Yuliya Pechonkina (née Nosova), Russia	2001–05	2	2	2	6
7 =	Inger Miller, USA	1997–2003	3	2	0	5
=	Marion Jones, USA	1997–99	3	1	1	5
=	Maria Lourdes Mutola, Mozambique	1993–2003	3	1	1	5
=	Eunice Barber, France	1999–2005	2	2	1	5

* Up to and including the 2007 Championships in Osaka, Japan

First held at Helsinki in 1983, the IAAF (International Amateur Athletics Federation) outdoor Championships were originally held every four years, but since 1993 have been held every two years. A record 1,981 athletes competed in 2007 at Osaka, Japan.

Cricket

TOP 10 **TEAM TOTALS IN THE 2007 ICC WORLD TWENTY20**

	COUNTRY	OPPONENTS	VENUE	TOTAL
1	Sri Lanka	Kenya	Johannesburg	260–6
2	India	England	Durban	218–4
3	South Africa	West Indies	Johannesburg	208–2
4	West Indies	South Africa	Johannesburg	205–6
5	England	India	Durban	200–6
6	New Zealand	India	Johannesburg	190
7	Pakistan	Sri Lanka	Johannesburg	189–6
8 =	England	Zimbabwe	Cape Town	188–9
=	India	Australia	Durban	188–5
10	India	New Zealand	Johannesburg	180–9

TOP 10 **MOST RUNS IN THE ICC WORLD CUP***

	PLAYER / COUNTRY	YEARS	MATCHES	INNINGS	RUNS
1	Sachin Tendulkar, India	1992–2007	36	35	1,796
2	Ricky Ponting, Australia	1996–2007	39	36	1,537
3	Brian Lara, West Indies	1992–2007	34	33	1,225
4	Sanath Jayasuriya, Sri Lanka	1992–2007	38	37	1,165
5	Adam Gilchrist, Australia	1999–2007	31	31	1,085
6	Javed Miandad, Pakistan	1975–96	33	30	1,083
7	Stephen Fleming, New Zealand	1996–2007	33	33	1,075
8	Herschelle Gibbs, South Africa	1999–2007	25	23	1,067
9	Aravinda de Silva, Sri Lanka	1987–2003	35	32	1,064
10	Viv Richards, West Indies	1975–87	23	21	1,013

*1975–2007

TOP 10 **INDIVIDUAL INNINGS IN THE 2007 ICC WORLD TWENTY20**

	BATSMAN / COUNTRY	OPPONENTS	VENUE	BALLS	RUNS
1	Chris Gayle, West Indies	South Africa	Johannesburg	57	117
2	Herschelle Gibbs, South Africa	West Indies	Johannesburg	55	90*
3	Justin Kemp, South Africa	New Zealand	Durban	56	89*
4	Sanath Jayasuriya, Sri Lanka	Kenya	Johannesburg	44	88
5	Kevin Pietersen, England	Zimbabwe	Cape Town	37	79
6	Gautam Gambhir, India	Pakistan	Johannesburg	54	75
7	Matthew Hayden, Australia	Bangladesh	Cape Town	48	73*
8	Junaid Siddique, Bangladesh	Pakistan	Cape Town	49	71
9	Yuvraj Singh, India	Australia	Durban	30	70
10	Virender Sehwag, India	England	Durban	42	68

* Not out

The inaugural championship was held in South Africa between 11–24 September 2007. India beat Pakistan by five wickets in the final. Matthew Hayden scored the most runs in aggregate, 245. The next championship will be held in England in 2009.

TOP 10 **MOST WICKETS IN TEST CRICKET**

	BOWLER / COUNTRY	YEARS	MATCHES	WICKETS
1	Muttiah Muralitharan, Sri Lanka	1992–2007	118	723
2	Shane Warne, Australia	1992–2007	145	708
3	Anil Kumble, India	1990–2007	122	591
4	Glenn McGrath, Australia	1993–2007	124	563
5	Courtney Walsh, West Indies	1984–2001	132	519
6	Kapil Dev, India	1978–94	131	434
7	Richard Hadlee, New Zealand	1973–90	86	431
8	Shaun Pollock, South Africa	1995–2007	107	416
9	Wasim Akram, Pakistan	1985–2002	104	414
10	Curtly Ambrose, West Indies	1988–2000	98	405

* As at 1 January 2008

The highest-placed Englishman is Ian Botham in 11th place with 383 wickets from 102 matches in the period 1977–92.

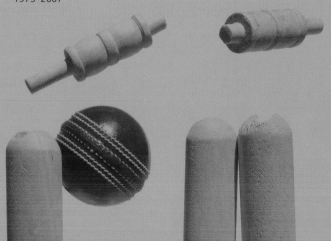

TOP 10 **MOST RUNS IN TEST CRICKET***

	BATSMAN / COUNTRY	YEARS	MATCHES	INNINGS	RUNS
1	Brian Lara, West Indies	1990–2006	131	232	11,953
2	Sachin Tendulkar, India	1989–2007	142	229	11,289
3	Allan Border, Australia	1978–94	156	265	11,174
4	Steve Waugh, Australia	1985–2004	168	260	10,927
5	Sunil Gavaskar, India	1971–87	125	214	10,122
6	Rahul Dravid, India	1996–2007	115	196	9,641
7	Ricky Ponting, Australia	1995–2007	112	186	9,508
8	Jacques Kallis, South Africa	1995–2007	111	189	9,197
9	Graham Gooch, England	1975–95	118	215	8,900
10	Javed Miandad, Pakistan	1976–93	124	189	8,832

* As at 5 December 2007

The Prince's reign
Nicknamed 'The Prince', Trinidadian batsman Brian Lara's statistics, in addition to his Test record, include 34 Test centuries – the most for a West Indian player – and 22,156 runs in First Class cricket.

TOP 10 **MOST CATCHES IN TEST CRICKET***

	PLAYER / COUNTRY	YEARS	TESTS	CATCHES
1	Mark Waugh, Australia	1991–2002	128	181
2	Brian Lara, West Indies & ICC	1990–2006	131	164
3	Stephen Fleming, New Zealand	1994–2007	106	161
4	Mark Taylor, Australia	1989–99	104	157
5	Rahul Dravid, India & ICC	1996–2007	116	160
6	Allan Border, Australia	1978–94	156	156
7=	Ricky Ponting, Australia	1995–2007	113	129
=	Mahela Jayawardene, Sri Lanka	1997–2007	93	129
9	Shane Warne, Australia	1992–2007	145	125
10	Greg Chappell, Australia	1970–84	87	122

* By an outfield player, as at 1 January 2008

The highest-placed Englishman is Ian Botham (12th) with 120 catches from 102 Tests in the period 1977–92.

Ball Games

TOP 10 MOST ALL-IRELAND GAELIC FOOTBALL TITLES*

	TEAM	FIRST WIN	LAST WIN	TOTAL WINS
1	Kerry	1903	2007	35
2	Dublin	1891	1995	22
3	Galway	1925	2001	9
4	Meath	1949	1999	7
5	Cork	1890	1990	6
6	= Wexford	1893	1918	5
	= Cavan	1933	1952	5
	= Down	1960	1994	5
9	= Tipperary	1889	1920	4
	= Kildare	1905	1928	4

* Gaelic Athletic Association (GAA) senior titles 1887–2007

The All-Ireland Final is played at Croke Park, Dublin on the third or fourth Sunday in September each year. The winning team receives the Sam Maguire Cup, named after the former player and senior member of the GAA who died in 1928. The province of Munster has provided a record 47 winners.

TOP 10 MOST WORLD POOL TITLES*

	PLAYER / COUNTRY	TITLE	YEARS	WINS
1	Sue Thompson, Scotland	Women's 8-Ball	1996–97, 2000, 2002–04, 2006–07	8
2	= Linda Leadbitter (née Moffat), England	Women's 8-Ball	1993–95, 1998	4
	= Allison Fisher, England	Women's 9-Ball	1996–98, 2001	4
4	Earl Strickland, USA	Men's 9-Ball	1990–91, 2002	3
5	= Robin Bell, USA	Women's 9-Ball	1990–91	2
	= Johnny Archer, USA	Men's 9-Ball	1992, 1997	2
	= Rob McKenna, Scotland	Men's 8-Ball	1994, 1997	2
	= Chao Fongpang, Chinese Taipei	Men's 9-Ball	1993, 2000	2
	= Lisa Quick, England	Women's 8-Ball	1999, 2001	2
	= Liu Hsinmei, Chinese Taipei	Women's 9-Ball	1999, 2002	2
	= Jason Twist, England	Men's 8-Ball	2000, 2002	2
	= Chris Melling, England	Men's 8-Ball	2001, 2003	2
	= Kim Ga-Young, South Korea	Women's 9-Ball	2004, 2006	2

* 8-Ball Pool World Championship (men and women) and 9-Ball Pool World Championships (men and women) up to and including all 2007 Championships

The first World 9-Ball Championships were held in 1990 and the inaugural 8-Ball Championships in 1993. The 9-Ball Championships are organized by the WPBA (World Pool-Billiard Association) while the 8-Ball event is under the aegis of the WEPF (World Eight Ball Pool Federation), but their championship is now also recognized by the WPBA.

TOP 10 MOST PBA* TITLES

BOWLER# / FIRST/LAST WINS† / TOTAL

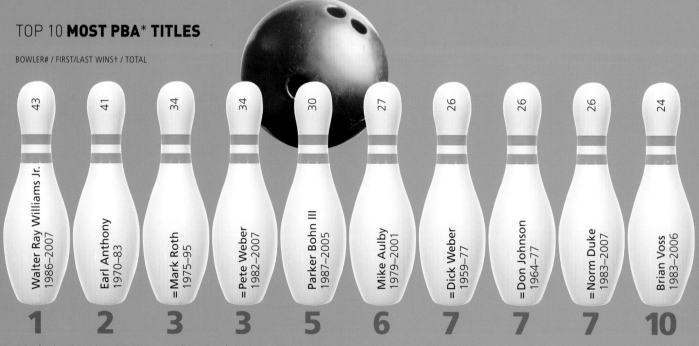

43	Walter Ray Williams Jr. 1986–2007	**1**
41	Earl Anthony 1970–83	**2**
34	= Mark Roth 1975–95	**3**
34	= Pete Weber 1982–2007	**3**
30	Parker Bohn III 1987–2005	**5**
27	Mike Aulby 1979–2001	**6**
26	= Dick Weber 1959–77	**7**
26	= Don Johnson 1964–77	**7**
26	= Norm Duke 1983–2007	**7**
24	Brian Voss 1983–2006	**10**

* Professional Bowlers Association # All bowlers from the USA † As at 1 January 2008 Source: PBA

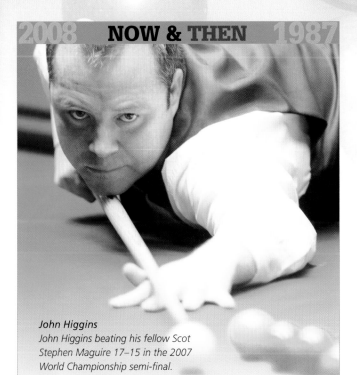

John Higgins
John Higgins beating his fellow Scot
Stephen Maguire 17–15 in the 2007
World Championship semi-final.

TOP 10 **SNOOKER RANKINGS**

2007–08 Season PLAYER / COUNTRY	**1987–88 Season** PLAYER / COUNTRY
1 John Higgins, Scotland	Steve Davis, England
2 Graeme Dott, Scotland	Jimmy White, England
3 Shaun Murphy, England	Neal Foulds, England
4 Ken Doherty, Ireland	Cliff Thorburn, Canada
5 Ronnie O'Sulllivan, England	Joe Johnson, England
6 Peter Ebdon, England	Terry Griffiths, Wales
7 Neil Robertson, Australia	Tony Knowles, England
8 Stephen Hendry, Scotland	Dennis Taylor, Northern Ireland
9 Ding Junhui, China	Alex Higgins, Northern Ireland
10 Stephen Maguire, Scotland	Silvino Francisco, South Africa

Only two players from the Top 10 ranked players of 1987–88 were still in the main tour rankings in 2007–08; Steve Davis was ranked No. 15 and Jimmy White was No. 60.

TOP 10 **MOST MEN'S MAJOR FAST PITCH SOFTBALL TITLES***

	TEAM / LOCATION	FIRST WIN	LAST WIN	TOTAL WINS
1	Clearwater Bombers, Florida	1950	1973	10
2	Raybestos Cardinals, Stratford, Connecticut	1955	1976	6
3	Sealmasters, Aurora, Illinois	1959	1967	4
4	= Zollner Pistons, Fort Wayne, Indiana	1945	1947	3
	= Briggs Beautyware, Detroit	1948	1953	3
	= Pay'n Pak, Seattle	1985	1987	3
	= Decatur Pride, Decatur, Illinois	1995	1999	3
8	= Kodak Park, Rochester, New York	1936	1940	2
	= Hammer Air Field, Fresno, California	1943	1944	2
	= Billard Barbell, Reading, Pennsylvania	1977	1978	2
	= Peterbilt Western, Seattle	1980	1982	2
	= Penn Corp, Sioux City, Iowa	1989	1990	2
	= National Health Care, Sioux City, Iowa	1992	1993	2
	= Meierhoffer, St Joseph, Missouri	1998	2000	2
	= Frontier Players Casino, St Joseph, Missouri	2001	2002	2
	= Farm Tavern, Madison, Wisconsin	2003	2004	2
	= Tampa Bay Smokers, Tampa Bay, Florida	1997	2005	2

* Amateur Softball Association of America (ASA) titles 1933–2007

TOP 10 **MOST WOMEN'S MAJOR FAST PITCH SOFTBALL TITLES***

	TEAM / LOCATION	FIRST WIN	LAST WIN	TOTAL WINS
1	Raybestos/Stratford Brakettes, Stratford, Connecticut	1958	2007	26
2	Orange Lionettes, California	1950	1970	9
3	Jax Maids, New Orleans	1942	1947	5
4	California Commotion, Woodland Hills	1996	1999	4
5	= Arizona Ramblers, Phoenix	1940	1949	3
	= Redding Rebels, California	1993	1995	3
7	= National Screw & Manufacturing, Cleveland	1936	1937	2
	= J. J. Krieg's, Alameda, California	1938	1939	2
	= Hi-Ho Brakettes, Stratford, Connecticut	1985	1988	2
	= Phoenix Storm, Phoenix, Arizona	2000	2001	2

* Amateur Softball Association of America (ASA) titles 1933–2007

Basketball

TOP 10 MEDAL-WINNING COUNTRIES IN THE BASKETBALL WORLD CHAMPIONSHIPS*

	COUNTRY	GOLD	SILVER	BRONZE	TOTAL
1	= Yugoslavia	5	3	2	10
	= USA	3	3	4	10
3	USSR/Russia	3	5	1	9
4	Brazil	2	2	1	5
5	= Argentina	1	1	0	2
	= Chile	0	0	2	2
7	= Croatia	0	0	1	1
	= Germany	0	0	1	1
	= Greece	0	1	0	1
	= Philippines	0	0	1	1
	= Spain	1	0	0	1

* Up to and including the 2006 Championships

The first FIBA World Championship was held at Buenos Aires, Argentina, in 1950. The Women's World Championship was first held at Santiago, Chile, in 1953.

Spain versus Greece
Spain won the 2006 World Championship with a comfortable 70–47 win over Greece in the final.

TOP 10 MOST POINTS IN A SINGLE NBA GAME*

	PLAYER / TEAM	OPPONENTS	DATE	POINTS
1	Wilt Chamberlain, Philadelphia Warriors	New York Knicks	2 Mar 1962	100
2	Kobe Bryant, Los Angeles Lakers	Toronto Raptors	22 Jan 2006	81
3	Wilt Chamberlain, Philadelphia Warriors	Los Angeles Lakers	8 Dec 1961#	78
4	= Wilt Chamberlain, Philadelphia Warriors	Chicago Packers	13 Jan 1962	73
	= Wilt Chamberlain, San Francisco Warriors	New York Knicks	16 Nov 1962	73
	= David Thompson, Denver Nuggets	Detroit Pistons	9 Apr 1978	73
7	Wilt Chamberlain, San Francisco Warriors	Los Angeles Lakers	3 Nov 1962	72
8	= David Robinson, San Antonio Spurs	Los Angeles Clippers	24 Apr 1994	71
	= Elgin Baylor, Los Angeles Lakers	New York Knicks	15 Nov 1960	71
10	Wilt Chamberlain, San Francisco Warriors	Syracuse Nationals	10 Mar 1963	70

* As at the end of the 2006–07 season # Including three periods of overtime

TOP 10 **MOST GAMES PLAYED IN THE NBA***

PLAYER / YEARS	GAMES
1 Robert Parish 1976–97	1,611
2 Kareem Abdul-Jabbar# 1969–89	1,560
3 John Stockton 1984–2003	1,504
4 Karl Malone 1985–2004	1,476
5 Kevin Willis† 1984–2007	1,424
6 Reggie Miller 1987–2005	1,389
7 Clifford Robinson 1989–2007	1,380
8 Gary Payton 1990–2007	1,335
9 Moses Malone 1976–95	1,329
10 Buck Williams 1981–99	1,307

* As at the end of 2006–07 season
# Lew Alcindor in 1971
† Active in 2007–08

Source: NBA

TOP 10 **NCAA MEN'S DIVISION 1 BASKETBALL CHAMPIONSHIPS***

	TEAM	FIRST WIN	LAST WIN	TOTAL WINS
1	UCLA	1964	1995	11
2	Kentucky	1948	1998	7
3	Indiana	1940	1987	5
4	North Carolina	1957	2005	4
5	Duke	1991	2001	3
6	=Oklahoma A&M#	1945	1946	2
	=San Francisco	1955	1956	2
	=Cincinnati	1961	1962	2
	=North Carolina State	1974	1983	2
	=Louisville	1980	1986	2
	=Kansas	1952	1988	2
	=Michigan State	1979	2000	2
	=Connecticut	1999	2004	2
	=Florida	2006	2007	2

* Since 1939
# Now Oklahoma State

Karl Malone
After 18 seasons starring for Utah Jazz between 1985 and 2003, Karl Malone finished his career with one season at Los Angeles Lakers in 2003–04.

TOP 10 **ALL-TIME CAREER SCORING LEADERS IN THE NBA***

	PLAYER	YEARS	GAMES	POINTS
1	Kareem Abdul-Jabbar#	1969–89	1,560	38,387
2	Karl Malone	1985–2004	1,476	36,928
3	Michael Jordan	1984–2003	1,072	32,292
4	Wilt Chamberlain	1959–73	1,045	31,419
5	Moses Malone	1976–95	1,329	27,409
6	Elvin Hayes	1968–84	1,303	27,313
7	Hakeem Olajuwon	1984–2002	1,238	26,946
8	Oscar Robertson	1960–74	1,040	26,710
9	Dominique Wilkins	1982–99	1,074	26,668
10	John Havlicek	1962–78	1,270	26,395

* As at the end of 2006–07 season
# Lew Alcindor in 1971

Source: NBA

Combat Sports

TOP 10 **GOLD MEDAL-WINNING COUNTRIES AT THE WORLD AMATEUR BOXING CHAMPIONSHIPS***

	COUNTRY	GOLD MEDALS
1	Cuba	62
2	Russia/USSR	29
3	USA	14
4	= Bulgaria	7
	= Romania	7
6	Kazakhstan	5
7	= Hungary	3
	= Germany	3
	= Uzbekistan	3
10	= France	2
	= South Korea	2
	= Turkey	2

* Men's, 1974–2007

The first World Amateur Boxing Championships were held at Havana, Cuba, in 1974 and since 1989 have been staged every two years.

THE 10 **LAST FIGHTS OF MUHAMMAD ALI**

	OPPONENT / COUNTRY	VENUE	RESULT	DATE
1	Trevor Berbick, Canada	Nassau, Bahamas	Lost – points, 10 rounds	11 Dec 1981
2	Larry Holmes, USA	Las Vegas, USA	Lost – retired, 10th round	2 Oct 1980
3	Leon Spinks, USA	New Orleans, USA	Won – points, 15 rounds	15 Sep 1978
4	Leon Spinks, USA	Las Vegas, USA	Lost – points, 15 rounds	15 Feb 1978
5	Earnie Shavers, USA	New York, USA	Won – points, 15 rounds	29 Sep 1977
6	Alfredo Evangelista, Uruguay	Landover, USA	Won – points, 15 rounds	16 May 1977
7	Ken Norton, USA	New York, USA	Won – points, 15 rounds	28 Sep 1976
8	Richard Dunn, UK	Munich, West Germany	Won – tko*, 5 rounds	24 May 1976
9	Jimmy Young, USA	Landover, USA	Won – points, 15 rounds	30 Apr 1976
10	Jean-Pierre Coopman, Belgium	San Juan, Puerto Rico	Won – knockout, 5 rounds	20 Feb1976

* tko = technical knockout

TOP 10 **OLYMPIC FENCING COUNTRIES***

	COUNTRY	MEDALS			
		GOLD	SILVER	BRONZE	TOTAL
1	Italy	42	37	26	105
2	France	36	35	31	102
3	Hungary	34	21	25	80
4	Russia/USSR/Unified Team	27	20	23	70
5	Germany/West Germany	11	15	10	36
6	Poland	4	8	8	20
7	United States	2	5	12	19
8	Romania	3	3	6	12
9	= Belgium	3	3	4	10
	= Great Britain	1	9	0	10

* Based on total medals won by men and women at all Olympics up to and including 2004

TOP 10 **OLYMPIC JUDO COUNTRIES***

	COUNTRY	MEDALS			
		GOLD	SILVER	BRONZE	TOTAL
1	Japan	31	14	13	58
2	Russia/USSR/Unified Team	7	8	20	35
3	= France	10	6	17	33
	= South Korea	8	12	13	33
5	Cuba	5	8	13	26
6	Germany/West Germany	3	5	14	22
7	= Netherlands	4	1	10	15
	= UK	0	6	9	15
9	China	5	2	7	14
10	Brazil	2	3	7	12

* Based on total medals won by men and women at all Olympics up to and including 2004

Judo was first contested at the Tokyo Olympics in 1964. However, it was not held four years later but returned in 1972, and has been featured ever since.

Crossing swords
Aldo Montano (left) of Italy and Zsolt Nemcsik (Hungary) in the sabre event at the Athens Olympic Games, 2004. Montano's 15–14 win added to his country's tally of gold medals, plus a silver as a member of his country's sabre team.

On Two Wheels

TOP 10 **MEDAL-WINNING COUNTRIES IN THE WORLD ROAD-RACE CYCLING CHAMPIONSHIPS***

	NATION	GOLD	SILVER	BRONZE	TOTAL
1	Italy	20	25	22	67
2	Belgium	31	17	15	63
3	France	17	16	17	50
4	Netherlands	14	12	11	37
5	Russia/Soviet Union	3	9	12	24
6	Germany/West Germany	6	8	7	21
7	Spain	5	5	9	19
8	Switzerland	5	8	4	17
9	USA	5	7	3	15
10	Great Britain	4	3	3	10

* Men 1927–2007; women 1958–2007

The first men's champion was Alfredo Binda of Italy, who won the inaugural race at the Nürburgring, Germany, in 1927. Britain's only winner of the men's race was in 1965 when Tommy Simpson won the title in San Sebastian, Spain.

World Championship
The 2007 event took place in Stuttgart, Germany. The men's Road Race was won by Paolo Bettini and the women's race by Marta Bastianelli, both of Italy, further confirming their country's overall pole position in the table.

TOP 10 **MOST FINISHERS IN THE TOUR DE FRANCE**

	YEAR	WINNING RIDER / COUNTRY	STARTERS	FINISHERS
1	1991	Miguel Indurain, Spain	198	158
2	1990	Greg LeMond, USA	198	156
3	2005	Lance Armstrong, USA	189	155
4	2002	Lance Armstrong, USA	189	153
5	1988	Pedro Delgado, Spain	198	151
6	=2004	Lance Armstrong, USA	188	147
	=2003	Lance Armstrong, USA	189	147
8	=2001	Lance Armstrong, USA	189	144
	=1985	Bernard Hinault, France	180	144
10	=1999	Lance Armstrong, USA	180	141
	=2007	Alberto Contador, Spain	189	141

The first time that 100 riders finished the race was in 1970, when Eddy Merckx (Belgium) headed the field of 150 starters. The 155 finishers from 189 starters in 2005 represents the highest percentage of finishers to starters – 82.01 per cent. The year with fewest finishers was 1919, when just 11 of the 69 starters completed the race, which was won by Firmin Lambot (Belgium).

Rossi and Hayden
Valentino Rossi handed Nicky Hayden his first world title when he crashed out in the final round of the 2006 MotoGP.

THE 10 **LATEST US RIDERS TO WIN MOTOR-RACING GRAND PRIX WORLD TITLES***

	RIDER	CLASS	YEAR			RIDER		
1	Nicky Hayden	MotoGP	2006	6	= Wayne Rainey	500cc	1990
2	Kenny Roberts Jr	500cc	2000		= John Kocinski	250cc	1990
3	Kevin Schwantz	500cc	1993	8	Eddie Lawson	500cc	1989
4	Wayne Rainey	500cc	1992	9	Eddie Lawson	500cc	1988
5	Wayne Rainey	500cc	1991	10	Eddie Lawson	500cc	1986

* Individual champions only; as at the end of the 2007 season

Freddie Spencer is the only US rider to win two world titles in one year, winning the 500cc and 250cc titles in 1985.

Surtees' Success

The only man to win world titles on two and four wheels is John Surtees (UK). Between 1956 and 1960 Surtees won seven world titles at both 350 and 500cc. He switched to Formula One and made his debut for Lotus at Monaco in 1960. He moved to Ferrari in 1963 and the following year was crowned world champion.

TOP 10 **COUNTRIES WITH THE MOST WORLD MOTOR-CYCLING CHAMPIONS***

	COUNTRY	MOTO GP/ 500CC	250CC	125CC	350CC	50/80CC	TOTAL
1	Italy	18	21	23	8	2	72
2	UK	17	9	4	13	–	43
3	Spain	1	6	12	–	12	31
4	USA	15	2	–	–	–	17
5	Germany/ West Germany	–	7	3	2	4	16
6	Australia	7	1	1	1	–	10
7	= Southern Rhodesia	1	2	–	5	–	8
	= Switzerland	–	–	4	–	4	8
9	Japan	–	2	4	1	–	7
10	South Africa	–	2	–	3	–	5

* Individual champions only; as at end of 2007 season

TOP 10 **RIDERS WITH THE MOST MOTOR-CYCLING GRAND PRIX WINS***

	RIDER / COUNTRY	YEARS	WINS
1	Giacomo Agostini, Italy	1965–76	122
2	Angel Nieto, Spain	1969–85	90
3	Valentino Rossi, Italy	1996–2007	88
4	Mike Hailwood, UK	1959–67	76
5	Mick Doohan, Australia	1990–98	54
6	Phil Read, UK	1961–75	52
7	Jim Redman, Southern Rhodesia	1961–66	45
8	= Anton Mang, West Germany	1976–88	42
	= 'Max' Biaggi, Italy	1992–2004	42
10	Carlo Ubbiali, Italy	1950–60	39

* Solo classes only; correct as at end of the 2007 season

Football

TOP 10 MOST POINTS IN A BARCLAYS PREMIER LEAGUE SEASON*

	TEAM	SEASON	POINTS
1	Chelsea	2004–05	95
2	Manchester United	1993–94	92
3	=Manchester United	1999–2000	91
	=Chelsea	2005–06	91
5	Arsenal	2003–04	90
6	=Blackburn Rovers	1994–95	89
	=Manchester United	2006–07	89
8	Manchester United#	1994–95	88
9	Arsenal	2001–02	87
10	=Manchester United	1992–93	84
	=Blackburn Rovers#	1993–94	84

* Up to and including 2006–07
# Team did not win the League title in season indicated

TOP 10 BARCLAYS PREMIER LEAGUE GOALSCORERS IN ONE SEASON*

	PLAYER / CLUB	SEASON	GOALS
1	=Andy Cole, Newcastle United	1993–94	34
	=Alan Shearer, Blackburn Rovers	1994–95	34
3	=Alan Shearer, Blackburn Rovers	1993–94	31
	=Alan Shearer, Blackburn Rovers	1995–96	31
5	=Kevin Phillips, Sunderland	1999–2000	30
	=Thierry Henry, Arsenal	2003–04	30
7	Robbie Fowler, Liverpool	1995–96	28
8	Thierry Henry, Arsenal	2005–06	27
9	=Chris Sutton, Norwich City	1993–94	25
	=Matt Le Tissier, Southampton	1993–94	25
	=Robbie Fowler, Liverpool	1994–95	25
	=Les Ferdinand, Newcastle United	1995–96	25
	=Alan Shearer, Newcastle United	1996–97	25
	=Ruud Van Nistelrooy, Manchester United	2002–03	25
	=Thierry Henry, Arsenal	2004–05	25

* Premier League matches only, up to and including 2006–07

The first Premier League goal was scored by Brian Deane of Sheffield United against Manchester United on the opening day of the 1992–93 season. The 1,000th goal was scored by Mike Newell of Blackburn Rovers against Nottingham Forest on 7 April 1993, and the 10,000th by Les Ferdinand of Tottenham Hotspur against Fulham on 15 December 2001. The latest milestone was the 15,000th goal, scored by Moritz Volz of Fulham against Chelsea on 30 December 2006.

TOP 10 GOALSCORERS IN THE FIFA WORLD CUP*

	PLAYER / COUNTRY	YEARS	GOALS
1	Ronaldo, Brazil	1998–2006	15
2	Gerd Müller, West Germany	1970–74	14
3	Just Fontaine, France	1958	13
4	Pelé, Brazil	1958–70	12
5	=Sándor Kocsis, Hungary	1954	11
	=Jürgen Klinsman, Germany	1990–98	11
7	=Helmut Rahn, West Germany	1954–58	10
	=Teófilo Cubillas, Peru	1970–78	10
	=Grzegorz Lato, Poland	1974–82	10
	=Gary Lineker, England	1986–90	10
	=Gabriel Batistuta, Argentina	1994–2002	10
	=Miroslav Klose, Germany	2002–06	10

* In the final stages, 1930–2006

Fontaine's 13 goals in the 1958 event is a record for one tournament.

Ronaldo

Ronaldo in action against France in the 2006 World Cup quarter-finals. In Brazil's previous game, against Ghana, Ronaldo's fifth-minute goal in a 3–0 victory, took him past Gerd Müller's all-time record of 14 goals in the World Cup final stages.

TOP 10 BARCLAYS PREMIER LEAGUE TRANSFERS IN 2007*

	PLAYER / TEAM	TO	FEE (£)
1	**Fernando Torres** Atlético Madrid, Spain	Liverpool	21,500,000
2	**= Anderson** Porto, Portugal	Manchester United	17,000,000
	= Owen Hargreaves Bayern Munich	Manchester United	17,000,000
4	**Darren Bent** Charlton Athletic	Tottenham Hotspur	16,500,000
5	**Nani** Sporting Lisbon, Portugal	Manchester United	14,000,000
6	**Florent Malouda** Lyon, France	Chelsea	13,500,000
7	**Ryan Babel** Ajax, Netherlands	Liverpool	11,500,000
8	**Yakubu** Middlesbrough	Everton	11,250,000
9	**Eduardo da Silva** Dinamo Zagreb, Croatia	Arsenal	10,000,000
10	**Craig Gordon** Hearts, Scotland	Sunderland	9,000,000

* Based on all reported transfers of players bought by Barclays Premier League teams in the calendar year 2007

TOP 10 COUNTRIES IN THE UEFA EUROPEAN CHAMPIONSHIP*

	COUNTRY	WINS	RUNNER-UP	SEMI-FINAL	POINTS
1	West Germany/Germany	3	2	1	14
2	Soviet Union	1	3	1	10
3	= Czechoslovakia/Czech Republic	1	1	3	8
	= France	2	0	2	8
5	= Italy	1	1	2	7
	= Netherlands	1	0	4	7
7	= Denmark	1	0	2	5
	= Spain	1	1	0	5
	= Yugoslavia	0	2	1	5
10	Portugal	0	1	2	4

* Based on 3 points for winning the tournament, 2 points for being the runner-up, and 1 point for being a losing semi-finalist; all tournaments 1960–2004

The leading UK country is England, with two points from two semi-final appearances. The first European Championship was played between 1958–60, with the Soviet Union beating Yugoslavia 2–1 after extra time in Paris to win the first final. England first entered in 1964 and were eliminated by France 6–3 on aggregate over two legs. The 5–2 second-leg defeat was Alf Ramsey's first game in charge of the national team.

Golf

TOP 10 **MOST POINTS IN THE RYDER CUP***

	PLAYER / COUNTRY#	TEAM(S)	YEARS	POINTS
1	Nick Faldo, England	GB & I/Europe	1977–97	25
2	Bernhard Langer, Germany	Europe	1981–2002	24
3	= Billy Casper, USA	USA	1961–75	23.5
	= Colin Montgomerie, Scotland	Europe	1991–2006	23.5
5	Arnold Palmer, USA	USA	1961–73	23
6	Seve Ballesteros, Spain	Europe	1979–95	22.5
7	Lanny Wadkins, USA	USA	1977–93	21.5
8	José María Olazábal, Spain	Europe	1987–2006	20.5
9	Lee Trevino, USA	USA	1969–81	20
10	Jack Nicklaus, USA	USA	1969–81	18.5

* Up to and including 2006
# Great Britain (GB): 1921 to 1971; Great Britain and Ireland (GB & I): 1973 to 1977; Europe (E): 1979 to 2006

TOP 10 **GOLF COURSES TO HOST THE MOST MAJORS**

	CLUB / LOCATION	YEARS	US MASTERS	BRITISH OPEN	US OPEN	US PGA	TOTAL
1	Augusta National, Georgia	1934–2007	71	0	0	0	71
2	St Andrews, Fife, Scotland	1873–2005	0	27	0	0	27
3	Prestwick, Ayrshire, Scotland	1860–1925	0	24	0	0	24
4	Muirfield, East Lothian, Scotland	1892–2002	0	15	0	0	15
5	Royal St George's, Sandwich, Kent	1894–2003	0	13	0	0	13
6	= Royal Liverpool, Hoylake	1897–2006	0	11	0	0	11
	= Oakmont, Pennsylvania	1922–2007	0	0	8	3	11
8	= Baltusrol, New Jersey	1903–2005	0	0	7	1	8
	= Oakland Hills, Michigan	1924–96	0	0	6	2	8
10	Southern Hills, Oklahoma	1958–2007	0	0	3	4	7

The Augusta National is the only course to play host to a Major every year, as the home of the US Masters since its inception in 1934.

TOP 10 **MONEY WINNERS ON THE PGA CHAMPIONS TOUR***

	PLAYER	WINNINGS ($)
1	Hale Irwin	24,654,218
2	Gil Morgan	18,383,634
3	Dana Quigley	13,956,074
4	Bruce Fleisher	13,513,100
5	Larry Nelson	13,049,347
6	Allen Doyle	12,590,476
7	Jim Thorpe	12,476,861
8	Jim Colbert	11,623,031
9	Tom Kite	11,593,910
10	Tom Jenkins	11,225,366

* As at 1 January 2008; all golfers from the USA

The Champions Tour was founded in 1980 as the Senior PGA Tour, and changed its name in 2002. Run by the PGA Tour, it is for professional golfers who have reached the age of 50 and many ex-stars of the regular Tour compete on the Champions Tour.

Augusta
The Augusta National in Georgia realized the dream of the top amateur golfer Bobby Jones and his friend Clifford Roberts. The course, designed by Scot Dr Alistair Mackenzie, opened in 1931. Horton Smith won the first Masters at Augusta in 1934.

TOP 10 **MOST WOMEN'S MAJORS***

	PLAYER# / COUNTRY	YEARS	A	B	C	D	E	F	G	TOTALS
1	Patty Berg	1937–58	–	–	1	–	–	7	7	15
2	Mickey Wright	1958–66	–	4	4	–	–	2	3	13
3	= Louise Suggs	1946–59	–	1	1	–	–	4	4	10
	= Annika Sörenstam, Sweden	1995–2006	3	3	3	1	–	–	–	10
	= Babe Zaharias	1940–54	–	–	3	–	–	3	4	10
6	Betsy Rawls	1951–69	–	2	4	–	–	–	2	8
7	= Juli Inkster	1984–2002	2	2	2	–	1	–	–	7
	= Karrie Webb, Australia	1999–2006	2	1	2	1	1	–	–	7
9	= Betsy King	1987–97	3	1	2	–	–	–	–	6
	= Kathy Whitworth	1965–75	–	3	–	–	–	2	1	6
	= Pat Bradley	1980–86	1	1	1	–	3	–	–	6
	= Patty Sheehan	1983–96	1	3	2	–	–	–	–	6

* As recognized by the Ladies Professional Golf Association (LPGA) up to and including 2007
# All from the USA unless otherwise stated

Women's championships: a – Kraft Nabisco Championship (previously Nabisco Dinah Shore, Nabisco Championship) 1983–2007; b – LPGA Championship 1955–2007; c – US Women's Open 1946–2007; d – Women's British Open 2001–07; e – du Maurier Classic 1979–2000; f – Titleholders Championship 1937–42, 1946–66, 1972; g – Western Open 1930–67

TOP 10 **MOST MEN'S MAJORS IN A CAREER***

	PLAYER / COUNTRY	YEARS	US MASTERS	US OPEN	BRITISH OPEN	US PGA	TOTAL
1	Jack Nicklaus	1962–86	6	4	3	5	18
2	Tiger Woods	1997–2007	4	2	3	4	13
3	Walter Hagen	1914–29	0	2	4	5	11
4	= Ben Hogan	1946–53	2	4	1	2	9
	= Gary Player, South Africa	1959–78	3	1	3	2	9
6	Tom Watson	1975–83	2	1	5	0	8
7	= Harry Vardon, England	1896–1914	0	1	6	0	7
	= Gene Sarazen	1922–35	1	2	1	3	7
	= Bobby Jones	1923–30	0	4	3	0	7
	= Sam Snead	1942–54	3	0	1	3	7
	= Arnold Palmer	1958–64	4	1	2	0	7

* Professional Majors only, up to and including 2007; All golfers from the USA unless otherwise stated

Above: Annika Sörenstam
In 2003 Annika Sörenstam made history as the first woman to play on the men's PGA Tour since 1945.

Below: Jack Nicklaus
Jack Nicklaus won his first major, the US Open, in 1962 at the age of 22 and his last, the Masters, in 1986.

Horse Sports

TOP 10 OLYMPIC EQUESTRIAN MEDALLISTS*

	RIDER / COUNTRY	YEARS	GOLD	MEDALS SILVER	BRONZE	TOTAL
1	Reiner Klimke, West Germany	1964–88	7	0	2	9
2	Hans-Günther Winkler, West Germany	1956–76	5	1	1	7
3	= Piero d'Inzeo, Italy	1956–72	0	2	4	6
	= Raimondo d'Inzeo, Italy	1956–72	1	2	3	6
	= Josef Neckerman, West Germany	1960–72	2	2	2	6
	= Michael Plumb, USA	1964–84	2	4	0	6
	= Isabell Werth, Germany	1992–2000	4	2	0	6
	= Anky van Grunsven, Holland	1992–2004	2	4	0	6
9	= Earl Thomson, USA	1932–48	2	3	0	5
	= André Jousseaumé, France	1932–52	2	2	1	5
	= Henri Chammartin, Switzerland	1952–68	1	2	2	5
	= Gustav Fischer, Switzerland	1952–68	0	3	2	5
	= Liselott Linsenhoff, West Germany	1956–72	2	2	1	5
	= Christine Stückelberger, Switzerland	1976–88	1	3	1	5
	= Mark Todd, New Zealand	1984–2000	2	1	2	5

* Up to and including the 2004 Olympics

Equine elegance
The Dutch dressage rider Anky van Grunsven.

TOP 10 TRAINERS IN THE BREEDERS' CUP*

	TRAINER#	YEARS	WINS
1	D. Wayne Lukas	1985 (2), 1986 (2), 1987 (2), 1988 (3), 1989, 1994 (2), 1996, 1999 (2), 2000, 2002, 2005	18
2	'Shug' McGaughey III	1988–89 (2), 1992–93, 1995 (2), 2002, 2005	9
3	= Neil Drysdale, UK	1984–85, 1989, 1992–93, 2000	6
	= Richard Mandella	1993 (2), 2003 (4)	6
5	= Bill Mott	1987, 1992, 1995, 1997–98	5
	= Bob Baffert	1992, 1998, 2002, 2007 (2)	5
	= Bobby Frankel	2001–02, 2004–05, 2007	5
8	= Ron McAnally	1989–90, 1992, 1995	4
	= André Fabre, France	1990, 1993, 2001, 2005	4
	= Aidan O'Brien, Ireland	2001–03, 2007	4

* Up to and including the 2007 Breeders Cup races
# All jockeys from the USA unless otherwise stated

Source: Breeders' Cup

D. Wayne Lukas has saddled 146 horses in the Breeders' Cup and is the only trainer to have had a starter at every meeting. He has had 53 first three finishers and won nearly $20 million in prize money. His last winner was in 2005.

TOP 10 CHAMPION JOCKEYS IN THE UK WITH THE MOST WINS IN A SEASON*

	JOCKEY / NATIONAL HUNT/FLAT	SEASON	WINS
1	Tony McCoy (NH)	2001–02	289
2	Gordon Richards (F)	1947	269
3	Gordon Richards (F)	1949	261
4	Gordon Richards (F)	1933	259
5	Tony McCoy (NH)	2002–03	256
6	Tony McCoy (NH)	1997–98	253
7	Fred Archer (F)	1885	246
8	Tony McCoy (NH)	1999–2000	245
9	Fred Archer (F)	1884	241
10	Frankie Dettori (F)	1994	233

* National Hunt (NH) jockeys to the end of the 2006–07 National Hunt season and Flat (F) jockeys to the end of the 2007 flat racing season

All jockeys are from the UK and Ireland except Frankie Dettori (Italy). Seb Sanders and Jamie Spencer each rode 190 winners in 2007. Gordon Richards rode over 200 winners in a season 12 times and was champion jockey a record 26 times. In the 1933 season, 12 of his 259 winners came in successive races. He rode Barmby to victory in the 4 o'clock at Nottingham on 3 October. The next day he won all six races at Chepstow and on Thursday 5 October he won the first five races, again at Chepstow. The run came to an end when he finished third in the last race of the day on Eagle Ray.

TOP 10 FASTEST WINNING TIMES OF THE KENTUCKY DERBY*

	HORSE	YEAR	TIME MINS:SECS
1	Secretariat	1973	1:59.40
2	Monarchos	2001	1:59.97
3	Northern Dancer	1964	2:00.00
4	Spend A Buck	1985	2:00.20
5	Decidedly	1962	2:00.40
6	Proud Clarion	1967	2:00.60
7	=Grindstone	1996	2:01.00
	=Fusaichi Pegasus	2000	2:01.00
9	War Emblem	2002	2:01.13
10	Funny Cide	2003	2:01.19

* Up to and including 2007

The Kentucky Derby is held on the first Saturday in May at Churchill Downs, Louisville, Kentucky. The opening leg of the Triple Crown, it was first raced in 1875 over a distance of one mile four furlongs.

TOP 10 JOCKEYS WITH THE MOST US TRIPLE CROWN WINS*

	JOCKEY / COUNTRY	YEARS	KENTUCKY DERBY	PREAKNESS STAKES	BELMONT STAKES	TOTAL WINS
1	Eddie Arcaro	1938–57	5	6	6	17
2	Bill Shoemaker	1955–86	4	2	5	11
3	=Bill Hartack	1956–69	5	3	1	9
	=Earl Sande	1921–30	3	1	5	9
	=Pat Day	1985–2000	1	5	3	9
6	=Jim McLaughlin	1881–88	1	1	6	8
	=Gary Stevens	1988–2001	3	2	3	8
8	=Angel Cordero Jr, Puerto Rico	1974–85	3	2	1	6
	=Charley Kurtsinger	1931–37	2	2	2	6
	=Ron Turcotte, Canada	1965–73	2	2	2	6

* Up to and including 2007; all jockeys from the USA unless otherwise stated

Eddie Arcaro won his first Triple Crown race, the Kentucky Derby, on Lawrin in 1938. He twice won the Triple Crown, on Whirlaway in 1941 and in 1948 on Citation. Arcaro won 4,779 out of 24,092 races, in which he won a then-record of more than $30 million in prize money. Arcaro retired in 1962 and died in 1997 at the age of 81.

Derby winner
Monarchos on his way to winning the 2001 Kentucky Derby. He raced only 10 times before retiring to stud. His only other major win was the 2001 Florida Derby.

Motor Sports

TOP 10 MOST RACE WINS IN A FORMULA ONE CAREER BY A DRIVER*

	DRIVER / COUNTRY	YEARS	WINS
1	Michael Schumacher, Germany	1992–2006	91
2	Alain Prost, France	1981–93	51
3	Ayrton Senna, Brazil	1985–93	41
4	Nigel Mansell, UK	1985–94	31
5	Jackie Stewart, UK	1965–73	27
6 =	Jim Clark, UK	1962–68	25
=	Niki Lauda, Austria	1974–85	25
8	Juan-Manuel Fangio, Argentina	1950–57	24
9 =	Nelson Piquet, Brazil	1980–91	23
=	Damon Hill, UK	1993–98	22

* Up to and including the 2007 season

The most career wins by a current driver is 19 by Fernando Alonso.

TOP 10 MOST CAREER WINS IN CHAMP CAR RACES*

	DRIVER#	CAREER	WINS
1	A. J. Foyt	1960–81	67
2	Mario Andretti	1965–93	52
3	Michael Andretti	1986–2003	42
4	Al Unser	1967–87	39
5	Bobby Unser	1966–81	38
6 =	Al Unser Jr	1984–95	31
=	Paul Tracy, Canada	1993–2007	31
8	Rick Mears	1978–91	29
9 =	Johnny Rutherford	1965–86	27
=	Sébastien Bourdais, France	2003–07	27

* Formerly CART (Championship Auto Racing Teams), Champ Car (short for 'Championship Car') was introduced in 2004; correct as at the end of the 2007 season
# All drivers from the USA unless otherwise stated

TOP 10 MOST FORMULA ONE GRAND PRIX RACE WINS IN A SEASON BY A DRIVER*

	DRIVER / COUNTRY	SEASON	WINS
1	Michael Schumacher, Germany	2004	13
2	Michael Schumacher, Germany	2002	11
3 =	Nigel Mansell, UK	1992	9
=	Michael Schumacher, Germany	1995	9
=	Michael Schumacher, Germany	2000	9
=	Michael Schumacher, Germany	2001	9
7 =	Ayrton Senna, Brazil	1988	8
=	Michael Schumacher, Germany	1994	8
=	Damon Hill, UK	1996	8
=	Mika Häkkinen, Finland	1998	8

* To the end of the 2007 season

TOP 10 MOST FORMULA ONE GRAND PRIX WINS BY A MANUFACTURER*

	MANUFACTURER / COUNTRY#	FIRST WIN	LAST WIN	TOTAL WINS
1	Ferrari, Italy	1951	2007	201
2	McLaren	1968	2007	156
3	Williams	1979	2003	113
4	Lotus	1960	1987	79
5	Brabham	1964	1985	35
6	Renault, France	1979	2006	33
7	Benetton, Italy	1986	1997	27
8	Tyrrell	1971	1983	23
9	BRM	1959	1972	17
10	Cooper	1958	1967	16

* To the end of the 2007 season
# All manufacturers from the UK unless otherwise stated

Michael Schumacher
Michael Schumacher winning at Imola in his final season, 2006.

Lewis Hamilton

Lewis Hamilton leading the field ahead of his McLaren team-mate Fernando Alonso in the United States Grand Prix at Indianapolis. Hamilton went on to win his second Formula One race.

THE 10 **LOWEST STARTING POSITIONS BY WINNERS OF THE INDIANAPOLIS 500***

	DRIVER#	YEAR	POSITION
1	= Ray Harroun	1911	28th
	= Louie Meyer	1936	28th
3	Fred Frame	1932	27th
4	Johnny Rutherford	1974	25th
5	= George Souders	1927	22nd
	= Kelly Petillo	1935	22nd
7	Lora Corum/ Joe Boyer†	1924	21st
8	= Tommy Milton	1921	20th
	= Frank Lockhart	1926	20th
	= Al Unser	1987	20th

* Based on the starting position on the grid
\# All drivers from the USA
† Joint drivers

Source: Indianapolis Motor Speedway

THE 10 **FIRST FORMULA ONE GRAND PRIX RACES OF LEWIS HAMILTON**

	GRAND PRIX	VENUE	POSITION	DATE
1	Australian	Albert Park, Melbourne	3rd	18 Mar 2007
2	Malaysian	Sepang, Kuala Lumpur	2nd	8 Apr 2007
3	Bahrain	Bahrain International Circuit, Sakhir	2nd	15 Apr 2007
4	Spanish	Circuit de Catalunya, Barcelona	2nd	3 May 2007
5	Monaco	Circuit de Monaco, Monte-Carlo	2nd	7 May 2007
6	Canadian	Circuit Gilles Villeneuve, Montreal	1st	10 Jun 2007
7	United States	Indianapolis Motor Speedway, Indianapolis	1st	17 Jun 2007
8	French	Circuit de Nevers, Magny-Cours	3rd	1 Jul 2007
9	British	Silverstone, England	3rd	8 Jul 2007
10	European	Nürburgring, Nürburg, Germany	9th	22 Jul 2007

In addition to his two wins here, Hamilton won two more races, in Hungary and Japan. In 17 races he failed to finish just once, was out of the points on only two occasions and achieved 12 podium finishes. His total points for the season was 109, one behind the eventual champion Kimi Räikkönen, who captured the title in the last race of the season in Brazil. Whilst Hamilton's 12 podiums is a record for a rookie, it falls five short of the record set by Michael Schumacher in 2002.

Rugby

TOP 10 **BIGGEST WINS IN THE SIX NATIONS CHAMPIONSHIP***

	WINNER / OPPONENT	YEAR	VENUE	SCORE
1	England v. Italy	2001	Twickenham	80–23
2	Ireland v. Italy	2000	Lansdowne Road	60–13
3	England v. Italy	2000	Rome	59–12
4	France v. Italy	2005	Rome	56–13
5	Ireland v. Wales	2002	Lansdowne Road	54–10
6	France v. Italy	2003	Rome	53–27
7	Ireland v. Italy	2007	Rome	51–24
8 =	England v. Ireland	2000	Twickenham	50–18
=	England v. Wales	2002	Twickenham	50–10
=	England v. Italy	2004	Rome	50–9

* Since 2000 when Italy joined the competition, based on the score of the winning team; up to and including the 2008 Championship

TOP 10 **BIGGEST CHALLENGE CUP WINS***

	WINNERS	LOSERS	YEAR	SCORE
1	Leeds Rhinos	London Broncos	1999	52–16
2	St Helens	Huddersfield Giants	2006	42–12
3	St Helens	Bradford Bulls	1996	40–32
4	Wakefield Trinity	Hull	1960	38–5
5	Huddersfield	St Helens	1915	37–3
6	Wigan	Warrington	1990	36–14
7	Featherstone Rovers	Bradford Northern	1973	33–14
8 =	Wigan	Halifax	1988	32–12
=	St Helens	Bradford Bulls	1997	32–22
=	St Helens	Wigan Warriors	2004	32–16

* Based on the score of the winning team in all finals, 1897–2007

Leeds' 52–16 win over London Broncos in 1999 was the last Rugby League Challenge Cup Final at the old Wembley Stadium. Leroy Rivett of Leeds became the first man ever to score four tries in a Challenge Cup final.

TOP 10 **MOST POINTS IN A WORLD CUP CAREER***

	PLAYER	COUNTRY	MATCHES	YEARS	POINTS
1	Jonny Wilkinson	England	15	1999–2007	249
2	Gavin Hastings	Scotland	13	1987–95	227
3	Michael Lynagh	Australia	15	1987–95	195
4	Grant Fox	New Zealand	10	1987–91	170
5	Andrew Mehrtens	New Zealand	10	1995–99	163
6	Gonzalo Quesada	Argentina	8	1995–99	135
7 =	Matt Burke	Australia	13	1995–99	125
=	Nicky Little	Fiji	11	2003–07	125
9	Thierry Lacroix	France	9	1991–95	124
10	Gareth Rees	Canada	13	1987–99	120

* Up to and including the 2007 tournament

Chris Paterson (Scotland), Percy Montgomery (South Africa), Frédéric Michalak (France) and Elton Flatley (Australia) are the only other men to have scored 100 points in a World Cup career. Grant Fox scored 126 points in 1995, which represents the biggest haul in a single tournament.

Jonny Wilkinson
Jonny Wilkinson made his England debut as an 18-year-old when he came off the bench against Ireland at Twickenham on 4 April 1998. He has spent his entire club career with Newcastle Falcons, which he joined in 1997.

Kevin Sinfield

Born in Oldham, Kevin Sinfield has spent his whole career at Leeds Rhinos, which he joined in 1996, and the following year made his debut at the age of 16.

TOP 10 **POINTS-SCORERS IN SUPER LEAGUE XII***

	PLAYER	CLUB	POINTS
1	Kevin Sinfield	Leeds Rhinos	249
2	Pat Richards	Wigan Warriors	242
3	Chris Thorman	Huddersfield Giants	234
4	Lee Briers	Warrington Wolves	221
5	Paul Deacon	Bradford Bulls	216
6	Jamie Rooney	Wakefield Trinity Wildcats	210
7	Danny Tickle	Hull FC	194
8	John Wilshere	Salford City Reds	170
9	Thomas Bosc	Catalans Dragons	142
10	Paul Sykes	Bradford Bulls	127

* In the 2007 regular season only

TOP 10 **MOST-CAPPED RUGBY UNION PLAYERS***

	PLAYER	COUNTRY	YEARS	CAPS*
1	George Gregan	Australia	1994–2007	139
2	Jason Leonard	England/Lions#	1990–2004	119
3	Fabien Pelous	France	1995–2007	118
4	Philippe Sella	France	1982–95	111
5	Gareth Thomas	Wales/Lions#	1995–2007	103
6	Stephen Larkham	Australia	1996–2007	102
7	= David Campese	Australia	1982–96	101
	= Alessandro Troncon	Italy	1994–2007	101
9	Raphael Ibañez	France	1996–2007	98
10	Colin Charvis	Wales/Lions#	1996–2007	96

* Of the 'Big 10' nations: Australia, Argentina, England, France, Italy, Ireland, New Zealand, Scotland, South Africa and Wales, as at 1 January 2008
# British and Irish Lions

Tennis

TOP 10 MOST WINS IN THE DAVIS CUP*

	COUNTRY	YEARS	WINS
1	USA	1978–79, 1981–82, 1990, 1992, 1995	8
2	Sweden	1975, 1984–85, 1987, 1994, 1997–98	7
3	Australia	1973, 1977, 1983, 1986, 1999, 2003	6
4	= Germany	1988–89, 1993	3
	= France	1991, 1996, 2001	3
6	= Spain	2000, 2004	2
	= Russia	2002, 2006	2
8	= South Africa	1974	1
	= Italy	1976	1
	= Czechoslovakia	1980	1
	= Croatia	2005	1

* Since the abolition of the Challenge system in 1972

The Davis Cup was first contested in 1900. From then until 1972 the winners were challenged for the title each year, but it became a knockout tournament between the top 16 nations in 1981.

TOP 10 MOST MEN'S GRAND SLAM TITLES*

	PLAYER / COUNTRY / YEARS	SINGLES	DOUBLES	MIXED	TOTAL
1	Roy Emerson, Australia 1959–71	12	16	0	28
2	John Newcombe, Australia 1965–76	7	17	2	26
3	= Frank Sedgman, Australia 1948–52	5	9	8	22
	= Todd Woodbridge, Australia 1988–2004	0	16	6	22
5	Bill Tilden, USA 1913–30	10	6	5	21
6	Rod Laver, Australia 1960–71	11	6	3	20
7	John Bromwich, Australia 1938–50	2	13	4	19
8	= Jean Borotra, France 1925–36	4	9	5	18
	= Ken Rosewall, Australia 1953–72	8	9	1	18
	= Neale Fraser, Australia 1957–62	3	11	4	18

* Up to and including 2007

THE 10 LONGEST SETS IN A GRAND SLAM FINAL*

	YEAR	TOURNAMENT	EVENT	SET WINNERS	OPPONENTS	SCORE
1	1946	US Open	Men's doubles	Gardnar Mulloy (US) Bill Talbert (US)	Don McNeil (US) Frank Guernsey (US)	20–18
2	1992	Wimbledon	Men's doubles	John McEnroe (US) Michael Stich (Germany)	Jim Grabb (US) Richey Reneberg (US)	19–17
3	= 1927	Australian Open	Men's singles	Gerald Patterson (Australia)	John Hawkes (Australia)	18–16
	= 1949	US Open	Men's singles	Ted Schroeder (US)	Pancho Gonzales (US)	18–16
	= 2000	Australian Open	Men's doubles	Ellis Ferrera (South Africa) Rick Leach (US)	Wayne Black (Zimbabwe) Andrew Kratzmann (Australia)	18–16
6	1959	Wimbledon	Men's doubles	Rod Laver (Australia) Bob Mark (Australia)	Roy Emerson (Australia) Neale Fraser (Australia)	16–14
7	= 1911	US Open	Men's doubles	Fred Alexander (US Harold Hackett (US)	Raymond Little (US) Gus Touchard (US)	15–13
	= 1930	US Open	Men's doubles	George Lott (US) Johnny Doeg (US)	Wilmer Allison (US) John Von Ryn (US)	15–13
	= 1959	US Open	Mixed doubles	Bob Mark (Australia) Janet Hopps (US)	Neale Fraser (Australia) Margaret Osborne duPont (US)	15–13
	= 1971	Wimbledon	Mixed doubles	Owen Davidson (Australia) Billie Jean King (US)	Marty Riessen (US) Margaret Court (Australia)	15–13

* Up to and including all 2007 Grand Slam events

The first-named player(s) won the set, not necessarily the match.

For Pete's sake
Pete Sampras won a record 14 Grand Slam singles titles – the most by a male player.

Below: Court's triumph
Margaret Court's four singles titles in a year and total of 24 remains an unbeaten record.

TOP 10 **MOST GRAND SLAM SINGLES TITLES***

	PLAYER / COUNTRY	YEARS	A	F	W	US	TOTAL
1	Margaret Court (*née* Smith), Australia	1960–73	11	5	3	5	24
2	Steffi Graf, Germany	1987–99	4	6	7	5	22
3	Helen Wills-Moody, USA	1923–38	0	4	8	7	19
4	= Chris Evert-Lloyd, USA	1974–86	2	7	3	6	18
	= Martina Navratilova, Czechoslovakia/USA	1978–90	3	2	9	4	18
6	Pete Sampras, USA	1990–2002	2	0	7	5	14
7	= Roy Emerson, Australia	1961–67	6	2	2	2	12
	= Billie Jean King, USA	1966–75	1	1	6	4	12
	= Roger Federer, Switzerland	2003–07	3	0	5	4	12
10	= Rod Laver, Australia	1960–69	3	2	4	2	11
	= Bjorn Borg, Sweden	1974–81	0	6	5	0	11

* Up to and including 2007

A = Australian Open; F = French Open; W = Wimbledon; US = US Open

Suzanne Lenglen (France) won eight Grand Slam singles titles, but if her total of four French singles titles (1920–23) were included, she would be in joint seventh place with 12. However, because the French Championships up to 1925 were for members of French clubs only, they are not regarded as official Grand Slam events.

Water Sports

TOP 10 MEDAL-WINNING COUNTRIES AT THE WORLD AQUATIC CHAMPIONSHIPS*

	COUNTRY	GOLD	MEDALS SILVER	BRONZE	TOTAL
1	USA	144	120	78	342
2	Australia	58	45	34	137
3	East Germany	50	40	25	115
4	Russia/USSR	31	38	38	107
5	Germany/West Germany	25	36	40	101
6	China	33	17	17	67
7	= Hungary	17	12	14	43
	= UK	6	10	27	43
9	Netherlands	7	16	17	40
10	Japan	3	10	24	37

* At the FINA World Long Course Championships 1973–2007

The first World Swimming Championships were held at Belgrade, Yugoslavia, in 1973 and held sporadically to 1998. Since 2001 they have been held every two years and the next championships will be in Rome, Italy, in 2009.

TOP 10 OLYMPIC ROWING COUNTRIES*

	COUNTRY	GOLD	MEDALS SILVER	BRONZE	TOTAL
1	USA	30	29	21	80
2	Germany/West Germany	26	21	21	68
3	East Germany	33	7	7	47
4	= UK	21	17	8	46
	= Russia/USSR/Unified Team	13	20	13	46
6	Italy	10	13	13	36
7	Romania	18	10	7	35
8	Canada	7	13	12	32
9	France	6	11	10	27
10	Australia	8	7	11	26

* Up to and including the 2004 Olympics

TOP 10 FASTEST WINNING TIMES OF THE MEN'S 100-METRES FREESTYLE FINAL AT THE OLYMPIC GAMES

	SWIMMER / COUNTRY	YEAR	TIME (SECS)
1	Pieter van den Hoogenband, Netherlands	2004	48.17
2	Pieter van den Hoogenband, Netherlands	2000	48.30
3	Matt Biondi, USA	1988	48.63
4	Aleksandr Popov, Russia	1996	48.74
5	Aleksandr Popov, Unified Team	1992	49.02
6	Rowdy Gaines, USA	1984	49.80
7	Jim Montgomery, USA	1976	49.99
8	Jörg Woithe, East Germany	1980	50.40
9	Mark Spitz, USA	1972	51.22
10	Mike Wenden, Australia	1968	52.20

* At all Olympic finals up to and including 2004

Pulling together
Lisa Schlenker and Stacey Borgman (USA), winners of the women's lightweight double sculls 'B' final at the 2004 Athens Olympics.

Record-breaker
In his semi-final at the 2000 Sydney Olympics, Pieter van den Hoogenband set a new world record time of 47.84 seconds, still standing in 2008.

TOP 10 **MOST GOLD MEDALS AT THE FINA WORLD AQUATICS CHAMPIONSHIPS***

	SWIMMER / COUNTRY	YEARS COMPETED	INDIVIDUAL GOLDS	RELAY GOLDS	TOTAL GOLDS
1	Michael Phelps, USA	2001–07	11	4	15
2	Ian Thorpe, Australia	1998–2003	6	5	11
3	Grant Hackett, Australia	1998–2005	7	3	10
4	= Kornelia Ender, East Germany	1973–75	4	4	8
	= Aaron Peirsol, USA	2001–07	6	2	8
	= Libby Lenton, Australia	2003–07	4	4	8
7	= Kristin Otti, East Germany	1982–86	3	4	7
	= Jenny Thompson, USA	1998–2003	3	4	7
	= Leisel Jones, USA	2001–07	4	3	7
10	= Aleksandr Popov, Russia	1994–2003	5	1	6
	= Brendan Hansen, USA	2001–07	4	2	6
	= Katie Hoff, USA	2005–07	4	2	6

* Individual medals at the FINA World Long Course Championships, 1973–2007

TOP 10 **OLYMPIC SWIMMING GOLD MEDALS***

	SWIMMER / COUNTRY	YEAR(S)	INDIVIDUAL	RELAY	TOTAL
1	Mark Spitz, USA	1968–72	4	5	9
2	= Matt Biondi, USA	1984–92	2	6	8
	= Jenny Thompson, USA	1992–2004	0	8	8
4	= Kristin Otto, East Germany	1988	4	2	6
	= Amy van Dyken, USA	1996–2000	2	4	6
	= Michael Phelps, USA	2004	4	2	6
7	= Charles Daniels#, USA	1904–08	4	1	5
	= Johnny Weismuller, USA	1924–28	3	2	5
	= Don Schollander, USA	1964–68	2	3	5
	= Tom Jager, USA	1984–92	0	5	5
	= Krizstina Egerszegi, Hungary	1988–96	5	0	5
	= Gary Hall Jr, USA	1996–2004	2	3	5
	= Ian Thorpe, Australia	2000–04	3	2	5

* Up to and including the 2004 Olympics
# Includes one gold medal won at the 1906 Intercalated Olympic Games in Athens

Winter Sports

TOP 10 **ICE HOCKEY NATIONS AT THE OLYMPIC GAMES***

1 Canada

2 = United States

= USSR/Russia

4 = Czechoslovakia/ Czech Republic

= Sweden

6 Finland

7 = Great Britain

= West Germany/ Germany

= Switzerland

10 Unified Team

GOLD

SILVER

BRONZE

* Up to and including the 2006 Turin Olympics

Ice hockey was first contested at the Summer Olympics in 1920, and at the Winter Olympics since 1924 for men and since 1998 for women.

TOP 10 **OLYMPIC BOBSLEIGH NATIONS***

	COUNTRY	GOLD	SILVER	BRONZE	TOTAL
1	Switzerland	9	10	11	30
2	Germany/West Germany	10	6	8	24
3	United States	6	6	6	18
4	East Germany	5	5	3	13
5	Italy	4	4	4	12
6	= UK	1	1	2	4
	= USSR/Russia	1	1	2	4
8	= Canada	2	1	0	3
	= Austria	1	2	0	3
10	Belgium	0	1	1	2

* Up to and including the 2006 Turin Olympics

The two-man bobsleigh event made its debut at the 1932 Olympics and has been held at every Games since, with the exception of 1960 as there was no bob run at Squaw Valley, California, USA. The four-man event made its debut at the 1928 Games in St Moritz. The two-women bobsleigh event was held for the first time at the 2002 Olympics, when it was won by the USA.

TOP 10 **MEDAL-WINNING COUNTRIES AT THE WINTER OLYMPICS***

	COUNTRY	GOLD	SILVER	BRONZE	TOTAL
1	Russia/USSR/Unified Team	122	89	86	297
2	Norway	96	102	84	282
3	USA	78	81	59	218
4	Germany/West Germany	76	78	57	211
5	Austria	50	64	71	185
6	Finland	42	57	52	151
7	Sweden	46	32	44	122
8	Canada	38	38	44	120
9	Switzerland	37	37	43	117
10	East Germany	39	37	35	111

* Up to and including the 2006 Turin Games

Totals include medals won at figure skating and ice hockey included in the Summer Olympics prior to the inauguration of the Winter Games in 1924. From 1924 to 1992, they were held in the same year as the Summer Olympics but since 1994 they have been held in the two years in between the Summer Games.

TOP 10 **MOST SKIING WORLD CUP RACE WINS IN A CAREER (MEN)***

	SKIER / COUNTRY	FIRST WIN	LAST WIN	TOTAL WINS
1	Ingemar Stenmark, Sweden	1974–75	1988–89	86
2	Hermann Maier, Austria	1997–97	2005–06	53
3	Alberto Tomba, Italy	1987–88	1997–98	50
4	Marc Girardelli, Luxembourg	1982–83	1995–96	46
5	Pirmin Zurbriggen, Switzerland	1981–82	1989–90	40
6	Bode Miller, USA	2001–02	2007–08	31
7	Benjamin Raich, Austria	1998–99	2007–08	30
8	Stephan Eberharter, Austria	1997–98	2003–04	29
9	Phil Mahre, USA	1976–77	1982–83	27
10	Franz Klammer, Austria	1973–74	1983–84	26

* Up to and including the 2007–08 season

TOP 10 **MOST SKIING WORLD CUP RACE WINS IN A CAREER (WOMEN)***

	SKIER / COUNTRY	FIRST WIN	LAST WIN	TOTAL WINS
1	Annemarie Pröll, Austria	1969–70	1979–80	62
2	Vreni Schneider, Switzerland	1984–85	1994–95	55
3	Renate Goetschl, Austria	1992–93	2006–07	46
4	Anja Paerson, Sweden	1998–99	2007–08	38
5	Katja Seizinger, Germany	1991–92	1997–98	36
6	Hanni Wenzel, Liechtenstein	1973–74	1983–84	33
7	Erika Hess, Switzerland	1980–81	1986–87	31
8	Janica Kostelic, Croatia	1998–99	2005–06	30
9	Michela Figini, Switzerland	1983–84	1989–90	26
10 =	Maria Walliser, Switzerland	1982–83	1989–90	25
=	Michaela Dorfmeister, Austria	1995–96	2005–06	25

* Up to and including the 2007–08 season

Alpine champion
Sweden's Anja Paerson has also won an Olympic gold medal, in the slalom in 2006, and won seven World Championship golds between 2001 and 2007 in slalom, giant slalom, super-g, combined and downhill.

Leisure Pursuits

TOP 10 HIGHEST-EARNING SPORTSMEN

	SPORTSMAN / COUNTRY*	SPORT	EARNINGS ($)
1	Tiger Woods	Golf	100,000,000
2	Oscar de la Hoya	Boxing	43,000,000
3	Phil Mickelson	Golf	42,200,000
4	Kimi Raikkonen, Finland	Motor racing	40,000,000
5	Michael Schumacher, Germany	Motor racing	36,000,000
6	David Beckham, UK	Football	33,000,000
7	Kobe Bryant	Basketball	32,900,000
8	Shaquille O'Neal	Basketball	31,900,000
9	= Michael Jordan	Basketball	31,000,000
	= Ronaldinho, Brazil	Football	31,000,000

* All from the USA unless otherwise stated

Source: *Forbes* magazine

Winner of 13 Majors and 61 Tour events (to 1 January 2008), Tiger Woods has won over $75 million since turning professional in 1996 – $25 million more than the second placed golfer. His annual income includes payments for endorsements for companies such as Nike.

$351-million team

Manchester United players celebrating after beating Chelsea 4-0 on penalties, after the game ended 1-1, to win the 2007 FA Community Shield at Wembley Stadium.

TOP 10 MOST VALUABLE SPORTS TEAM BRANDS

	TEAM / COUNTRY	SPORT	VALUE 2007 ($)
1	Manchester United/UK	Soccer	351,000,000
2	Real Madrid/Spain	Soccer	288,000,000
3	Bayern Munich/Germany	Soccer	255,000,000
4	New York Yankees/USA	Baseball	217,000,000
5	Arsenal/UK	Soccer	185,000,000
6	AC Milan/Italy	Soccer	184,000,000
7	Dallas Cowboys/USA	American football	175,000,000
8	Barcelona/Spain	Soccer	130,000,000
9	Boston Red Sox/USA	Baseball	125,000,000
10	Washington Redskins/USA	American football	120,000,000

Source: *Forbes* magazine

Manchester United has one of the biggest fans bases with supporters in all corners of the globe. It is estimated that more than 50 per cent of their supporters are based in Asia. Their estimated merchandise revenue was nearly $25 million in 2007, but their overall value falls well short of the most valuable sports brand, ESPN, which is estimated to be worth $7.5 billion.

TOP 10 **MOST SPORTS, GAMES AND PHYSICAL ACTIVITIES IN THE UK**

ACTIVITY	% PARTICIPATION 2005–06*	
	WOMEN	MEN
1 = Gym	13	13
= Indoor swimming/ diving	18	13
= Snooker, pool, billiards	3	13
4 = Outdoor football	1	12
= Recreational cycling	6	12
6 Golf	1	9
7 Jogging, running	3	7
8 Darts	2	6
9 = Keep-fit, aerobics, dance exercise	10	4
= Tenpin bowling	3	4

* 16 and over, ranked by male percentage

Source: *Social Trends 2007*

$200-million film
Hillary Swank, as Maggie Fitzgerald, a waitress who decides to change her life by becoming a boxer, in Million Dollar Baby. Directed by Clint Eastwood, it won four Oscars, including those for Best Picture, Best Director and Best Actress – and earned over $200 million worldwide.

THE 10 **LATEST WINNERS OF THE BBC SPORTS PERSONALITY OF THE YEAR AWARD**

	WINNER	SPORT	YEAR
1	Joe Calzaghe	Boxing	2007
2	Zara Phillips	Eventing	2006
3	Andrew Flintoff	Cricket	2005
4	Kelly Holmes	Athletics	2004
5	Jonny Wilkinson	Rugby Union	2003
6	Paula Radcliffe	Athletics	2002
7	David Beckham	Soccer	2001
8	Steve Redgrave	Rowing	2000
9	Lennox Lewis	Boxing	1999
10	Michael Owen	Soccer	1998

Source: BBC

TOP 10 **SPORT FILMS**

	FILM	YEAR	SPORT
1	Cars*	2006	Car racing
2	Rocky IV	1985	Boxing
3	Million Dollar Baby	2004	Boxing
4	Space Jam*	1996	Basketball
5	The Longest Yard	2005	American footbal
6	The Waterboy	1998	American footbal
7	Dodgeball: A True Underdog Story	2004	Dodgeball
8	Days of Thunder	1990	Stock car racing
9	Talladega Nights: The Ballad of Ricky Bobby	2006	NASCAR racing
10	Rocky Balboa	2006	Boxing

* Animated

Further Information

THE UNIVERSE & THE EARTH

Astronautics
www.astronautix.com
Spaceflight news and reference

Caves
www.caverbob.com
Lists of long and deep caves

Disasters
www.emdat.be
Emergency Events Database covering major disasters since 1900

Elements
www.webelements.com
Detailed data on every element

Islands
islands.unep.ch
Information on the world's islands

Mountains
peaklist.org
Lists of the world's tallest mountains

NASA
www.nasa.gov
The main website for the US space programme

Oceans
www.oceansatlas.org
The UN's resource on oceanographic issues

Planets
www.nineplanets.org
A multimedia tour of the Solar System

Space
www.space.com
Reports on events in space exploration

LIFE ON EARTH

Animals
animaldiversity.ummz.umich.edu
A wealth of animal data

Birds
www.bsc-eoc.org/avibase
A database on the world's birds

Conservation
iucn.org
The leading nature conservation site

Endangered
www.cites.org
Lists of endangered species of flora and fauna

Environment
www.unep.ch
The UN's Earthwatch and other programmes

Fish
www.fishbase.org
Global information on fish

Food and Agriculture Organization
www.fao.org
Statistics from the UN's FAO website

Forests
www.fao.org/forestry
FAO's forestry website

Insects
ufbir.ifas.ufl.edu
The University of Florida Book of Insect Records

Sharks
www.flmnh.ufl.edu/fish/sharks
The Florida Museum of Natural History's shark data files

THE HUMAN WORLD

Crime, international
www.interpol.int
Interpol's crime statistics

Crime, UK
www.homeoffice.gov.uk
Home Office crime and prison population figures

Leaders
www.terra.es/personal2/monolith/00index.htm
Facts about world leaders since 1945

Military
www.globalfirepower.com
World military statistics and rankings

Population and names
www.statistics.gov.uk
The UK in figures and naming trends for the UK population

Religions
www.worldchristiandatabase.org
World religion data

Royalty
www.royal.gov.uk
The official site of the British Monarchy, with histories

Rulers
rulers.org
A database of the world's rulers and political leaders

US presidents
www.whitehouse.gov/history/presidents
Biographies, facts and figures from the White House

World Health Organization
www.who.int/en
World health information and advice

TOWN & COUNTRY

Bridges and tunnels
en.structurae.de
Facts and figures on the world's buildings, tunnels and other structures

Countries
www.theodora.com/wfb
Country data, rankings, etc.

Country and city populations
www.citypopulation.de
A searchable guide to the world's countries and major cities

Country data
www.cia.gov/library/publications/the-world-factbook
The CIA World Factbook

Country populations
www.un.org/esa/population/unpop
The UN's worldwide data on population issues

Development
www.worldbank.org
Development and other statistics from around the world

Population
www.census.gov/ipc/www
International population statistics

Steel bridges
www.sbi.se/default_en.asp
A downloadable list of the world's steel bridges

Skyscrapers
www.emporis.com/en
The Emporis database of high-rise buildings

Tunnels
home.no.net/lotsberg
A database of the longest rail, road and canal tunnels

CULTURE & LEARNING

The Art Newspaper
www.theartnewspaper.com
News and views on the art world

The British Library
www.bl.uk
The route to the catalogues and exhibitions in the national library

Education
www.dfes.gov.uk/statistics
Official statistics relating to education in the UK

Languages of the world
www.ethnologue.com
Online reference work on the world's 6,912 living languages

Library loans
www.plr.uk.com
Public Lending Right's lists of the UK's most-borrowed books

The Man Booker Prize
www.themanbookerprize.com
Britain's most prestigious literary prize

Museums and galleries
www.24hourmuseum.org.uk
A guide to exhibitions and events at the UK

Oxford English Dictionary
www.oed.com
The online version of the *OED*, accessible via most public libraries

Translations
databases.unesco.org/xtrans/stat/xTransList.a
UNESCO's lists of the most translated books and authors

UNESCO
www.unesco.org
Comparative international statistics on education and culture

MUSIC

All Music Guide
www.allmusic.com
A comprehensive guide to all genres of music

Billboard
www.billboard.com
US music news and charts data

The Brit Awards
www.brits.co.uk
The official website for the popular music awards

The British Phonographic Industry Ltd
www.bpi.co.uk
Searchable database of gold discs and other certified awards

Grammy Awards
www.naras.org
The official site for the famous US music awards

Launch
uk.launch.yahoo.com
UK music charts and news from Yahoo

MTV
www.mtv.co.uk
The online site for the MTV UK music channel

New Musical Express
www.nme.com
The online version of the popular music magazine

The Official UK Charts Company
www.theofficialcharts.com
Weekly and historical music charts

VH1
www.vh1.com
Online UK music news

ENTERTAINMENT

Academy Awards
www.oscars.org
The official 'Oscars' website

BAFTAs
www.bafta.org
The home of the BAFTA Awards

BBC
www.bbc.co.uk
Gateway to BBC TV and radio, with a powerful Internet search engine

Film Distributors' Association
www.launchingfilms.com
Trade site for UK film releases and statistics

Golden Globe Awards
www.hfpa.org
Hollywood Foreign Press Association's Golden Globes site

Internet Movie Database
www.imdb.com/
The best of the publicly accessible film websites; IMDbPro is available to subscribers

London Theatre Guide
www.londontheatre.co.uk
A comprehensive guide to West End theatre productions

Screen Daily
www.screendaily.com
Daily news from the film world at the website of UK weekly *Screen International*

Variety
www.variety.com
Extensive entertainment information (extra features available to subscribers)

Yahoo! Movies
uk.movies.yahoo.com
Charts plus features, trailers and links to the latest film UK releases

THE COMMERCIAL WORLD

The Economist
www.economist.com
Global economic and political news

Energy
www.bp.com/
Online access to the *BP Statistical Review of World Energy*

Gold
www.gold.org
The website of the World Gold Council

Internet
www.internetworldstats.com
Internet World Stats

Organisation for Economic Co-operation and Development
www.oecd.org
World economic and social statistics

Rich lists
www.forbes.com
Forbes magazine's celebrated lists of the world's wealthiest people

Telecommunications
www.itu.int
Worldwide telecommunications statistics

UK tourist attractions
www.alva.org.uk
Information and visitor statistics on the UK's top tourist attractions

The World Bank
www.worldbank.org
World development, trade and labour statistics

World Tourism Organization
www.world-tourism.org
The world's principal travel and tourism organization

ON THE MOVE

Air disasters
www.airdisaster.com
Reports on aviation disasters

Airports
www.airports.org
Statistics on the world's busiest airports

Air speed records
www.fai.org/records
The website of the official air speed record governing body

Balloons
www.eballoon.org
History and information on hot air ballooning

Car manufacture
www.oica.net
The International Organization of Motor Vehicle Manufacturers' website

Land and water speed records
www.bluebird-electric.net/bluebird_site_navigator.htm
Wide range of resources, 1901–

Railways
www.railwaygazette.com
The world's railway business in depth from *Railway Gazette International*

Shipwrecks
www.shipwreckregistry.com
A huge database of the world's wrecked and lost ships

Water speed records
www.geocities.com/Colosseum/Sideline/8707
List of record-holders, 1919 to the present

Yachts
powerandmotoryacht.com
The annual *Power & Motoryacht* guide to the world's megayachts

SPORT & LEISURE

Athletics
www.iaaf.org
The world governing body of athletics

Cricket
www.cricinfo.com
Cricinfo, launched in 1993, since merged with the online version of *Wisden*

Cycling
www.uci.ch
The Union Cycliste Internationale, the competitive cycling governing body

FIFA
www.fifa.com
The official website of FIFA, the world governing body of soccer

Football
www.football-league.co.uk
The official site of the Football League

Formula One
www.formula1.com
The official F1 website

Olympics
www.olympic.org/uk
The official Olympics website

Premier League
www.premierleague.com
The official web site of soccer's Premier League

Rugby
www.itsrugby.co.uk
Comprehensive rugby site

Skiing
www.fis-ski.com
Fédèration Internationale de Ski, the world governing body of skiing and snowboarding

Index

Acknowledgements

Special research: Ian Morrison (sport); Dafydd Rees (music)

Peter Bond
Richard Braddish
Thomas Brinkhoff
Hannah Conduct
Philip Eden
Christopher Forbes
Russell E. Gough
Robert Grant
Bob Gulden
Dr Benjamin Lucas
Phil Matcham
Chris Mead
Roberto Ortiz de Zarate
Emil Pocock
Robert Senior
Lucy T. Verma

Academy of Motion Picture Arts and Sciences
 – Oscar statuette is the registered trademark
 and copyrighted property of the Academy
 of Motion Picture Arts and Sciences
Advertising Age
Airports Council International
Alexa
Amnesty International
Artnet
The Art Newspaper
Association of Leading Visitor Attractions
 (ALVA)
Association of Tennis Professionals
Audit Bureau of Circulations Ltd (ABC)
BBC
Billboard
Box Office Mojo
BP Statistical Review of World Energy 2007
Breeders' Cup
British Academy of Film and Television Awards
 (BAFTA)
The BRIT Awards
British Film Institute
British Library
British Phonographic Industry (BPI)
British Video Association
BusinessWeek
Cameron Mackintosh Ltd
Central Intelligence Agency, *World Factbook*
Channel Swimming Association
Checkout
Chinese Academy of Sciences
Christie's
Computer Industry Almanac
Criminal Statistics England & Wales
Death Penalty Information Center
De Beers
Department for Environment, Food and Rural
 Affairs (DEFRA)
Department of Trade and Industry
The Diamond Registry
EarthTrends
The Economist

EM-DAT, CRED, University of Louvain
Emporis
Environmental Performance Index (EPI)
Ethnologue
Euromonitor International, Global Market
 Information Database
Federal Bureau of Investigation
Fédération Internationale de Football Association
Fédération Internationale de Motorcyclisme
Fédération Internationale de Ski
Food and Agriculture Organization of the
 United Nations (FAO)
Forbes magazine
Fortune
The Gallup Organization
General Register Office for Scotland
Global Education Digest (UNESCO)
Gold Fields Mineral Services, *Gold Survey 2007*
HM Prison Services
HM Treasury
Home Office
Human Development Report (United Nations)
Imperial War Museum
Index Translationum (UNESCO)
Indianapolis Motor Speedway
Interbrand
International Air Transport Association
International Association of Athletics
 Federations
International Centre for Prison Studies
International Federation of Audit Bureaux of
 Circulations
International Game Fish Association
The International Institute for Strategic
 Studies, *The Military Balance 2008*
International Hydrographic Organization
International Iron & Steel Institute
International Labour Organization
International Monetary Fund (IMF)
International Obesity Task Force
International Olympic Committee
International Organization of Motor Vehicle
 Manufacturers
International Shark Attack File, Florida
 Museum of Natural History
International Telecommunication Union
International Union for Conservation of
 Nature and Natural Resources (IUCN)
Internet Movie Database
Internet World Stats
Kirin
Ladies Professional Golf Association
Leisure Accident Surveillance System (LASS)
Man Booker Prize
Metropolitan Opera House, New York
MRIB
MTV
Music Information Database
National Academy of Recording Arts and
 Sciences (NARAS) (Grammy Awards)
National Aeronautics and Space
 Administration (NASA)
National Basketball Association (NBA)

National Football League (NFL)
National Phobics Society
National Statistics
Nationwide Mercury Prize
Natural History Museum, London
AC Nielsen
Nobel Foundation
NSS GEO2 Committee on Long and Deep
 Caves
The Official UK Charts Company
Open University
Ordnance Survey
Organisation for Economic Co-operation and
 Development (OECD)
Organisation Internationale des Constructeurs
 d'Automobiles
Oxford English Dictionary
Periodical Publishers Association
Point Topic
Population Reference Bureau
Power & Motoryacht
Professional Golfers' Association
Public Lending Right
River Systems of the World
Royal Aeronautical Society
Royal Astronomical Society
Royal Opera House, Covent Garden
Screen Digest
Screen International
Siemens, *International Telecom Statistics*
The Silver Institute, *World Silver Survey 2007*
Social Trends 2007
Sony Radio Academy Awards
Sotheby's
Stockholm International Peace Research
 Institute (SIPRI)
Stores
Top500
UIC Railisa Database
United Nations
United Nations Educational, Scientific and
 Cultural Organization (UNESCO)
United Nations Environment Programme (UNEP)
United Nations Office on Drugs and Crime
United Nations Population Division
Universal Postal Union
US Census Bureau
US Census Bureau International Data Base
US Geological Survey
Ward's Motor Vehicle Facts & Figures 2007
Wine Institute
World Association of Newspapers
World Christian Database
World Conservation Monitoring Centre
World Development Indicators (World Bank)
World Gold Council
World Health Organization
World Nuclear Association
World of Learning
World Population Reference Bureau
World Tennis Association
World Tourism Organization

Picture Credits

AKG Images: 75t Ullstein Bild, 158 Walt Disney Pictures/Album, 165tr Disney Enterprises/Album.

Catherine Benson: 7

Christie's Images Limited: 114l.

Corbis: 10-11 Farhad Parsa/zefa, 11b, 95c, 121, 211, 231b, 239b Bettmann, 16 Michael S. Lewis, 18, 22t Galen Rowell, 19 George Steinmetz, 21 Wayne Lawler; Ecoscene, 23tr David Muench, 27t & b, 62l Corbis, 30t Louie Psihoyos, 31t Theo Allofs, 32b Denis Scott, 34b (inset) Stephen Frink, 35t, 39t Paul Souders, 35b Renee Lynn, 37r Serge Kozak/zefa, 38b Manfred Danegger/zefa, 40b, 84b Yann Arthus-Bertrand, 42b Ricardo Azoury, 43b, 63tr, 128c, 134t, 191t, 196, 209t, 215t, 232tl, 233b, 239t Reuters, 45br Phil Schermeister, 46-47, 47t Rickey Rogers/Reuters, 53br Pierre Perrin Sygma, 56t Ali Jarekji/Reuters, 59tl Larry Williams, 59bl Jack Hollingsworth, 60br, 171c Michel Setboun, 61 epa, 65tl PoodlesRock, 66 Ted Spiegel, 67tr Kieran Doherty/Reuters, 68br Creasource, 71t Matt Rainey/Star Ledger, 73b Scott Houston, 76b KCNA/epa, 78b Eyal Ofer, 79b Punit Paranjpe/Reuters, 82-83b Hamid Sardar, 83t, 86 Kevin R. Morris, 85tr Gideon Mendel/ActionAid, 87 China Daily Information Corp - CDIC/Reuters, 88b Ken Straiton, 89 Peter Adams, 91l Ladislav Janicek/zefa, 91r Nick Smyth; Cordaiy Photo Library Ltd., 92-93t Momatiuk - Eastcott, 92-93b, 115t Nik Wheeler, 94 Juergen Effner/dpa, 95b Anwar Mirza/Reuters, 99tr Martin Ruetschi/epa, 103 Keren Su, 107bl John Springer Collection, 108tl Nancy Kaszerman/ZUMA, 108-109t & b Jim Zuckerman, 109r Massimo Listri, 110b Simon Marcus, 112b Tony Kurdzuk/Star Ledger, 113b Mike Segar/Reuters, 118cl Contographer ®, 120c Neal Preston, 124tl Gary Hershorn/Reuters, 125b John Hayes/Reuters, 126 Federico Gambarini/epa, 127 Bruno Bebert/Pool/Reuters, 130 Jose Manuel Ribeiro/Reuters, 131 Alessia Pierdomenico/Reuters, 135c Robbie Jack, 142cl Phil McCarten/Reuters, 150-151 Patrik Giardino, 160b Jutta Klee, 161 Lester Lefkowitz, 168l China Newsphoto/Reuters, 169r Sherwin Crasto/Reuters, 171b Lynsey Addario, 173tl Jodi Hilton, 177t Raj Patidar/Reuters, 180 José Fuste Raga/zefa, 181 Gideon Mendel, 183 Dave G. Houser, 185t Emilio Suetone/Hemis, 186 Tokyo Space Club, 187t David Pillinger, 188cr Owen Franken, 189cr Jose Fuste Raga, 190br Rick Wilking/Reuters, 192-193t Du Huaju/Xinhua Press, 192-193b Karl-Heinz Haenel/zefa, 194ct Gilles Sabrié, 195t Jeremy Horner, 197 Sergio Dorantes/Sygma, 200t Wolfgang Deuter/zefa, 200b Skyscan, 202b Matthias Hiekel/dpa, 203 Jim Sugar, 205t Fred Derwal/Hemis, 206b Chris Helgre/Reuters, 207b Robert Sciarrino/Star Ledger, 214tr Duomo, 215b Jean-Yves Ruszniewski/TempSport, 216c Kimimasa Mayama/epa, 222b Franck Robichon/epa, 223b Eric Miller/Reuters, 224-225 Jason Reed/Reuters, 230b Tony Roberts, 231t Greg Fiume/NewSport, 234b Schlegelmilch, 235 Gero Breloer/epa, 236b Christian Liewig/Liewig Media Sports, 243b Eddy Risch/epa, 244b Andy Rain/epa.

Fotolia: 20t Imageman Rez, 22-23c Nikolay Titov, 24b Georgios Alexandris, 25tr Antony McAulay, 26 Robert Paul van Beets, 32t Zampa, 33b Olivier Lantzendörffer, 34t Fotoflash, 38t Ichtor, 40tl, 233tl Edsweb, 40tr Stefan Hermans, 41tl

Luchschen, 41tr EastWest Imaging, 41b Jody Snelgrove, 46t Andrzej Tokarski, 46b Piter PKruger, 51bl Olga Lyubkina, 51br Stephen Finn, 52-53 Karin Lau, 56b Nymph, 60l Roman Dekan, 62-63 Granitepeaker, 64t Nikolay Okhitin, 64tr Mikhail Perfilov, 64-65b Irmine van der Geest, 66tl Mashe, 68 PhotoBristol, 68tl Photlook, 69 Kmit, 70tl, 175b Irochka, 70c Sergey Lavrentev, 71c Sascha Burkard, 74b Slobodan Djajic, 77l, 156b Kirsty Pargeter, 77tr Xygo, 78tl Drizzd, 78tr Georgios Kollidas, 79tl, 175t Jean-Louis Bouzou, 79tc Dmitry Rukhlenko, 79tr MM, 84-85t Leslie Hender, 88t Robert, 90b Claudio Baldini, 96-97b ManicBlu, 102t Douglas Freer, 102bl Gudellaphoto, 106-107, 129b Mr. Lightning, 110-111t Jo Ann Snover, 111br Paul Turner, 112t JChMedinger, 113t Andrey Chmelyov, 118b Dino O., 118-119t Mark Huls, 119br Marlee, 120t Pierre-Jean G., 120b Carsten Reisinger, 122-123, 245b Franck Boston, 124b, 129t OH, 124-125t U.P.images, 128t Vladimir Mucibabic, 128b, 178t Dotshock, 135t, 142l, 143r Ferenc Szelepcsenyi, 135b Alex Staroseltsev, 138-139 James Steidl, 140l Milosluz, 141, 244t ktsdesign, 144t, 145r Olga Mishyna, 144-145 Joyful_Girl, 148-149 Lorelyn Medina, 152-153b Tritooth, 156t Michanolimit, 157b Tatyana Nyshko, 160t Adam Gryko, 162-163 Laura, 163br Ljupco Smokovski, 165 Claudio Divizia, 165br Adam Borkowski, 170t Ploum1, 170b Stachu343, 171t Georgios Kollidas, 172t Mikhail Tolstoy, 172cl Gino Santa Maria, 172-173b Orlando Florin Rosu, 174tl PhotoCreate, 174tr Sir_Eagle, 174b Aleksandr Ugorenkov, 179b Objectsforall, 182tl Tom Perkins, 182tc Joe Gough, 182tr Elnur, 184t Celso Pupo, 184cl Steve Cukrov, 184cr Luka, 184-185b Pandore, 187b Sdraskovic, 188-189 Mathieu Viennet, 190bl Stefano Maccari, 190-191 Juan Jose Gutierrez Barrow, 194t Hazel Proudlove, 194cb Clivia, 194b BilderBox, 195 Nickos, 205b Gina Sanders, 206-207t Stephanie Bandmann, 210 Stasys Eidiejus, 214b TFphotos, 216t Jeffrey van Daele, 216b jStock, 220b Jean-Luc Cochonneau, 220b TimurD, 221b Bryce Newell, 222t, 223t Albo, 230t Ant Clausen, 232 Sean Gladwell, 236t Martine Coquilleau, 238t Vincenzo Novello, 242-243 Imagine-Nation.

Getty Images: 51t Hank Walker/Time Life Pictures, 55 Per-Anders Pettersson, 63br Alex Wong, 69tc Time Life Pictures/FBI/Time Life Pictures, 73t Ruslan Alkhanov/AFP, 74t Mansell/Time & Life Pictures, 75b Topical Press Agency, 96-97t Liu Song/ChinaFotoPress, 104t Choo Youn-Kong/AFP, 106bl Popperfoto, 119c Alexander Tamargo, 122bl, 129c Michael Ochs Archives, 122br Ed Clark/Time & Life Pictures, 123b Frank Driggs Collection, 173tr Fotos International, 179t AFP, 217 Hugo Philpott/AFP, 219 Jewel Samad/AFP, 221c Laurence Griffiths, 226 David Hecker/AFP, 227 Teh Eng Koon/AFP, 229 Stuart Franklin/Bongarts, 237 Matthew Lewis, 240br Robert Laberge, 241t Phil Walter.

Ivan Hissey: 66t, 174b, 177cr, 187l, 240bl

iStockphoto: 10br Carolina K. Smith, 11c, 16-17 Shawn Gearhart, 20b Edwin van Wier, 22-23b Dmytro Korolov, 23t Mikael Damkier, 24t Amanda Rohde, 24c John Rodriguez, 25cl & cr Fred De Bailliencourt, 25b Ilker Canikligil, 30b Victor Soares, 31b, 43tl, tcll, tclr, tc & tr Eric Isselée, 34b Michal Rozanski, 39b Scott Morgan, 42tl Editorial12, 42tr Narvikk, 43crl Jiri Vaclavek, 43crr Chepko Danil, 44t Ceneri, 44cl Christine Balderas,

44cr Spauln, 44b Bluestocking, 45t Naphtalina, 45bl Jaroslaw Wojcik, 52bl Ferran Traite Soler, 54t & b Corey Weiner, 54c Cole Vineyard, 57 Rob Blackburn, 58 Sandramo, 59tr, 69tl & tr, 71b, 202tr, 238-239 iStockphoto.com, 59br Blackred, 60bc Stefan Hermans, 65tl Michel de Nijs, 66b Tatiana Morozova, 70tr & br Andrew Brown, 70bl Robyn Mackenzie, 72 Christian Pound, 76t, 77br Simon Spoon, 77 Phil Morley, 90t Anton Seleznev, 92l, 93r, 105b Lisa Thornberg, 95t DaddyBit, 98-99 Andrea Sturm, 102br Milos Luzanin, 104-105 Perefu, 114-115 Laura Eisenberg, 134b Oscar Durand, 147b Izabela Habur, 154t Kirill Putchenko, 164l Steve Jacobs, 168r Chris Schmidt, 168-169t Ryan KC Wong, 172cr Vik Thomas, 176tl, tr & br Mark Evans, 177b Scott Maxwell, 178b Hans F. Meier, 182b, 245t YinYang, 187cr Matt Knannlein, 188t Vito Elefante, 189t Lidian Neeleman, 193br Svetlana Tebenkova, 202tl kkgas, 209b Goldmund, 214tl Brian Wilke, 218 Tom Brown, 221t Slawomir Kruz, 228tr Simon Askham, 228bl Nikada, 234t Kativ, 238b Sean Warren, 240bl Neeley Spotts, 240-241 Peter Evans.

The Kobal Collection: 132-133 New Line/James, David, 133r MGM/UA, 141t Walt Disney/ Mountain, Peter, 142-143t Marvel/Sony Pictures, 142-143b Dreamworks/Paramount, 144b New Line/Avery Pix/Cartwright, Richard, 145l Bonne Pioche/Buena Vista/APC/Maison, Jerome, 146 New Line, 147t Sony/Columbia/Bennett, Tracy, 148tr 20th Century Fox/Paramount, 149t Paramount/Miramax, 152t Warner Bros./Gordon, Melinda Sue, 154tl New Line/Saul Zaentz/Wing Nut/Vinet, Pierre, 155 Warner Bros./James, David, 156t (inset) Columbia/Mein, Simon, 157t Warner Bros/DC Comics, 159 20th Century Fox/Groening, Matt, 150tl MGM/ Bull, Clarence Sinclair, 151t Paramount/Vantage, 164r Warner Bros./Cooper, Andrew, 245c Warner Bros./Wallace, Merie W.

Mary Evans Picture Library: 65tr, 208.

Moviestore Collection Ltd.: 140tl, 151br, 153t.

NASA: 10bl, 83c Goddard Space Flight Center, 12 European Space Agency and A. Nota (STScI/ESA), 13tl, bl, bcr & br, 192t Jet Propulsion Laboratory, 13tc European Space Agency, J. Clarke (Boston University), and Z. Levay (STScI), 13tr Solar and Heliospheric Observatory (European Space Agency & NASA), 13ct, 201 NASA, 13cb & bcl Headquarters - Great Images in NASA, 13bc Steve Lee University of Colorado, Jim Bell Cornell University, 14 Kennedy Space Center, 14br, 15 Marshall Space Flight Center.

Naturepl: 33t Doug Perrine, 36 Daniel Gomez.

Photolibrary: 37l Howard Hall.

Science Photo Library: 30c Joe Tucciarone, 50 Scott Camazine.

TopFoto: 138tl Marilyn Kingwill/ArenaPAL, 139t Michael le Poer Trench/ArenaPAL.

Publisher's Acknowledgements
Cover design: Ron Callow at Design 23.

Packager's Acknowledgements
Palazzo Editions would like to thank Richard Constable and Robert Walster for their design contributions.